From ABBOTTS to ZURICH

Counties of New York State

From
ABBOTTS
to
ZURICH

*New York State
Placenames*

Ren Vasiliev

SYRACUSE UNIVERSITY PRESS

Copyright © 2004 by Syracuse University Press
Syracuse, New York 13244–5160

All Rights Reserved

First Edition 2004
04   05   06   07   08   09   6   5   4   3   2   1

All photographs courtesy of, and copyrighted © 2004 by, Jon Crispin.

The paper used in this publication meets the minimum requirements
of American National Standard for Information Sciences—Permanence
of Paper for Printed Library Materials, ANSI Z39.48–1984.∞™

Library of Congress Cataloging-in-Publication Data

Vasiliev, Ren.
From Abbotts to Zurich : New York State placenames / Ren Vasiliev.— 1st ed.
p. cm.
Includes bibliographical references.
ISBN 0-8156-0798-9 (pbk. : alk. paper)
1. Names, Geographical—New York (State) 2. New York (State)—History,
Local. I. Title.
F117.V37 2004
917.47—dc22
2004000153

Manufactured in the United States of America

Contents

Ren Vasiliev is associate professor and chair of the Geography Department at the State University of New York, College at Geneseo.

Preface

THIS BOOK DID NOT EXIST when I needed it more than a decade ago as I was working on my master's thesis. That work was a study of the geographic and temporal diffusion of all the places in the United States that were named Moscow. The references that proved most helpful then were the placename books for many of the individual states. When I discovered that there was no one book for the state of New York, I vowed that someday I would write it. That day is now.

Of course, very few projects are ever completed without the help of others, especially one of this extent. In chronological order, then, I would like to thank a number of people and institutions. Back from my master's days, I must thank my thesis committee and readers who were willing to stand up for my subject: David Mark, Mike Woldenberg, and Babs Buttenfield. The American Name Society was invaluable as a source of support for this kind of toponymic research. In particular, I want to thank Ed Callary, Tom Gasque, and Alan Rayburn for always being enthusiastic about my placename research. At the same time and in conjunction with the ANS, Roger Payne and Donald Orth at the United States Geological Survey (USGS) and the Board on Geographic Names provided help and instruction in the use of the Geographic Names Information System (GNIS), as well as encouragement through their continuing enthusiasm for my work over the years.

During my doctoral work at Syracuse University's Department of Geography, I veered off into other geographic and cartographic realms. When that was done, and after a number of other projects, I came back to toponymy—never having really left it (I had kept up my ANS membership over the years and become a member of the New York State Committee on Geographic Names)—because I was asked, by Carol Kammen of Ithaca, to write an essay about placenames for *The Encyclopedia of Local History.* Carol then championed my idea for this book by arranging a contact with Syracuse University Press. I thank her for this. At the press,

Sally Atwater took my project under her wing until a contract was signed. I thank her for the time she spent on this while at the press and for her editing comments.

Since then, during the research and the writing of the book, the following have been extremely helpful: at my home institution, the State University of New York, College at Geneseo, the people at Milne Library were generous in their time when I was searching for materials. Harriet Sleggs in the Interlibrary Loan Department was tireless in tracking down documents. The sabbatical leave committee granted me a semester's leave so that I could have several months of uninterrupted writing time. The Geography Department is also to be thanked for allowing me to take that sabbatical. At the New York State Archives and Library, I must thank Phil Lord, the chair of the New York State Geographic Names Committee, for his support of the project. Through a grant from the 2000 Larry J. Hackman Research Residency Program, I was able to spend a few weeks that summer collecting information in the archives. I thank Jill Rydberg for helping administer that grant, and Jim Folts and his staff in the archives for toting boxes of papers back and forth for me. They were all interested in the project and very helpful.

Have I forgotten anyone? Most probably. It is difficult to keep track of everyone who expressed interest, who told stories, and who sent me on the path to find some obscure reference. I thank them wholeheartedly even as I cannot remember all of them. And, through all the dark days of thinking that I would never get this done; through my days of writing that were sometimes manic, other times just crazy; and through the good times when I knew that this would be finished and that I would like the result, Peter Jones, who himself knows the loneliness of writing, was always quietly supportive.

There are probably errors in this work. They are all mine; they are the fault of no one else.

Abbreviations

A&K	Aber and King, *The History of Hamilton County*
Albany	Amasa J. Parker, *Landmarks of Albany County*
Allegany	*History of Allegany County, New York*
Amana	http://www.amanacolonies.com
Anderson	Anderson, Glengarry Historical Society, Internet posting
APN	Stewart, *American Place-Names*
Bayles	Bayles, *Historical and Descriptive Sketches of Suffolk County with a Historical Outline of Long Island*
Bedell	Bedell, *Now and Then and Long Ago in Rockland County*
Beers	Beers, *Gazetteer and Biographical Record of Genesee County, New York, 1788–1890*
Blake	Blake, *The History of Putnam County, New York*
Bolton	Bolton, *The History of the Several Towns, Manors and Patents of the County of Westchester from Its First Settlement to the Present Time*, vols. 1 and 2
Bowen	Bowen, *History of Lewis County, New York, 1880–1965*
Bruce	Bruce, *Onondaga's Centennial*
Child	Child, *Gazetteer and Business Directory of Sullivan County, New York*
Churchill	Churchill, *Landmarks of Oswego County, New York*
Clark	J. M.Clark, "The Place Names of Schenectady County"
Clark-O	Joshua V. H. Clark, *Onondaga; or Reminiscences of Earlier and Later Times*, vol. 2
Clayton	Clayton, *History of Onondaga County, New York*
Cleveland	Cleveland, *History and Directory of Yates County*, Vols. 1 and 2
Cole	Cole, *History of Rockland County, New York*
Cowles	Cowles, *Landmarks of Wayne County, New York*
C&V	Chernow and Vallasi, *The Columbia Encyclopedia*, 5th ed.
Curtis	Curtis, *Our County and Its People: A Memorial Record of St. Lawrence County, New York*

D&H	Downs and Hedley, *History of Chautauqua County, New York, and Its People*
D&P	Durant and Pierce, *History of Jefferson County, New York*
Delaware	*History of Delaware County*
Donaldson	Donaldson, *A History of the Adirondacks,* vols. 1 and 2
Doty	Doty, *A History of Livingston County, New York*
Doty-G	Doty, *History of the Genesee Country*
Ellis	Ellis, *History of Cattaraugus County, New York*
Ellis-C	Ellis, *History of Columbia County, New York*
Flick	Flick, *History of the State of New York*, vol. 10, *The Empire State*
French	French, *Gazetteer of the State of New York*
Fried	Fried, *The Early History of Kingston and Ulster County, New York*
Frothingham	Frothingham, *History of Montgomery County, New York*
Fulton	*History of Montgomery and Fulton Counties, New York*
Gannett	Gannett, *The Origin of Certain Place-Names of the United States*
Gay	Gay, *Historical Gazetteer of Tioga County, New York*
Goodwin	Goodwin, *Pioneer History, or, Cortland County and the Border Wars of New York*
Green	Green, *The History of Rockland County*
Greene	*History of Greene County*
Grumet	Grumet, *Native American Place Names in New York City*
Hakes	Hakes, *Landmarks of Steuben County, New York*
Harder	Harder and Smallman, *Claims to Name: Toponyms of St. Lawrence County*
Herkimer	*History of Herkimer County, New York*
Hough-J	Hough, *A History of Jefferson County in the State of New York from the Earliest Period to the Present*
Hough-L	Hough, *A History of Lewis County in the State of New York*
Hough-SLF	Hough, *A History of St. Lawrence and Franklin Counties, New York*
Howell	Howell, *Bicentennial History of Albany: History of the County of Albany, N.Y., from 1609 to 1886*
Hurd-C&F	Hurd, *History of Clinton and Franklin Counties*
Hurd-O	Hurd, *History of Otsego County, New York*
Jackson	Jackson, *The Encyclopedia of New York City*
Johnson	Johnson, *History of Washington County, New York*
Johnson-O	Johnson, *History of Oswego County, New York*
Johnstown	Workers of the Writers' Program Works Projects Administration. *Johnstown in New York State's Mohawk Valley*
Landon	Landon, *The North Country: A History Embracing Jefferson, St. Lawrence, Oswego, Lewis, and Franklin Counties, New York*, vol. 1
Lederer	Lederer, *The Place-Names of Westchester County, New York*
Lounsbury	Lounsbury, *Iroquois Place-Names in the Champlain Valley*

Mc-M	McIntosh, *History of Monroe County, New York*
Mc-W	McIntosh, *History of Wayne County, New York*
McMahon	McMahon, *Chautauqua County: A History*
Melone	Melone, *History of Central New York*
Milliken	Milliken, "Ontario County Place Names"
Minard	Minard, *Allegany County and Its People*
Montgomery	*History of Montgomery and Fulton Counties, New York*
Morgan	Morgan, *League of the Iroquois*
Munsell	Munsell, *History of the County of Schenectady, New York, from 1662 to 1886*
Murray	Murray, *Delaware County: History of the Century, 1797–1897*
Norris	Norris, *The Origins of Place Names in Tompkins County*
North	North, *Our County and Its People; a Descriptive and Biographical Record of Genesee County, New York*
Noyes	Noyes, *A History of Schoharie County*
Oneida	*History of Oneida County*
Orleans	Lynch, Gibson, and Pratt, *Orleans County History*
P&H-C	Peirce and Hurd, *History of Chemung County, New York*
P&H-S	Peirce and Hurd, *History of Schuyler County, New York*
P&H-T	Peirce and Hurd, *History of Tompkins County, New York*
P&H-Ti	Peirce and Hurd, *History of Tioga County, New York*
Parker	Arthur C. Parker, "Indian Place Names of the Genesee Country"
Peck	Peck, *Landmarks of Monroe County, New York*
Pelletreau	Pelletreau, *History of Putnam County, New York*
Pool	Pool, *Landmarks of Niagara County*
Quinlan	Quinlan, *History of Sullivan County*
R&C	Ruttenber and Clark, *History of Orange County, New York*
Roberts	Roberts, *Historical Gazetteer of Steuben County, New York*
Roscoe	Roscoe, *History of Schoharie County, New York*
S&S	Shonnard and Spooner, *History of Westchester County, New York, from Its Earliest Settlements to the Year 1900*
Selkreg	Selkreg, *Landmarks of Tompkins County, New York*
Seneca	*History of Seneca County, New York*
Sias	Sias, *A Summary of Schoharie County*
Signor	Signor, *Landmarks of Orleans County*
Smith-B	Smith, *History of Broome County*
Smith-C&M	Smith, *History of Chenango and Madison Counties*
Smith-D	Smith, *History of Dutchess County, New York*
Smith-E	Smith, *History of the City of Buffalo and Erie County*, vol. 1
Smith-Ex	Smith, *History of Essex County*
Smith-W	Smith, *History of Warren County*

Stewart — Stewart, *Names on the Land*

Stone — Stone, *Washington County, New York: Its History to the Close of the Nineteenth Century*

Storke — Storke, *History of Cayuga County, New York*

Suffolk — *History of Suffolk County, New York* (The page numbers in this reference are not continuous; each town history starts over with 1. So the references read: Suffolk/town name:page number.)

Syl-S — Sylvester, *History of Saratoga County, New York*

Syl-U — Sylvester, *History of Ulster County, New York, Part Second*

Vedder — Vedder, *Official History of Greene County, New York, 1651–1800*

Weise — Weise, *History of the Seventeen Towns of Rensselaer County*

Williams — Williams, *Niagara County, New York*, vol. 1

Winsche — Winsche, Richard A. 1999. *The History of Nassau County Community Place-Names*

WPANY — Writer's Program of the Work Projects Administration. 1940. *New York: A Guide to the Empire State*

WPANYA — Writer's Program of the Work Projects Administration of New York State research papers in the New York State Archives.

WPANYC — Writer's Program of the Work Projects Administration. 1939. *New York City Guide*

WPANYD — Writer's Program of the Work Projects Administration. 1937. *Dutchess County*

WPANYS — Writer's Program of the Work Projects Administration. 1940. "A Survey of New York State Place-Names." Unpublished manuscript in the New York State Archives.

WPAPA — Writer's Program of the Work Projects Administration. 1940. *Pennsylvania: A Guide to the Keystone State*

WPARM — Writer's Program of the Work Projects Administration. 1937. *Rochester and Monroe County*

WPAW — Writer's Program of the Work Projects Administration in the State of New York. 1942. *Warren County: A History and Guide*

Wyoming — *History of Wyoming County* 1841.

Introduction

PLACENAMES TELL STORIES. They are not just labels for locations but are cultural and historical guideposts to past events and ideas. This book is primarily a compilation of placenames and their origins, the "whys" of their naming. Within those origins are embedded ways of thinking, methods of decision making, and exotic influences that open the way to seeing how people lived in the early United States.

New York State was a prime mover in the early days of the nation. Pivotal battles were fought there in several wars, before and after the Revolution. Its Erie Canal helped open the way west for people, their ideas, and their goods, as well as providing a faster way for resources from the west to reach the cities on the East Coast. New York City was the hub around which new immigrants circled, deciding on what to do with their lives: stay in the urban swarm or go west to find a new destiny. New York State placenames tell the stories of all these events and decisions, and commemorate the influential people, famous and local, involved in them—some long forgotten except for their names.

However, the placenames do not trace events and people within New York State only: as the country grew, people from New York began to move to other parts of the new, emerging United States—and they took their placenames with them. Lansing, Michigan; Syracuse and Manhattan, Kansas; Geneseo, Illinois; Oneonta Park, California; Wyoming—these are just a few of the names transplanted from New York State.

Placenames are also labels, and, as such, must follow some rules so that they can serve this function well. Each must be unique so that mail, trains, and now FedEx deliveries and responses to 911 calls can get where they are supposed to go. To that end, early in the country's history, the Post Office Department gave each new post office a name that was not duplicated anywhere else in the state. Often, the post office name was different from the name of the settlement's that it served. This policy was not meant, as some have contended, to change the local placename; it was designed simply to preserve the singularity of each post office. In practice, however, the policy did generate confusion, eventually leading many settlements to change their names to match those of the post offices serving them.

The railroads were another huge influence on placenames, systematically imprinting the landscape with names not only in New York State but all across the country. The railroads would set up stations in locations that were appropriate and convenient to them. Like the post offices, the stations needed names to distinguish them from one another, so a railroad official would name them, often without regard to local placenames. As with the post offices, when the name of a station differed from the name of the nearest settlement, often the settlement would eventually change its name to match that of the station. Decisions over names were most complicated when a single place had different names for its settlement, post office, and train station; there would come a time when a decision would be made to use just one name for all three institutions.

Neither the Post Office Department nor the railroads had any real system for assigning names. Office and station names had to be different from others around them, so they came from local people—the first postmaster at a new post office, for example—or they complimented someone—perhaps the daughter of the president of the railroad. Sometimes they were picked out of thin air—just as long as they were short, euphonius, and different.

Throughout the book, the reader will find name origins from the post office, from the railroads, from the various canals built to facilitate the movement of goods and people between the interior and the Atlantic, as well as commemorative names for local citizens or prominent national and international figures.

New York State set the trend for naming in the rest of the country, but it followed general fashions as well. Exotic names were often used because they were different from nearby names and because they were, well, exotic. They evoked images of places and events that most people at that time would never see or participate in, but which were interesting or appealing to them. When France's Marquis de Lafayette, a prominent friend to the colonies during the Revolution, toured the United States soon after its formation, he generated an excitement that resulted in a number of names: Fayette, Fayetteville, LaFayette. During various South American revolutions, places in New York State were named for Peru, Bolivar, Mexico, Montezuma. When Napoleon was marching his armies across Europe and around the Mediterranean, more names appeared: Moscow, Borodino, eventually even Waterloo and Austerlitz.

The Bible provided many names. It was the one book that most people read and it contains a plethora of names, each with some meaning attached. The Bible is a source of names signaling hope (Bethlehem), describing similar geographic locations (Jericho and Egypt), or teaching lessons to the next generation (Sodom).

Probably the most famous New York State trend was that of naming places with classical names. After the Revolutionary War, the state government set aside a large tract of land in the central part of the state to be used as payment to veterans of the war. This Military Tract was subdivided into sections that later became towns. In 1790, the land commissioners responsible for the tract were charged with naming it and dispensing parcels to veterans after it had been surveyed. They approved the classical names that were written on the map of the survey: those of Roman tribunes, Greek gods and goddesses, philosophers and poets and orators, battles and cities. Simeon DeWitt, the state's surveyor general, was first blamed for this naming theme. He denied it. The land commissioners were blamed. They denied it. Finally, it was found that a deputy secretary of state, a man named Robert Harpur, was responsible. But it seems that he was under the orders of the land commissioners, so they must share the blame. The classical naming, however, was not such a strange event. The New World was new: it was rugged and perceived to be uncivilized by the recognized civilizations of the Old World. Naming settlements with classical names was an assertion that the people in this new, rough, untamed place were themselves not rough and untamed but educated, literate, and civilized.

Much of the later naming of places in New York State was done by people originally from England. However, other nationalities had quite an influence. The Dutch and the French held parts of what became New York State for many years before the British took over. Their names are everywhere: Dutch in the Hudson River Valley and Long Island; French in the Adirondacks and in the western part of the state. Enclaves of German settlers named many places in the Hudson and Mohawk River Valleys. The Irish and the Scottish also contributed names. But, of course, people were already living in the area long before any Europeans showed up. We now call them Native Americans, indigenous peoples, Indians, but they had their own names for themselves and their places. Many of these names were recorded by the early European explorers and traders and used, although often in changed forms. The Native American names all had meanings, many of which are now lost or are conjectures. It is difficult to know how much credence to put into the meanings that were recorded, but until a comprehensive, detailed study is done on Native American placenames in the United States, we will have to rely on the sources that we have.

Which Names Were Chosen, Why, and How the Research Was Done

The writing of any book requires making decisions about what to include—and what to exclude. In my case this task was complicated by the sheer wealth of names within the state. According to the United States Board on Geographic Names (USBGN, a section of the U.S. Geological Survey that is the official name authority for the country), there are about 6,800 populated places in New York State. The board defines a populated place as "a place or area with clustered or scattered buildings and a permanent human population (city, settlement, town, village)." In New York State, the legal designations for local settlements are *county, city, town, hamlet,* and *village.* A town may contain one or more villages or hamlets, and a county may contain a number of towns and cities. These various legal entities may share a name or their names may differ. Although the USBGN's list covers the thousands of names given other kinds of places within the state, such as natural features (rivers and mountains) and man-made ones (airports, malls, and highways), these will have to be addressed in another book.

To reduce this list to manageable proportions, I first decided to limit the discussion to names of populated places, knowing that, since many settlements are named for natural features, I would thus be able to include brief discussions of the names of at least some of those features. However, that still left nearly 7000 names. My choices within that list were guided by the consideration that any book is written for the edification and benefit of its readers. While lovers of placenames might not care about the size and accessibility of the settlements whose names I was recording, travelers would. I therefore decided to exclude the names of populated places not visited by general travelers in the state, many of which are not even listed on road maps. So, using three road maps of New York State—the *Rand McNally Road Atlas* (1999), the *National Geographic Road Atlas* (1999), and an AAA "Map of New York State" (1999)—I narrowed the list of names that I had received from the Geographic Names Information System (the computerized arm of the USBGN) to those appearing on at least two of the three maps. This brought the number down to a manageable figure of about 2,500. I am hopeful that I will be able to include the names of the other populated places, as well as the names of natural features, in later, revised editions of this book. Placename research never ends.

Once I had a list of names, I needed to find their origins. A number of people have written books on placenames in parts of New York State, but there has been no one reference book for placenames in the entire state. Histories or gazetteers often contain much placename information, but recording placenames is not their primary purpose.

The bibliography contains the complete list of the references that I used. There are several, though, that I want to highlight as extremely useful sources. Back in 1860, J. H. French published *The Historical and Statistical Gazetteer of New York State.* In it, he included many name origins when discussing the organizations of counties, towns, and villages.

In the late nineteenth century, there was a fashion to publish histories of counties. Many were published by the same companies; Munsell, Everts and Ensign, D. Mason, and F. W. Beers are just a few of the more prominent publishers. These histories contain a good deal of information, much of which is probably true and some of which is apocryphal but makes a good story. In many cases, these are the best references left about the nineteenth century that contain detailed information on the naming of places.

In the 1930s, the Writers' Program of the Works Projects Administration (WPA) published guidebooks to all of the states. In compiling the information for these guidebooks, many offices also collected information on placename origins. A few states published separate placename books in addition to the guidebooks, but many did not have the resources to do so; in those cases, the placename information was either included in the guidebooks or the notes and manuscripts were simply left unpublished. The New York State Archives in Albany have all the notes and the almost-finished manuscript for a book on the placenames of New York State. Most of the information collected by the WPA workers was from the same county histories that I had direct access to. However, there were some references that I could not find, so this secondhand information became invaluable as the only documentation about those books. Working with the WPA notes, incidentally, opened a window onto conditions for workers in the 1930s, who did some very tedious work. With some of them, it showed. Some made up name origins but provided page numbers to references so that I could verify whether information was in fact there. Others did not provide page numbers but did cite a book title. Still others were very meticulous and conscientious, so that if there were no name origin recorded, they said so. This WPA work constitutes a story that needs to be told in more detail than I can assign space to here.

I also found invaluable several more general sources, including George R. Stewart's *American Place-Names* and Henry Gannett's *The Origin of Certain Place-Names of the United States,* that contained much information on New York State placenames. The fifth edition of *The Columbia Encyclopedia* was likewise helpful tracing more general source information, such as identifying the Greek and Roman gods and goddesses and keeping track of which president served when. The third edition of *Merriam-Webster's Geographical Dictionary* was very useful in determining past spellings and locations of some of the more exotic names used in New York State.

Format of Entries

Each entry contains the name of the place and the county in which it is located. The place itself might be a town, a village, a city, or some other sort of settlement, and the type is indicated in the entry. Some entries are for multiple settlements in the same county, usually those with variations of the same name (such as "West Edmeston" or "Old Chatham") that derive from the same origin. Places with the same name that are in different counties are listed separately because they often have different origins.

I tried to include as much information as possible in each entry, especially about past names for each place. It is interesting to trace the succession of names by which a place is known as they progress from local appellations—Hog's Hollow, for instance—to something more elegant, going through a number of local residents' names in the process.

Dates of post office establishment, town organization, or village incorporation are included where they were available. These dates help to illuminate trends in naming, as well as providing a location on the state's historical timeline.

At the end of each entry is an abbreviated list of sources with page numbers linked to the bibliography at the end of the book. These citations are provided for those readers interested in seeking more information about a place than just the name origin.

In some cases, very little is known about *why* a place was given its name. We may know when the name was adopted, we might even know the source of the name (if it is an exotic name, for example), but we do not know why a particular name was chosen. That information is lost to us. We may speculate on the reason the name was used, but doing so is dangerous. In plenty of cases, we do know why a name was chosen, yet had we speculated on the reason from the name alone, we would have guessed wrong. For this reason, when I have been unable to document the reason for a choice of placename, I have refrained from speculation.

Included in an appendix to the book is a list of placenames (drawn from my edited list of 2,500 placenames) about which I could find no information at all. I include this list in the hope that anyone having or finding information about a name on it will share that information with me, so that I can include it in a later edition.

Finally, I wanted to write each entry as a story, not as a dry compilation of facts. To this end, the reader will find that I tried to avoid using the phrases "Named for . . ." or "This place was named . . ." in favor of a more direct approach. "So-and-so built a bridge here in some year" tells a better story and contains all the relevant information. This method sometimes requires the reader to make the link between "So-and-soburg" and the fellow's name without it being explicitly stated, but I expect that the readers of this book are intelligent enough not to need everything spelled out for them.

I must make a note here that the USGS Geographic Names Information System (a compilation of all the names that appear on the USGS topographic maps) listed no names in New York State beginning with *X*. I almost made one up, just to have one—but then people would not trust the rest of my work, so the *X* slot remains empty.

From ABBOTTS to ZURICH

Auburn © *2004 by Jon Crispin*

Abbotts. Cattaraugus. This place used to be called Abbott's Corners. [Ellis:498]

Accord. Ulster. When it came time to ask for a post office, the citizens could not agree on a name. Someone sent in the petition with the name Discord; the post office department returned it with a post office named Accord. [Syl-U:218; WPANY:404]

Adams, Adams Center. Jefferson. The town of Adams was formed in 1802 and named for President John Adams. The post office in the village of Adams was established in 1806. Adams Center was formerly called Adams Five Corners. [APN:3; D&P:242, 249, 255; French:355; Gannett:18; Hough-J:71, 75]

Adams Basin. Monroe. This place on the Erie Canal was named for the Adams family and for the enlargement of the canal at this point to allow for docking and maintenance. [French:400; WPANYS]

Addison. Steuben. The town was formed in 1796 as Middletown. The early settlers called the place Tuscarora. The name was changed in 1808 for that of the village, which was named for Joseph Addison, an English writer. The post office was opened in 1804, and the village was incorporated in 1854. [APN:3; French:621; Gannett:19; Roberts:92, 96; Steuben:39, 305]

Adirondack. Warren. The hamlet was called Mill Brook. Then the name was changed for the mountains in which the town is located. The word *adirondack* is a Native American word that means "wood or tree eaters." The story is that the Iroquois had come into the area and took it over from previous occupants, driving them northward and taunting them with the derogative "tree eater," meaning that the conquered were no longer strong or brave enough to kill game and would be reduced to eating bark and trees. [APN:3; Gannett:19; WPANYS; Smith-W:32]

Adrian. Steuben. Nathan Crosby and his family settled here in 1790, and the place became known as Crosbyville. The post office and railroad station were named Adrian when they were established, and the hamlet soon followed suit. [Steuben:78; WPANYA]

Afton. Chenango. In 1857, the town of Afton was separated from the town of Bainbridge. The towns were rivals, and the new town decided to have a name that started with the letter "A" in order to be ahead of Bainbridge. Afton is a river in Britain that the Scottish poet Burns described in "Flow Gently Sweet Afton." Before the separation of the towns, the post office and village at Afton were called South Bainbridge. [APN:3; Smith-C&M:134, 144; WPANY:452]

Airmont. Rockland. Named for its geographic location as the highest settled point in the county. [WPANYA]

Akron. Erie. The village had been referred to as the Corporation, but when time came to get a post office, about 1836, Sylvester Goff, who became the first postmaster, suggested the name Akron, from the Greek *akros*, meaning "extreme" or "highest," for the hills in the area. There is no evidence that it was named for the city in Ohio. The Seneca village that had been here was called Gaskosada, "waterfall." [Parker:298; Smith-E:370]

Alabama, South Alabama. Genesee. The town was formed in 1826 as Gerrysville. It was intended to be named for David Gary, one of the early settlers, but it ended up inadvertently being named for Elbridge Gerry, a former vice president and the fellow after whom the word *gerrymandering* was coined. In 1828, the name was changed for the state of Alabama, whose name comes from the Choctaw *alba aya mule*, "I clear the thicket," although other references say it means "Here I rest." South Alabama was the name of the post office in the village of Smithville, which had been named for Dr. Smith who settled here from Vermont. [Beers:117; French:324; Gannett:20; North:457, 459; Parker:300]

Albany. Albany. This place has had many names by many different people over the years because of its favorable location on the Hudson River. It was called Pempotuwuthut, "place of the council fires," by the Mohicans; Schenegh-tada, "through the pine woods," by the Iroquois; Gaishtinic by the Minci; Fuyck, "hoop net," for the shape of the bend in the river where fish were caught, by the Dutch. The Dutch then changed the name. From 1634 to 1664, the settlement was referred to as Beverwyck or Beverswyck, "a place for beavers." After the English took over in 1664, it went through a number of names. It became Fort Orange, in honor of William, Prince of Orange and Nassau; Rensselaerwyck, for the Van Rensselaers, a preeminent family of patroons; Aurania, another name for Orange; Williamstadt, for William; New Orange, for the Duke of Orange; and finally Albany, in honor of James, Duke of York, Albany, and Ulster (who later became King James II), the brother of King Charles II. [Albany:283; APN:7; French:159; Gannett:20; Howell:460; WPANY:182; WPANYS]

Albertson. Nassau. The Long Island Railroad named this station in 1874 for the Albertson family, who had settled here in the mid-1800s. [Winsche:13]

Albion. Orleans. This village was called Newport (or, according to one reference, Freeport), until 1828, when a post office was established. Because there was another Newport in New York State, the post office was named with the ancient name for England. The town was formed in 1875 and named for the village. [APN:7; French:456, 513; Gannett:21; Orleans:48; Pool:273; Signor:216]

Alcove. Albany. The settlement was first called Stephensville for Archibald Stephens, who owned mills here. The post office was called Alcove, which later became the name of the settlement. [Albany:482; Howell:830; WPANYS]

Alden. Erie. The post office was established here in 1823 as Alden, named by one of the village's citizens for his wife's mother. [Gannett:21; Smith-E:443]

Alder Creek. Oneida. This settlement was named for the creek, a tributary of the Black River, which is named for the trees. [Oneida:125; WPANYS]

Alexander. Genesee. The town was formed in 1812. It took its name from the village, which was named for Alexander Rea, a surveyor for the Holland Land Company, through which he bought land here in 1802. Rea founded the village, then built a sawmill in 1804. [Beers:144; French:324; Gannett:21; North:461–2]

Alexandria Bay. Jefferson. The town of Alexandria was formed in 1821 and named for Alexander LeRay, son of James LeRay de Chaumont who fought in the war with Texas and then died in a duel in 1836. The village on the shore of the St. Lawrence River was surveyed and laid out as a village for LeRay in 1818. [D&P:268; French:355; Gannett:21; Hough-J:79]

Alfred, Alfred Station. Allegany. The town was formed in 1808 and named for Alfred the Great because of the similarity of this landscape to that of England. The village of Alfred was first called Alfred Center. The post office was established in about 1848. In 1894, the village and the post office names were changed to Alfred. Alfred Station had been called Bakers Bridge, named for the Baker family who built a pole bridge across the creek. Later, the settlement took the name of the town and the railroad station. [Allegany:147; French:169; Minard:643–4; WPANYS]

Allegany. Cattaraugus. The name of the town and village comes from the name of the river, which is a derivation of a Native American word, *welhikhana,* meaning "the best or the fairest river" or "long river." The town was organized in 1831 as Burton, but the name was changed in 1851. The village is on the Allegheny River. When the post office was established in the village in 1851, it was called Burton, but that changed when the town name changed. [APN:9; Ellis:445, 446; French:187; Gannett:22; Morgan:466; Parker:285]

Allens Hill. Ontario. Named either for Moses Allen, possibly the first white settler here in 1796, or for Nathaniel Allen, amother early settler, who started the first blacksmith's shop and later served as sheriff of Ontario County. He went on to serve as a member of the state Assembly in 1812, as paymaster during the War of 1812, and as an elected member of Congress in 1819. [Milliken:103; French:498]

Allentown. Allegany. The town of Allen was formed in 1823 and may have been named for Ethan Allen, a hero of the Revolution who, with his Green Mountain Boys, won the first American victory of the war by capturing Fort Ticonderoga. The entire Allen family lived in the area and could have been the source for the community's name: Solomon Allen was an early settler, Myron Allen a later one, and Riley Allen was an early oil producer/businessman. [French:170; Minard:498, 550–1, 555; WPANYA]

Alloway. Wayne. Captain Henry Towar came here from Alloa, Scotland, built a sawmill, a gristmill, and two stores, and named the place for his original home. [Cowles:246]

Alma. Allegany. The town was formed in 1854, the year Russian troops were defeated by the English, French, and Turkish armies on the Alma River during the Crimean War. The name became popular then as both a placename and as a name for girl babies. The settlement had been called Honeoye Corners, Honeoye, and Shongo, for James Shongo, a grandson of Mary Jemison. She was called the White Woman of the Genesee after she was adopted by two Seneca women when she was captured during the French and Indian War. She was given land in western New York in 1797. [Allegany:156; APN:10; French:170; Minard:551; WPANYS]

Almond, West Almond. Allegany. The town of Almond was formed in 1821. The name was suggested to Judge Crandall, who chose it, by a plate of almonds that was being passed around while the placename discussion was under way. The town of West Almond was formed in 1833, named for its location. [Allegany:159; French:170, 176; Minard:511]

Aloquin. Ontario. The name might be a shortening of Algonquin. Earlier, the settlement was known as Lewis Station and as Ennerdale. [Milliken:103]

Alpine. Schuyler. This place was named for its geographic location in a pretty, hilly part of the state. The post office was established in about 1852. [French:610; P&H-S:88; WPANYS]

Alplaus. Schenectady. The hamlet was named for the stream, the name of which comes from the Dutch *aalplaats,* "a place for eels." [Clark:57; French:597; Munsell:2; WPANYA]

Alps. Rensselaer. Named after the Swiss mountain range because of the physical character of the landscape. [APN:11; Weise:126; WPANYA]

Altamont. Albany. This was first called Knowerville for the Knower family who settled here in about 1792. In 1887, the name was changed to a romantic description of its mountainous location: *alta* is "high" in Italian; *mont* is "mountain" in French. [Albany:521, 523; APN:11; Howell:853; WPANYS]

Altay. Schuyler. This was first known as Kendall Hollow for Abel Kendall, who bought the land in 1813. When the post office was established, it was called Tobehanna for Big Tobehanna Creek on which the settlement was sited. There is no record of the current name origin. [French:612; P&H-S:221; WPANYA]

Altmar. Oswego. There is no record of name origin for this village. It might have been Alkmaer or Sand Bank or Pineville before changing its name to the present one. [Johnson-O:210, 278–9]

Alton. Wayne. A Mr. Gates settled here from Alton, Connecticut, and suggested the name. [Cowles:214; WPANYS]

Altona. Clinton. The town was formed in 1857 and named for a city in Germany, which is now part of Hamburg. [APN:11; French:235]

Amagansett. Suffolk. The name of this place comes from the Algonquian word for "a place with a well." [APN:12; Bayles:414; WPANYA]

Amawalk. Westchester. This place took its name from a Native American word meaning "people gathering up a little hill." [Lederer:8]

Amber. Onondaga. This "snug, pleasant little village" was probably named for a popular personal name. [APN:12; Clark-O:345; Clayton:350]

Amboy, Amboy Center, West Amboy. Oswego. The town of Amboy was organized in 1830 and named for the town in New Jersey. The name is a Native American term meaning "hollow inside, like a bowl." Amboy Center and

West Amboy were named for their locations in the town. [APN:12; French:520; Gannett:24; Johnson-O:348; Churchill:474, 477, 480]

Amenia, South Amenia, Amenia Union. Dutchess. The town was formed in 1788; its name comes from Young's *Conquest of Quebec* and means "pleasant" or "lovely" in Latin. The village of Amenia Union had been called Hitchcock's Corners for Solomon Hitchcock and his family, who came here from Norwalk, Connecticut, in about 1800. The post office was established in 1823. [French:269; Gannett:24; Smith-D:335; WPANYS]

Ames. Montgomery. This village was named for Fisher Ames (1758–1808), American statesman and orator. [French:412; Frothingham:248; Gannett:24; Montgomery:98]

Amherst, East Amherst. Erie. The town and the village were named for Amherst, Massachusetts, which was named for Lord Jeffrey Amherst, commander of the English forces in America in 1759–60 during the French and Indian War. [APN:13; French:282; Smith-E:400]

Amity. Orange. When the Presbyterian Church was formed, the name of the place was changed from Pochuck for something more euphonius and friendly. [French:510; R&C:579]

Amityville. Suffolk. Before 1840, this village was called West Neck South and Sweet Hollow. Its new name was to present it as a friendly place. [Bayles:173; French:636; Suffolk/Babylon:13; WPANYS]

Amsterdam. Montgomery. The town was organized in 1793 and named by Emanuel E. DeGraff, an early settler who had come from the Netherlands. The village that became the city had formerly been called Veedersburgh or Veddersburg for Albert (or Aaron) Vedder, who settled here during the Revolutionary War and built a sawmill and a gristmill. It was first called Vedder's Mills, then Veddersburg, then, in 1804, the name was changed to that of the Dutch city at the insistence of many settlers with ties to Holland. [APN:13; French:411; Frothingham:176, 184; Gannett:24; Montgomery:88]

Ancram, Ancramdale. Columbia. This area in which this settlement was located was originally part of Livingston Manor in Massachusetts, but became part of New York in 1853 after the residents petitioned Massachusetts in 1848. The town was formed in 1803 as Gallatin, named for Albert Gallatin, Thomas Jefferson's secretary of the treasury. In 1814, however, the name was changed to Ancram, after Ancaram, Scotland, the native home of the Livingston family. In 1830, a section was formed into a separate town, which then took the name of Gallatin. [Ellis-C:405; French:242–3; WPANYA]

Andover. Allegany. The town was formed in 1824. Many early settlers were from Connecticut and brought placenames from New England. The village was first known as Bakertown for Alpheus and Thaddeus Baker, who settled here in about 1807. [Allegany:186; French:171; Minard:585]

Angelica. Allegany. The town was formed in 1805 and named for the village, which was started in about 1801 and was named by Captain Philip Church for his mother, Angelica, the eldest daughter of General Philip Schuyler of the Revolutionary War. [Allegany:195; French:171; Minard:405]

Angola, Angola-on-the-Lake. Erie. The village of Angola was first called Evans Station for being in the town of Evans on the Erie Railroad. In about 1854, the post office was established as Angola and the village took that name. It might have been named for the country in Africa as a pleasant sounding name. The Seneca name for this place was Dyoahista, "depot place." [APN:15; French:290; Parker:297; Smith-E:580]

Annadale. Richmond. This place was named in about 1860 for Anna Seguine, a member of a prominent family in the area. [Jackson:38]

Annandale-on-Hudson. Dutchess. John Bard owned an estate in this area that was called Annandale. He donated land to St. Stephen's College, later called Bard College, here in the 1860s. The post office was established in 1865. [Smith-D:198–9]

Annsville. Westchester. Named for Ann Van Cortlandt de Lancey, a member of the prominent landowning Cortlandt family in the area. [French:698; Lederer:9]

Antwerp. Jefferson. The town was formed in 1810 and named for the Antwerp Company, a European land company. The village was called Indian River; the post office opened in 1809. The village was incorporated as Antwerp in 1853. [D&P:277–8; French:355; Hough-J:85]

Apalachin, South Apalachin. Tioga. The settlement was named for Apalacon or Apalachin Creek, which flows from Pennsylvania. The word might be related to Appalachian, the name given to the mountains, which comes from the name of a people, meaning "those by the sea." [APN:18; Gannett:26; Gay:398; P&H-Ti:145]

Apex. Delaware. The name indicates a summit or a high point, but there is no record of the origin of the name. [APN:18; WPANYS]

Appleton. Niagara. The settlement was first called Hess Road for the road cleared by Peter and James Hess in the 1820s. The post office was established as Hess Road, but the name of the settlement was changed to Appleton in 1896. [French:454; Pool:329; Williams:373, 390]

Apulia, Apulia Station. Onondaga. Named for the southern region in Italy. [APN:19; Gannett:27; WPANYA]

Aquebogue. Suffolk. In 1860, there were two places, Old or Lower Aquebogue and Upper Aquebogue. The first used the Jamesport post office and was a station on the Long Island Railroad. The second had its own post office. The name comes from an Algonquian word that means "head of the water" or "at the end of a small pond." [APN:19; French:637; Gannett:27; WPANYS]

Arcade. Wyoming. The town was known as China until 1866 when it took the name of its principal village. The village was named for the arches formed by the trees over its streets, and possibly with the allusion to Arcadia, a pastoral region of Greece. The post office was established when the village was incorporated, around 1871. [APN:20; WPANYS; Wyoming:116]

Arden. Orange. This hamlet was first established as the Greenwood Iron Works, in 1811, that became the Parrott Iron Company in 1880. E. H. Harriman had a twenty-thousand-acre estate here at the beginning of the twentieth century that was named for the forest in Shakespeare's *As You Like It*. The village took the name of the estate. [APN:21; WPANY:385; WPANYS]

Ardonia. Ulster. Named for Caleb's third son in the Hebrew Bible. [WPANYA]

Ardsley, Ardsley-on-Hudson. Westchester. The village of Ardsley had been called Ashford, for the English birthplace of an early settler, Captain King, who ran a pickle factory. But when petitioning for a post office in the early 1880s, it was found that there already was an Ashford post office in the state, so the new name was chosen to honor Cyrus W. Field's ancestral home in England. He had organized the company that laid the telegraph cable across the Atlantic and lived in the village. Ardsley-on-Hudson had started out as the Ardsley Casino of the Ardsley Country Club. The train station here was called "on Hudson"; this phrase was added to "Ardsley" to distinguish this place from the other. [Lederer:10–11; S&S:627]

Argusville. Schoharie. This settlement was formerly known as Molicks Mills, but then changed its name for the Albany newspaper, which was named for the all-seeing Greek mythological giant. The post office was established in 1840. [APN:21; French:604; Gannett:28; Noyes:156; Roscoe:313; WPANYA]

Argyle, North Argyle, South Argyle. Washington. The town was first granted by patent to Scottish immigrants in 1764. It was formed as a town in 1786. Its name comes from the Scottish duke of Argyle. The villages are named for their locations in the town, although North Argyle had been called Stevenson's Corner for the first postmaster, Daniel Stevenson. [French:679; Gannett:28; Johnson:230, 243; Stone:414, 425]

Arkport. Steuben. The ark was a type of canal boat or river craft used in the early nineteenth century. In 1800, Christopher Hurlbut started to transport grain from this region to Baltimore on the Canisteo River and the canal system using the ark, and the place's name reflected this activity. [APN:22; Roberts:412; Steuben:120–1, 307]

Arkville. Delaware. A house owned by Noah Dimmick, built on a hill, was the only one left standing after the Bush Kill flooded, sometime in the late 1700s. The house became known as the Ark; the settlement name followed. The post office was opened in 1837. [Delaware:261, 264; Murray:508; WPANYS]

Arkwright. Chautauqua. The town and the hamlet were named for Sir Richard Arkwright, the inventor of the water frame, a type of spinning machine. The place was known for the first cooperative cheese factory in the state, established by Asahel Burnham in 1862. [D&H:117; McMahon:289, 290]

Arlington. Dutchess. This suburb of Poughkeepsie was named for an English village. [APN:23; WPANYD:103]

Armonk. Westchester. This place on the Byram River was called Mill or Mile Square until 1853. At that time, it took a part of the Native American name of the river, Chaubunkongamaug, meaning "fishing place." [APN:22; Bolton(1):713; French:703; Gannett:28; Lederer:11, 29]

Arverne. Queens. This was a neighborhood developed by Remington Vernam in 1882. His signature he used on his checks—R. Vernam—inspired the name of the community. [Jackson:60]

Asharoken. Suffolk. This village was settled in about 1646. The name is said to come from that of a local Native American chief whose land this had been. The village was incorporated in 1925. [WPANYS]

Ashland. Greene. When the town was formed in 1848, it was named for the home of Henry Clay, American statesman from Kentucky, 1777–1852. The village was first called Scienceville because the families who first settled there were very interested in higher education. Then it was called Windham. Finally, its name came to match that of the post office. [French:331; Gannett:29; Vedder:13, 16; WPAW]

Ashokan. Ulster. Named for the Algonquian word for "little mouth," meaning the outlet of a small stream. [APN:24]

Ashville. Chautauqua. Named for the four asheries that were located here. The first one was built in 1822. Ashes were created by burning hardwood and were used in the making of soap and glass. The ashes were leached with water to create lye, then the boiled lye was quickly cooled to create a hard lump called potash, which was used in the manufacture of glass. [D&H:198; McMahon:85–6, 290]

Astoria. Queens. This place was formerly called Hallett's Cove. Stephen A. Halsey, a fur merchant who developed this area starting in 1839, proposed that the place be named for John Jacob Astor, who built his fortune in the 1820s and 1830s in the fur trade. [French:548; Gannett:30; Jackson:63; WPANYC:563]

Athens. Greene. The village was settled in 1686 and called Loonenburgh, for Jan Van Loon, a patent holder. Between 1790 and 1840, New Englanders moved in just on the outskirts of Loonenburgh and called their part of the village Esperanza, "hope." They had a dream of making this village a prosperous rival to Hudson on the opposite bank of the river. They laid out streets with names such as Liberty, Equality, Beer, Art, Happiness, and so on. Both parts of the village were merged when they were incorporated as the village of Athens, named for the Greek city. [French:331; Gannett:30; Vedder:24, 26; WPANY:591; WPANYS]

Athol. Warren. This place was called Thurman, when it was settled in about 1795, for the town in which it is located. But the name was changed for the birth-place of many of the early settlers, the Athol district in Scotland. [APN:26; WPANYA; WPANYS; WPAW:176, 210]

Athol Springs. Erie. Named for the district in Scotland and the springs in the area. [APN:26]

Atlanta. Steuben. The settlement had been called Bloods for Calvin Blood, an early resident. Sometime between 1891 and 1896, the name was changed for the more pleasant-sounding name of the city in Georgia, which was coined by railroad builder J. E. Thompson in 1845 for the terminus of the Western and Atlantic Railroad. [APN:27; French:624; Roberts:248; Steuben:308–9; WPANYS]

Atlantic Beach. Nassau. This village was known as Long Beach in 1678, later as Long Beach West. It took its name for its location after about 1889. [Win-sche:13]

Atlantique. Suffolk. This is an alternative spelling for Atlantic, the body of water on which the village sits.

Attica, Attica Center. Wyoming. The town was formed in 1811 and was named for the district in ancient Greece during the time of much classical naming. The village was formerly known as Phelps Settlement for Zerah Phelps who came here from Connecticut in 1802. The Native American name for the place was Gwehtaanetecarnundodeh, meaning "the red village." [APN:27; Gannett:31; Morgan:467; WPANYS; Wyoming:131]

Attlebury. Dutchess. This railroad station and post office of the 1860s was prob-ably named for Attleboro, England. [APN:27; French:277; Gannett:31; Smith-D:292]

Auburn. Cayuga. John L. Hardenbergh came from Ulster County in 1792 to set-tle on land he had first seen as a surveyor of the military lands. His cabin even-tually drew others who opened stores, mills, and inns. This settlement, soon known as Hardenbergh's Corners, displaced the native peoples who had been living in the area. In June 1803, the name of Hardenbergh's Corners was changed to Auburn. The place had grown and been designated as a county seat for which residents thought a more dignified name would suit the place better. After some discussion, the name chosen was Auburn, from Oliver Goldsmith's poem "The Deserted Village," which begins, "Sweet Auburn! loveliest village of the plain," and goes on to decry the movement of youth from the rural villages in England in the 1700s to the growing industrial cities, such as Manchester and London. The irony here is that Auburn, New York, grew into an industrial center itself by the early twentieth century and no longer would look like the village for which it was named. [APN:27; Storke:139–44; WPANY:198]

Augusta. Oneida. General Augustus Van Horn promised a new military hat to Thomas Cassety, an early settler here from New England, if the town, organized in 1798, would be named for him. Looks like Tom got his hat. [French:462; Oneida:119]

Auriesville. Montgomery. This place, the site of the memorial shrine to Isaac Jogues and other Jesuits who were missionaries here in the 1630s (and who were killed and later canonized as the first North American Catholic saints), is named for Auries Creek, on whose mouth into the Mohawk River it sits. The name is said to be that of a Native American warrior. [APN:28; French:413; Frothingham:280, 285; WPANY:479]

Aurora. Cayuga. General Benjamin Ledyard had come to what became Cayuga County as an agent and clerk for the apportionment of Military Tract lands in the 1790s. After serving as clerk of Onondaga County, he became clerk for Cayuga County when that was sectioned from Onondaga County in 1799. He had been a captain in the army during the American Revolution. He named this village for the Latin word for "dawn." It seems that he was impressed with the view of Cayuga Lake, on the eastern shore of which the village sits, at dawn. The Native American name for this place was Deawendote, which meant "constant dawn." [APN; Morgan:470; WPANY:428]

Ausable Chasm, Au Sable Forks. Clinton. The town of Ausable took its name from the river, which was named by the French. The word meant "sandy" or "river of sand," said to derive from a sand bar in the river. Au Sable Forks lies at the junction of the east and south branches of the Au Sable River. The first bridge over the chasm was built at Ausable Chasm in 1805. [APN:28; French:235; Gannett:32; Hurd-C&F:247; WPANYA]

Austerlitz. Columbia. The town was formed in 1818 and was to be named New Ulm. But upon hearing that another town was being named Waterloo, after the site of Napoleon's famous defeat to the British, Martin Van Buren, then a state senator, instead named this town Austerlitz, after the site of a victory of Napoleon's, with the words, "There's an Austerlitz for your Waterloo!" The village was formerly called Upper Green River, but that name became applied to another locality and this one took that of the town. [APN:28; Ellis-C:381, 383; French:243; WPANY:543]

Ava. Oneida. The town was organized in 1846 and named for the city that was Burma's capital at the time of this town's naming. The village had been called

Ava Corners, but the post office was Ava. [French:462; Gannett:32; Oneida:123; WPANYS]

Averill Park. Rensselaer. In 1880, what was the western part of the village of Sand Lake became a separate place with its own post office, at that time called Averill. The name comes from a local prominent family. [Weise:141]

Avoca. Steuben. The village had been called Buchanan for the first settler, Michael Buchanan, who had come here in about 1800. In 1843, when the town was formed, it needed a name. At the request of Sophia White, a young woman on her deathbed (or so the story goes), the town was named for the place in Ireland that was commemorated by Thomas Moore in his poem "Sweet Vale of Avoca." [APN:29; French:622; Gannett:32; Roberts:112; Steuben:44, 319–20]

Avon, East Avon. Livingston. The town was formed as Hartford in 1789. Its name was changed in 1808 for Shakespeare's river. [APN:29; Doty-L:485; French:382; Gannett:32]

B

Buffalo © *2004 by Jon Crispin*

Babylon, West Babylon. Suffolk. The village and town were named for the ancient Middle Eastern city by the mother of Nathaniel Conklin, who had built a house here and placed an inscription on the chimney calling it New Babylon. The village is on a neck of land, the Native American name of which was Sampowans, Sampaoms, Sumpwans, or Sunquams. It was known as South Huntington until Conklin's name became popular. [APN:31; Bayles:177; Gannett:32; Suffolk/Babylon:9; WPANY:707; WPANYS]

Bainbridge. Chenango. When the town was formed in 1791, its name was Jericho, for the city in the Bible. The name was changed in 1814 to honor Commodore William Bainbridge, a hero of the U.S. Navy in the War of 1812. [APN:32, 227; French:225; Smith-C&M:155, 167; WPANYS]

Baiting Hollow. Suffolk. This settlement was once called Fresh Pond, but there is no record of how the present name came about. [Suffolk/Riverhead:5]

Bakers Mills. Warren. The original settlers here, in about 1860, were the Baker family. In 1936, Samuel Coplon, the "Santa Claus of the North Country," moved his toy distribution center here from North Creek. He had been giving gifts to children in the area for thirty years; his last Christmas was in 1937. [WPANY:493; WPANYA; WPANYS; WPAW:193]

Baldwin, Baldwin Harbor. Nassau. This settlement was originally named Hick's Neck in 1671, for John Hicks, an early settler. Just after the Revolutionary War, it became Milburn Corners, named for Milburn Creek. In 1810, the name was changed to Bethel for the Bethel Chapel. In 1825 Thomas Baldwin bought land here, built a hotel—the Baldwin House—and ran a general store—T. Baldwin and Sons. The place became known as Baldwinville until 1868 when the railroad named the station Fox Borough for Charles Fox, president of the South Side Railroad of Long Island. In 1897, after much discussion about what the name should be, the place became Baldwins. In 1900, the name lost the *s*. [French:547; Winsche:14–5]

Baldwinsville. Onondaga. When Dr. Jonas Baldwin came here in 1807, the place was called Columbia. When the post office was established in 1817, it was called Baldwin's Bridge for the bridge that he had built over the Seneca River. Soon that name was changed to the present one. [Bruce:744–5; Clark-O:160; Clayton:315, 317; Gannett:33]

Ballston Center, Ballston Lake, Ballston Spa. Saratoga. Reverend Eliphalet Ball came here with others in about 1777. As the settlement grew, it took his name and was called Balltown. Eventually an *s* was added to the spelling. The town was organized in 1788 as Ballston. The village of Ballston Spa took its named from the medicinal springs in the area, being first called Ballston Springs. [French:586; Gannett:34; Syl-S:246, 250; WPANYS]

Balmat. St. Lawrence. This place was named for Jean de Balmat, also written as John D. Balmat, who married a daughter of one of the officers who accompanied General Lafayette in 1777 in the American Revolution. [Harder:8]

Balmville. Orange. This place was first called Hampton, but the name was changed for a large tree that was locally called the Balm of Gilead. [R&C:279]

Bangall. Dutchess. This was a post village on Wappingers Creek in the 1860s; tradition has its name coming from the phrase "bang all," uttered when things go wrong, in this case when a peddler's horse was killed by some local boys. [French:277; Smith-D:295]

Bangor, North Bangor, West Bangor. Franklin. The town was organized in 1812 and named for a place in Wales. West Bangor was first known as Pottersville for Levi Potter, a tavernkeeper. [APN:34; Gannett:34; Landon:228; WPANYS]

Barcelona. Chautauqua. At one time, this place on the shores of Lake Erie was called Portland Harbor. In the 1820s, a lighthouse was built here that was lighted with natural gas from a gas spring just under a mile away. In 1831, the Barcelona Company, a developer, laid out a city at this location, and named it after the city in Spain. [APN:35; D&H:245; McMahon:99; WPANY:475]

Barker. Niagara. This village is named for David Barker, who owned the land here in the 1830s. For a while, it was called Somerset Station for its stop on the Rome, Watertown, and Ogdensburg Railroad. The village was incorporated in 1908 as Barker for the early landowner. [Pool:319; Williams:386–8; WPA-NYS]

Barnes Corners. Lewis. Elisha Barnes came here in 1805 from Middletown, Connecticut. [Bowen:458; Hough-L:206]

Barneveld. Oneida. The village of Trenton was incorporated in 1819 as Oldenbarnevelt, a name given the place by Gerrit Boon for a Dutch patriot who was hanged in 1619 at the age of eighty-two. In 1833, the name of the village was changed to Trenton, but mail was being sent to Trenton, New Jersey, instead, so a petition to change the post office and train station name back to Barneveld was granted in 1903. The village name, however, was not officially changed from Trenton until 1975. The Native American name for the village of Trenton was Oseteadaque, "in the bone." [French:467; Morgan:472; Oneida:191]

Barre Center, West Barre. Orleans. The town of Barre was formed in 1818 and named by John Lee, who came here from Barre, Massachusetts, which had been named for Colonel Isaac Barre, a friend to the American colonists while a member of the British parliament. Barre Center was named for its geographic location in the town. West Barre was first known as Manchester's Corners for Benson Manchester, a resident there. Then it was called Jackson's Corners for Ralph Jackson, but it became West Barre when the post office opened. [APN:36; French:513; Gannett:35; Orleans:82; Signor:461–2, 504, 506]

Barrytown. Dutchess. Named for William T. Barry, postmaster general of the United States during the term of President Andrew Jackson (1829–37). [Gannett:35; WPANYA]

Barryville. Sullivan. Named for William T. Barry, postmaster general of the United States under President Andrew Jackson. [Quinlan:320; WPANYS]

Barton. Tioga. On an early map of Tioga County, published by the surveyor general of New York, there were numbered lots. The word Barton was printed in Lot #175, presumably in reference to this being a manor—the old meaning of the word "barton." This word was taken to be a proper name although no one named Barton ever lived there. The town was formed with this name in

1824. The village was called Barton City. [French:650; Gay:71; P&H-Ti:72; WPANYS]

Basket. Sullivan. This settlement has a complex naming history. It was known as Long Eddy by the boatmen on the Delaware River because of the nature of the water here. The village itself was called Douglass Village, for an early settler. When the post office was established in 1855, it was called Long Eddy. In 1857, a depot was built here for the New York and Erie Railroad, and that was called Basket Station for nearby Basket Creek. All three names were used simultaneously until finally Basket prevailed. [Child:148; French:645; Fremont:645; Quinlan:293]

Basom. Genesee. The Basom post office was opened in 1889 and named for the Basom family, who settled here in 1825. Samuel Basom, born in 1835, was a prominent citizen. [Beers:121–3; North:459]

Batavia. Genesee. The town was formed in 1802. It and the eventual city were named for the Dutch district. Joseph Ellicott had wanted the place to be named Bustia or Bustiville for Paul Busti, the general agent of the Holland Land Company. Busti objected, saying that the name was too "ferocious," and proposed the name of Batavia. The early village was previously known as the Bend for its location on Tonawanda Creek. [APN:37; Beers:172–4; French:314, 325; Gannett:36; WPANY:472]

Batchellerville. Saratoga. Ambrose Batcheller and his family came here from West Brookfield, Massachusetts, and were instrumental in the development of the hamlet and the surrounding area. [Syl-S:371; WPANYA]

Bath. Steuben. When the town was formed in 1796, it was named for Lady Henrietta, Countess of Bath, daughter of Sir William Pulteney who owned much of the land here. The Native American name of the place was Donatagwenda, meaning "opening in an opening." [French:622; Gannett:36; Morgan:469; Roberts:126]

Bath Beach. Kings. Named for the English city. [APN:37; Jackson:86]

Battenville. Washington. Bartholomew Van Hogeboom, a Dutchman, was the first to settle in 1815 on the stream that runs through here. He was called Bart or Bat and the stream became known as Battenkill, as did the settlement that grew up on both banks of it. The name eventually changed to Battenville. The Native American name for the stream was Dionoondehowee. [Johnson:352; Stone:105; WPANYS]

Baychester. Bronx. Real estate developers named this place in the 1890s with a neutral name that sounded sophisticated. [Jackson:90]

Bayport. Suffolk. This was formerly called Middle Road and Midroadville. Its present name reflects its location on the water. [Bayles:221; French:636; Suffolk/Islip:7]

Bay Ridge. Kings. This suburb of Brooklyn used to be called Yellow Hook for the color of the clay in the area. In 1853, after the yellow fever epidemic of 1848–49, the name was changed so as not to be associated with the disease. The present name comes from the place's geographic location on the bay and along a glacial ridge. [French:373; Jackson:90]

Bay Shore. Suffolk. This settlement was first called Mechanicville, then Penataquit, a Native American name for a small stream in the neighborhood. Finally it was named for its location between the South Side Railroad and Great South Bay. [Bayled:210; French:636; Suffolk/Islip:7; WPANY:708]

Bayside. Queens. Named for its location on Little Neck Bay. [French:546; Jackson:90; WPANYC:571]

Bayville. Nassau. The village was made up of two places, Oak Neck, for all the oak trees in the area, and Pine Island. The name was changed to Bayville in about 1859 for its location, surrounded by water. [Winsche:18]

Beach Ridge. Niagara. This place's name is spelled both as Beach Ridge and Beech Ridge in the histories. It sits on a ridge of land and probably takes its name from the Beach family who were prominent influential residents in the county. The first settlement was in 1824 and, for a while, was called Hall's Settlement for Silas Hall who owned the land. The post office was established in 1853 as Beech Ridge. [French:455; Pool:242, 333–5; Williams:391]

Beacon. Dutchess. Mount Beacon is a high point, a good observation spot on the Hudson, named for its use as a signal station during the Revolutionary War. The city took its name from the hill. [APN:38; WPANY:575–6]

Bearsville. Ulster. C. Bear was a businessman here early on. [Syl-U:320; WPANYA]

Beaver Dams. Schuyler. The settlement was first called West Catlin but then took its name from two beaver dams on Post Creek on which the place was located. [P&H-S:104; WPANYS]

Beaver Falls. Lewis. Jacob Rohr had built a sawmill here on the Beaver River sometime before 1850 and the place was called Rohr's Mills. But at some point it was also called Castorville when it was settled by the French. *Castor* is French for "beaver," an animal that was ubiquitous in the area. The river was named for the animal. The settlement took its final name from the waterfalls. [APN:81; Bowen:113; Gannett:65; Hough-L:196]

Beaverkill. Sullivan. This name means "beaver creek," from the name of the animal and the Dutch term *kil,* meaning "creek" or "stream." The settlement is named for the nearby Beaverkill river. [Child:196-B; French:647]

Beaver Meadow. Chenango. When Ebenezer Hill settled here in 1800, there was a beaver dam across a stream that flooded about one hundred acres. [Smith-C&M:481; WPANYS]

Beckers Corners. Albany. Named for the Becker family, early settlers here. [Parker:495; WPANY:446]

Bedford, Bedford Hills. Westchester. The town was first formed in 1697 as part of Connecticut. It became part of New York State in 1704 and organized as a town in 1788. Its name, and that of the village, came from Bedfordshire, England, in an early naming move to keep English places in memory. Bedford Hills had been Bedford Station, a stop on the railroad, but this was changed in 1910 because the residents thought Bedford Hills was a better sounding name. [Bolton(1):1, 3; French:698; Gannett:38; Lederer:16; S&S:221]

Bedford-Stuyvesant. Kings. Named for the neighboring communities of Bedford and Stuyvesant Heights. [Jackson:94]

Beechhurst. Queens. The Shore Acres Realty Company laid out this area as a residential park in 1906 and named it for the beech tree. [APN:40; Jackson:96]

Beekmantown. Clinton. The town was named, in 1820 when it was formed, for William Beekman, one of the original owners of the land that was granted to them in 1769. [French:236; Gannett:39; Hurd-C&F:238–9; WPANYS]

Belden. Broome. The post office was established in 1868 when the Albany and Susquehanna Railroad was opened. [Smith-B:339]

Belfast. Allegany. The town was formed in 1824 as Orrinsburgh. In 1825, the name was changed for Belfast, Maine, the birthplace of John McKeen, an early justice of the peace. The town in Maine had been named by James Miller, an early settler there, for his native city in Ireland. [Allegany:212; French:171; Gannett:39; Minard:677; WPANYS]

Belfort. Lewis. A post office called Monterey was established here sometime in the late 1830s but was soon discontinued. Many of the early settlers were French; this settlement is named for a city in France. [APN:41; French:376; Hough-L:78]

Belgium. Onondaga. Named for the European country. [APN:41; Bruce:828; French:481; WPANYA]

Belle Harbor. Queens. Named for its location on the Atlantic Ocean and Jamaica Bay with the French word for "beautiful." [Gannett:39; Jackson:98]

Bellerose, Bellerose Terrace. Nassau. This name was meant to attract settlers in the 1890s. Bellerose Terrace was first called Bellerose Gardens West, but in 1927 a fire company called Bellerose Terrace Chemical Engine and Hose Company bought land here for a station. Eventually the village took the fire company's name. [Winshe:19–20]

Belle Terre. Suffolk. Incorporated in 1931, this village's name is of French origin and means "beautiful land." [WPANYS]

Belleville. Jefferson. Giles Hall ran mills here, lending his name to the place as Hall's Mills. The name was later changed for that of Belleville, Canada,

French for "beautiful city." [APN:41; D&P:362; French:357; Gannett:39; Hough-J:159]

Bellmont Center. Franklin. The town of Bellmont was named for William Bell, an early proprietor. The hamlet takes its name from its location and the post office, which was opened in 1879. [French:309; Hough-SLF:481; Hurd-C&F:441, 442]

Bellmore, North Bellmore. Nassau. This was called New Bridge for the bridge that was built across a creek in 1818. The name was changed by the South Side Railroad of Long Island. [Winshe:20; WPANYS]

Bellona. Yates. The settlement began to grow from about 1815 and was known as Slab Hollow, Pinkneyville, Wood's Hollow, and Benton, the last for the town that was the post office name until 1868 when it was finally changed to Bellona, its local name. That name was given by Samuel G. Gage back in 1818, inspired, it is said, by a fight between John McDermott and his wife, fueled by large quantities of alcohol, which the woman won. Bellona was the Roman goddess of war. [APN:42; Cleveland:176–7]

Bellport, North Bellport. Suffolk. The brothers Thomas and John Bell were responsible for much of the village's growth here in the 1830s. It is located on Great South Bay on a neck of land that the Native Americans called Accombamack or Occombomock. North Bellport was called Bellport Station when the Long Island Railroad first established the station. [Bayles:261, 272; Suffolk/Brookhaven:53]

Bellvale. Orange. Named for its quiet and scenic location. [R&C:580]

Belmont. Allegany. The village was first known as Philipsburgh for the Philipsburgh Mill Reserve, which owned the land and had the village surveyed and platted in 1833, and for Judge Philip Church, who owned the Philipsburgh Mill Reserve. In 1853, the village was incorporated as Philipsville, and again as Belmont in 1871. This name was derived from the hills in which the village sits: *belle*, "beautiful"; *mont*, "mountain." [Allegany:174, 176; French:170; Minard:446]

Belvidere. Allegany. In about 1835, the first post office here was called Hobbyville for the postmaster named Hobbie. When the Erie Railroad came through, it named the station Belvidere, Italian for "beautiful view," for the homestead of Judge Philip Church about a mile from the village. He owned much of the land here through his Philipsburgh Mill Reserve. [APN:42; Allegany:173; Gannett:40; Minard:454–5; WPANYA]

Bemis Heights. Saratoga. Jonathan Bemis kept a tavern in this hilly place at the time of the Revolutionary War. [French:593; Gannett:40; Syl-S:288, 295; WPANYA]

Bemus Point. Chautauqua. This village was a major resort on Lake Chautauqua named for William Bemus, the son-in-law of William Prendergast, the first property owner in the region. [D&H:157; McMahon:292]

Bennettsburg. Schuyler. Phineas Bennett bought 300 acres here in 1828 and built a gristmill and a sawmill on Cranberry Creek. [P&H-S:149]

Bennettsville. Chenango. This place was named for Bennett's Creek, which was named for Caleb Bennett who settled here in 1786 and was one of the first settlers. [Smith-C&M:178]

Bennington. Wyoming. When the town was formed in 1818, it was named, by early settlers from there, for Bennington, Vermont, which had been named for General Benning Wentworth of New Hampshire. Bennington Center was first called the Loomis Settlement for Chauncey Loomis who settled there in 1807. [APN:43; Gannett:40; WPANYS; Wyoming:146, 152]

Benson. Hamilton. The town was formed in 1860 and named for the Benson Tract, land that was owned by Egbert Benson in the early days of settlement. [A&K:14, 368; Donaldson(1):81]

Bensonhurst. Kings. In the late 1880s, James Lynch, a developer, bought land here from the Benson family and built a suburb that he called Bensonhurst-by-the-Sea. [Jackson:102]

Benson Mines. St. Lawrence. Named for the owner of the iron mine here. [WPA-NYA; WPANYS]

Benton Center. Yates. The town was formed as Vernon in 1803. The name was changed to Snell in 1808 for Jacob Snell, a state senator from Montgomery County. The local folks were not satisfied with this name, so in 1810 they changed it to Benton in honor of Levi Benton, the first settler here. The village was named for its location in the town. [Cleveland:168; French:719]

Bergen, West Bergen. Genesee. The town was formed in 1812 and named for Bergen, Norway. [French:325; Gannett:41]

Bergholtz. Niagara. The area where this settlement is located was settled by Germans from Prussia in the 1840s. It was first called New Bergholtz for the town in Prussia. The post office was established as Bergholtz in 1850 and the place eventually took that name. [French:456; Gannett:41; Pool:342–3; Williams:392]

Berkshire. Tioga. The town was first known as Brown's Settlement for a family that lived here from 1791 to about 1808. Later the name was changed for that of the Berkshire Mountains in Massachusetts because of the geographic resemblance of this place to them. [Gay:113; P&H-Ti:86, 90]

Berlin, Center Berlin. Rensselaer. The town was named for the German city when it was formed in 1806. Center Berlin takes its name from its geographic location. [APN:44; French:554; Gannett:41; Weise:118]

Berne, East Berne, South Berne, West Berne. Albany. The town of Berne (spelled Bern, at the time) was formed in 1795 and named for the Swiss city, possibly through the influence of the first settler in 1750, Jacob Weidman. The settlement of Berne had been called Beavertown; then it was called Corporation for the tavern, Corporation Inn, that Henry Engle opened in 1817. When the post office was established in 1825, it was called Berne for the town, and so the village took that name. East Berne was first called Warner's or Werner's Mills for the owner of the mills there. Sometimes the place was called Philadelphia or Philley: in about 1820, the tavern was run by Elnathan Stafford who got his liquor from Philadelphia, Pennsylvania. In 1825, the post office was opened here and named East Berne. South Berne had been called Centreville before 1825 for its equidistance from the three larger villages. It was also locally known as Mud Hollow for its swampy soil. The post office gave it the name South Berne. From about 1830 to 1835, West Berne was called Mechanicville for the large number of factory workers (then called mechanics) who lived there. Then Paul Settle, a miller, named the place Peoria for land he owned in Peoria, Illinois. When the post office was opened, it was called West Berne. [Albany:501, 507–9; APN:44; French:162; Gannett:41; Howell:72, 802, 817–9; WPANY:445]

Bernhards Bay. Oswego. John Bernard settled here in 1795 with his wife. [Johnson-O:288, facing 290; Churchill:494; WPANYA]

Best. Rensselaer. Jacob Best lived here on the east side of the Hoosick River. [French:558; Weise:98]

Bethany, East Bethany. Genesee. The town was formed in 1812 and named for the biblical village. [APN:45; French:325; Gannett:42]

Bethel. Sullivan. The town was formed in 1809 and named for the city in the Bible, meaning "house of God." [APN:45; Gannett:42]

Bethlehem Center, South Bethlehem, North Bethlehem. Albany. The town was named for the biblical town when it was formed in 1793, with a name meaning "house of bread," for the fertility of the soil here. Bethlehem Center was called Babcock's Corners for an early settler, Joshua Babcock. South Bethlehem had been called Jane's Corners for early settler William Janes and for Elishama Janes who ran a tavern. The post office was opened in 1874 and named South Bethlehem. [Albany:487, 492; APN:45; French:163; Gannett:42; Howell:778, 780; WPANYS]

Bethpage. Nassau. Thomas Powell, a Quaker, named this place for its location between Jericho and Jerusalem (the early name for Wantaugh) for the place in the Bible that was similarly located, then spelled Bethphage. The village became Central Park in 1867. In 1926, the name was changed back to Bethpage to avoid confusion with Central Park in Manhattan and to link it with the newly opened Bethpage State Park nearby. [APN:45; French:551; Winsche:21; WPANYS]

Big Flats. Chemung. The town and the village take their name from the broad flats that extend through the area. [P&H-C:189; WPANYS]

Big Indian. Ulster. There is a legend that a Native American "of enormous stature and strength" lived in this area. [Syl-U:308; WPANYA]

Big Moose. Herkimer. This village is probably named for the animal that used to roam through here. [WPANYS]

Big Tree. Erie. In the mid—to late 1800s, this place was called Big Tree Corners. The name comes from the Native American village that had occupied the site previously, Deonundaga, meaning "a big tree." [French:291; Gannett:43; Smith-E:523]

Billings. Dutchess. John Billings was elected as overseer of the poor in the first town of LaGrange elections in 1821. He was an influential citizen whose name was used for this settlement. [Smith-D:467; WPANYA]

Binghamton. Broome. The village was first called Chenango Point, but the name was changed in 1855 to honor William Bingham, the original proprietor of much of the land and a benefactor of the town, which was named after the village, which has since grown into a city. [APN:47; French:180; Gannett:43; Smith-B:197, 205; WPANY:203]

Birdsall. Allegany. When the town was formed in 1829, it was named for Judge John Birdsall, the circuit judge of the Eighth Judicial District in 1828–29. [Allegany:214; French:171; Gannett:43; Minard:507; WPANYS]

Bishopville. Allegany. A cheese factory was built here in 1891, but there is no record of the name origin. [Minard:565]

Black Brook. Clinton. The town was named for its principal stream when it was formed in 1839. The post office was established in 1840. [French:236; Hurd-C&F:243, 247; WPANYS]

Black Creek. Allegany. The settlement was called New Hudson Corners until after the post office was opened as Black Creek, named for the nearby stream. [French:175; WPANYA]

Black River. Jefferson. The village was named for the river, but it was locally known as Lockport. [D&P:425, 501; French:359, 361; Hough-J:239]

Blakeley. Erie. The Willink post office was established here when the place was called Osborn, for Elias Osborn, an early settler. Later the town and the post office took the name of a local prominent family. [Smith-E:539, 540]

Blasdell. Erie. The village was named for the Blaisdell family with a spelling change occurring at some point. [Smith-E:662]

Blauvelt. Rockland. This place was previously called Greenbush, but then took its name from Judge Cornelius I. Blauvelt, a prominent citizen, and became Blauveltville. The name was later shortened. [Cole:243; French:571; Green:333–4]

Bleecker. Fulton. Barent Bleeker, Cornelius Glen, and Abraham G. Lansing bought land here in 1793 that became known as the Bleeker and Lansing Patent. [French:316; Fulton:212; Gannett:45]

Bliss. Wyoming. The village was named for Sylvester Bliss, who bought the land from the Loomis family after the first settler, Justin Loomis, went insane in 1823. [WPANYS; Wyoming:188]

Blodgett Mills. Cortland. Nathan Blodgett and Jonathan Hubbard were early settlers here who built grist—and sawmills in the 1790s. [French:252; Goodwin:252; WPANYA]

Bloomfield. West Bloomfield, Ontario. The original town of Bloomfield was formed in 1789 and named for the natural beauty of the area, which consists of rolling and wooded hills. It was divided into several towns later, including East and West Bloomfield. East Bloomfield, North Bloomfield, and West Bloomfield developed in these towns, as did other settlements. The Native American name for West Bloomfield had been Ganundaok, meaning "the village on the top of a hill." In the 1990s, East Bloomfield and Holcomb were joined together by a vote to become the village of Bloomfield. Holcomb had been named for Hiram Holcomb, a prominent businessman. At this writing, there are still residents of what used to be East Bloomfield who refuse to use Bloomfield as their postal address. There is an entire block of post office boxes that uses the old zip code through the indulgence of the local postmaster. Bloomfield acquired Holcomb's old zip code and so does not fall into its correct numerical place, based on alphabetical order, in the zip code listings. [Milliken:105, 106, 110; Morgan:469]

Bloomingburg. Sullivan. The descriptive name for this village was selected by the residents here in about 1812. [Child:173; French:646; Quinlan:438]

Bloomingdale. Essex. A committee of three came up with this name for the post office in about 1852 when it was established. [Smith-Ex:654]

Blooming Grove. Orange. The community took this descriptive name to distinguish it from its neighbor, Hunting Grove. When the town organized in 1799, it took the name of the community. [French:504; R&C:633, 636]

Bloomville. Delaware. The settlement was first called Four Corners, then just the Corners. Judge Keeler and Lewis Bussy were early settlers and were responsible for the name Bloomville, describing the flowers in the area. [Delaware:235, 241; WPANYS]

Blossvale. Oneida. This place used to be known as Taberg Station on the Rome, Watertown, and Ogdensburg Railroad. It was named for the Bloss family, early settlers in the area. John Bloss was the first postmaster in about 1812. [Oneida:116; WPANYA]

Blue Mountain Lake. Hamilton. John G. Holland built the first hotel on the shore of the lake, then called Tallow Lake, in 1874. He thought the name of the lake was unattractive for his business, so he took the local name of the nearby mountain, Blue Mountain, officially called Mount Emmons for the geologist who had surveyed the area earlier, and applied it to the lake and to the hotel. The post office, when established, took the new name. [A&K:471; Donaldson(2):101; WPANY:496]

Blue Point. Suffolk. The Native Americans called this place on Great South Bay Manowtussquott. The vast oyster bed here took its name from this community of fishermen. [Bayles:2667; French:634; Suffolk/Brookhaven:51]

Blue Ridge. Essex. Named for the color of the mountains in the area. [WPANYA]

Bluff Point. Yates. The ridge that separates the two branches of Keuka Lake was called Bluff Point. It is about 400 feet high, 2 miles wide, and 8 miles long. The settlement was called Kinney's Corners, but its post office, established in 1850, was called Bluff Point, which eventually became the name of the settlement as well. [Cleveland:513, 567; French:719, 720; WPANYS]

Boght Corners. Albany. The place was sometimes called Groesbeck Corners for William G. Groesbeck, a settler here. The Dutch called it Boght, "bend," for the shape of the Mohawk River at this point. [Albany:405; APN:52; French:166; Howell:934]

Bohemia. Suffolk. Germans settled here and named the place for their former home. [APN:52; Bayles:207; Gannett:46; WPANYA]

Boiceville. Ulster. Z. P. Boice and his family lived here; he operated a mill. [Syl-U:297; WPANYA]

Bolivar, South Bolivar. Allegany. The town was formed in 1825, the time that Simon Bolivar, "the Liberator of South America," was a popular hero in the United States. South Bolivar had been locally called Honeoye Corners and Honeoye Forks. [APN:53; Allegany:220–1; French:172; Gannett:46; Minard:903; WPANY:391]

Bolton, Bolton Landing. Warren. This area was settled by New Englanders starting in about 1792. They probably brought the name with them; Bolton, Massachusetts, is named after Charles Powlet, third Duke of Bolton. [APN:53; French:673; Gannett:47; WPANYS; WPAW:167–8]

Bombay, South Bombay. Franklin. Named by Michael Hogan whose wife had lived in Bombay, India. [French:309; Gannett:47; Hough-SLF:482; Landon:251; WPANYS]

Boonville. Oneida. Gerrit Boon, an agent for the Holland Land Company, settled here in 1796. In 1805, the village was called Kortenaer, but soon it became known as Boon's Upper Settlement and was finally incorporated as Boonville in 1855. [French:462; Gannett:48; Oneida:125, 127; WPANY:12]

Boquet. Essex. Named for the Boquet River on which it sits and for which there is no name origin recorded. [Smith-Ex:557]

Borden. Steuben. Named for the creek, which was probably named for early settlers. [French:624]

Border City. Seneca. Named for its location on the border with the city of Geneva. [WPANYA]

Borodino. Onondaga. Named for the place in Russia, about seventy miles west of Moscow, at which Napoleon battled the Russian army in 1812. [APN:55; Gannett:48; Clark-O:352]

Borough Park. Kings. In the 1880s, this place was developed by Edwin C. Litchfield, who called it Blythebourne. In the boom of the 1920s, its name was changed. [Jackson:129; WPANYC:470]

Boston, North Boston. Erie. Named for the city in Massachusetts. The village that had been Boston Corners changed its name to Patchin. [Gannett:48; Smith-E:594, 598]

Boston Corner. Columbia. This part of New York State was part of Massachusetts when the place was named for the Massachusetts city. It became a part of New York State in 1857; the post office opened before 1860. [Ellis-C:407; French:243]

Bouckville. Madison. This place was first known as McClure Settlement for the McClure tavern that was here. At the same time, it was known as the Hook. Later, as the result of a drunken celebration, it was renamed Johnsville for John Edgarton, the first settler here. When the post office was established in the 1830s, it was named for William C. Bouck, who was then the canal commissioner and went on to become governor. [French:392; Gannett:48; Smith-C&M:621; WPANY:635]

Bovina, Bovina Center. Delaware. The town was named by General Erastus Root with the Latin word for cattle, indicating that the place was good for dairying. The settlement of Bovina was locally known as Butt End in the 1860s. [Delaware:123; French:259, 260; Gannett:49; Murray:293]

Bowens Corners. Oswego. Benjamin Bowen bought land here in about 1818. [Churchill:531; Johnson-O:393]

Bowmansville. Erie. In 1808, Daniel Robinson built a sawmill that he sold to Benjamin Bowman in 1811. Bowman then added a gristmill to his works and the settlement took his name. [Smith-E:453, 464]

Braddock Heights. Monroe. This place is above Braddock Bay, which was named for General John Prideaux who was accidentally killed near here in 1759. The namers had confused this death with that of General Edward Braddock in Pennsylvania in 1755. [APN:57; French:395]

Bradford. Steuben. The town was formed in 1836 and named for General Robert Bradford. [French:622; Gannett:50; Roberts:167; Steuben:64]

Bradley. Sullivan. Named for an early settler. [WPANYS]

Braeside. Rensselaer. In the Scottish dialect, this meant "hillside" or "bank of a stream." It was a term that was considered romantic in the mid-nineteenth century when used for naming places. [APN:57]

Brainard. Rensselaer. Joseph Brainard built a bridge over Kinderhook Creek here. The place was called Brainard's Bridge. Later the name was changed to Brainard in honor of Rev. David Brainard, a missionary. [French:557; Weise:126; WPANY:416]

Brainardsville. Franklin. Lawrence Brainard, first settler and a mill operator, came here in about 1869. [WPANYS]

Branchport. Yates. The early settlers named this place Esperanza, the Spanish for "hope." However, this name was thought to be too poetical for such a rugged place, so it was named for its location at the head of the west branch of Keuka Lake. This name was suggested by Spencer Booth, a local resident. [Cleveland:563; Gannett:50]

Brant. Erie. Named for Joseph Brandt or Brant, the Mohawk chief. His name was Thayandaneegah, which means "wood that is partially burned" or "a brand." [French:283; Smith-E:626]

Brantingham. Lewis. The town of Greig was first organized as Brantingham in 1828. The name was changed in 1832, but the settlement had kept the name of Thomas H. Brantingham who had owned land here. [French:375–7; Hough-L:32]

Brant Lake. Warren. The settlement was first called Horicon, for the town. Its name was changed for that of the lake on which it sits. The lake was named for Joseph Brant, the Mohawk chief who fought for the British in the American Revolution. [WPANY:56; WPANYS; WPAW:170]

Brasher Center, Brasher Falls, Brasher Iron Works. St. Lawrence. The town was named for Philip Brasher of Brooklyn, part owner of the land here. Brasher Falls was named for the rapids and waterfalls on the St. Regis River. Brasher Iron Works was the site of an iron furnace built by Stillman Fuller in 1836, who had come here the previous year to work the ore. [Curtis:632, 636, 638; French:575; Gannett:50; Hough:268]

Brasie Corners. St. Lawrence. Alonzo Brasie was the first postmaster here in 1879. [Harder:24]

Breakabeen. Schoharie. Named for the Dutch word for the rushes that grew along the creek here. [APN:58; French:605; Gannett:51; Noyes:151; Roscoe:183; WPANYA]

Breesport. Chemung. John Brees came here with his wife and eight children from Somerset, New Jersey, in 1787. In 1789, they moved to the town of Horseheads and built the first log house. The village was laid out in 1854 on land owned by William and Ulysses Brees, and the plat was surveyed by Azariah Brees. William Brees opened the first store, and Ulysses Brees was instrumental in establishing the first post office in 1851. [French:221; P&H-C:225, 238–9]

Breezy Point. Queens. Named for its location on the western tip of Rockaway Peninsula. [Jackson:135]

Brentwood. Suffolk. In 1851, this place was called Modern Times. It was an experiment in communal living, founded by Joseph Warren, Stephen Pearl Andrews, and others who believed in "The Sovereignty of the Individual," which included elements of the Free Love movement. The experiment failed, and a typical community village remained that changed its name to the more innocuous Brentwood in 1864. [Bayles:205; French:637; WPANY:705]

Brewerton. Onondaga. This place was settled opposite Fort Brewerton, which had been named for Captain Brewerton in the 1760s. The Native American name of the fort's location was Ohsahaunytahseughka, "where the water runs out of Oneida Lake," for the lake's outlet into the Oneida River. [Bruce:808; Clayton:338–9; French:481]

Brewster. Putnam. In about 1820, Samuel Brewster came to Putnam County from Rockland County. He died in 1871, but had had several sons, two of whom—William F. and James—bought the old Bailey farm on which the village of Brewster grew. They reopened the iron mine that was on the farm property, then sold it to Harvey Steel and Iron Company. The railroad came through, and for a time, the village was called Brewsters Station. [French:543; Gannett:51; Pelletreau:455, 462]

Briarcliff Manor. Westchester. In 1890, Walter W. Law bought land here and called it Briarcliff Farm. He later bought more land and called it Briarcliff Manor. The post office had been called Whitson, for Charles H. Whitson who owned 164 acres and was the first station agent of the railroad when the station was built. The post office name was changed in 1879 and that of the station soon after. The village was incorporated in 1902. [Lederer:20, 156]

Bridgeport. Madison. This place, located on Chittenango Creek about two miles from Oneida Lake, may have been named for Bridgeport, Connecticut, by settlers from there, or it might be named for its location. [Smith-C&M:757]

Bridgeville. Sullivan. In 1807, a bridge was built over the Neversink River here. [Child:196-I]

Bridgewater. Oneida. The place was settled in 1790 and the town organized in 1797. It was named for the town in Massachusetts that was the former home of some of the settlers, which itself was named for the town in England. [APN:59; French:462; Gannett:52; WPANY:420; WPANYS]

Brier Hill. St. Lawrence. Named for the shrubbery in the area. [Harder:25; WPANYA]

Brighton. Monroe. The town was formed in 1814 and named for the English town. [APN:60; Gannett:52]

Brighton Beach. Kings. The place was first developed in 1868 by William A. Engeman. It was named for the resort town in England by Henry C. Murphy and other businessmen who, in 1878, bought land here to build the Hotel Brighton. [Jackson:140; WPANYC:471]

Brightwaters. Suffolk. The village was incorporated in 1916 and was a "city of gardens," probably taking its descriptive name from the play of green on the water. [WPANY:708; WPANYS]

Brinckerhoff. Dutchess. Derick Brinckerhoff came here from Long Island in 1718. He kept a store during the Revolutionary War. The place was first called Brinckerhoffville, then, when the railroad came through, Brinckerhoff Station, and finally shortened to the present name. [French:272; Smith-D:533; WPANYD:132]

Briscoe. Sullivan. An early settler by this name built the Briscoe Sawmill. Soon a post office was established. [Child:111]

Bristol, Bristol Center, Bristol Springs, South Bristol. Ontario. Named after either Bristol, Connecticut, or Bristol, Massachusetts (which were named for the city in England), from which early settlers had come. Bristol Springs was first called Cold Springs for the temperature of the flowing water. [French:495; Gannett:52; Milliken:103]

Broadalbin, North Broadalbin. Fulton. The town was named for Broadalbin (sometimes spelled Breadalbane), Scotland, by Scottish settlers when it was organized in 1793. Before the Revolutionary War, the village had been called Kennyetto for the creek on which it sat, said to mean "snake trying to swallow its tail." The place was later called Fonda's Bush for Major Jelles Fonda, who owned land here. When the post office was established in 1804, the Scottish residents got it to be called Broadalbin. The village was incorporated in 1815 as Rawsonville for Dr. E. G. Rawson, the first physician here, but the name was never used. North Broadalbin used to be called Benedict's Corners. [APN:60; French:212; Fulton:214–6; Gannett:52; WPANY:489]

Broad Channel. Queens. This neighborhood on an island in Jamaica Bay was named for the waterway to its east, which is called Broad Channel. [Jackson:141; WPANYC:590]

Brockport. Monroe. Hiel Brockway came here after the War of 1812 and was the largest landowner. The Native American name was Gwehtaanetecarnundoteh, meaning "red village." [French:405; Gannett:52; Mc-M:158; Morgan:468; Peck:414; WPARM:318]

Brockville. Orleans. Hiel Brockway was an early settler here. [Gannett:52; Signor:408]

Brocton. Chautauqua. The village was called Salem-on-Erie or Salem Cross Roads. The post office was established in 1835. In 1857, the name of both the post office and the village was changed to Brocton. This was the birthplace of George Pullman, who invented the sleeper train car. [D&H:222; French:215; McMahon:292; WPANY:673]

Brodhead. Ulster. Conrad Brodhead and his family lived here in about 1820. The place was first called Brodhead's Bridge. [Syl-U:297; WPANYA]

Bronx. Bronx. Generally referred to as the Bronx, the name comes from Jonas Bronck, a Dutchman who had a farm here. People would say that they were going to the Broncks' to visit. After the British took over, the name stuck with the new spelling and retention of the definite article. [APN:61; Gannett:52; WPANYC:510]

Bronxville. Westchester. The village was first called Underhill's Crossing for John Underhill, who had dammed the Bronx River here to power a gristmill. He also built a bridge below the dam that gave this place its name. The name of the village was changed in 1847 at the suggestion of James Swain, a cutlery manufacturer, for its location on the Bronx River, which was named for Jonas or Jacob Bronck, an early Dutch settler. [Gannett:52; Lederer:22, 148; S&S:627; WPANYS]

Brookdale. St. Lawrence. This place was called Scotland in the 1890s. [Curtis:523]

Brookfield, North Brookfield. Madison. When the town was formed in 1795, it was named for its abundant water sources. [French:390; Smith-C&M:525]

Brookhaven. Suffolk. The town was organized in 1788, but the area had been inhabited much longer. The Brookhaven patent had been granted in 1600 and might have taken its name from the former home of some settlers from Massachusetts. The village had been called Fire Place until 1875 when it took the name of the town. [Bayles:274; Suffolk/Brookhaven:54; WPANYS]

Brooklyn, Brooklyn Heights, South Brooklyn. Kings. The Dutch had a settlement here in 1646 that they called Breukelen, meaning "broken land," for the geography. The Canarsee Indians called the area of Brooklyn Heights Ihpetonga, "high sandy bank." South Brooklyn was named for its location. [APN:61; French:367; Gannett:52; Jackson:148, 156; WPANYC:433, 441, 463]

Brooktondale. Tompkins. This settlement has been through several name changes since its beginning as Cantine's Mill (sometimes Cantinesburgh, Cantine's Little Location, or Cantinesville) after John Cantine Jr., who was the first settler in 1798. Later, William Mott and his family moved here and opened a number of establishments, including a store and a mill. The place became known as Mott's Corners (and Mottsville, Mott's Hollow, Mott's Mill). When they left, the name was changed to Brookton. The first railroad station, in 1873, was known as Mott's Corners, then was also changed to Brookton. The post office changed the name in 1926 to Brooktondale to avoid confusion with Brockton and Brooklyn. [Norris:17–8; P&H-T:139; Selkreg:290–1]

Brookview. Rensselaer. This place was formerly called Schodack Depot, for the town, when it was a station on the Boston and Albany Railroad. The current name is descriptive of the place. [French:559; Weise:74; WPANYS]

Brookville. Nassau. The Underhill family settled here in 1712 and named the place Wolverhampton. This became corrupted into Wolver Hollow, a name that was changed in 1848 to Brookville by a vote of the residents. [Winsche:22]

Brownsville. Kings. Charles S. Brown built 250 frame houses here starting in 1865. [Jackson:163; WPANYC:498]

Brownville. Jefferson. Jacob Brown, a general in the War of 1812, owned land here. The town was named for him when it was formed in 1802. The Brown family lived in the village of Brownville, incorporated in 1828. [D&P:294, 300; French:356; Gannett:53; Hough-J:95, 98; WPANY:641]

Brunswick, Brunswick Center. Rensselaer. The town was formed in 1807 and named by its German settlers for the place in Germany. [APN:62; French:554; Weise:102]

Buchanan. Westchester. Alexander F. Buchanan started the manufacture of oil-cloth here in 1874. The village was incorporated in 1920. [Lederer:23]

Bucks Bridge. St. Lawrence. Isaac Buck came here from Shoreham, Vermont, in 1807. [Curtis:502; French:582; Hough:438]

Buffalo. Erie. The name of the city comes from the name of Buffalo Creek, although when it was first laid out by Joseph Ellicott for the Holland Land Company, he had called it New Amsterdam. The people who were already living there preferred the name of the creek. The creek name has several possible origins. One theory is that it is a corruption of the French *beau fleuve,* "beautiful river," applied to the geographic location. Another is that the animal had been present in abundance here and used the stream as a watering place. The Seneca name for the creek and the land around it was Doshowey, meaning "basswood." White settlers found several Native American villages on the creek, one of which was headed by a man whose name was Degiyahgo, meaning "buffalo." The new settlers then referred to the place by his translated name. [APN:64; French:288; Gannett:55; Parker:295–6; Smith-E:57; WPANY:209]

Bullville. Orange. Thomas Bull lived here for many years. [R&C:418]

Burdett. Schuyler. The village was previously called Hamburg, but the name was changed when it was incorporated in 1898 for Sir Francis Burdett, who owned land here. [P&H-S:149; WPANYS]

Burgoyne. Saratoga. Named for the British general who surrendered in 1777 after the Battle of Saratoga. [WPANY:65]

Burke, Burke Center. Franklin. The town was organized in 1844 and named for Edmund Burke, a British statesman. The post office at Burke Center was established in 1829 when the village was known as West Chauteaugay. [French:309; Gannett:55; Hurd-C&F:453]

Burlingham. Sullivan. Walter Burling was a director of one of the turnpike companies that built a road through here. [WPANYS]

Burlington, Burlington Flats, West Burlington. Otsego. The town was formed in 1792 and named for Burlington, Vermont, the home of many early settlers. The Burlington post office was opened in the settlement of Burlington Green, which later dropped the Green. [French:531–2; WPANYS]

Burns. Allegany. The town was formed in 1826 and named for the Scottish poet Robert Burns. The settlement had been known as DeWittsburgh or De-Wittsville for S. DeWitt Brown who built a hotel here in 1826. When the railroad came through, it named its depot Burns Station. The settlement changed its name for that of the town in 1848. [Allegany:224, 228; French:172; Minard:615, 619; WPANYS]

Burnside. Orange. The community was called Otterville and named for Otter Kill, the creek on which it sits, but the post office was named Burnside, so the settlement eventually became that too. [French:507, R&C:655]

Burnt Hills. Saratoga. About the time that white settlers began coming in, this area had been burned by the Native Americans to clear the place of underbrush. [French:587; Syl-S:253]

Burrs Mills. Jefferson. John Burr and his sons settled here in about 1803. The place was first called Burrville. [D&P:227; French:362; Gannett:56; Hough-J:261]

Burt. Niagara. When the Rome, Watertown, and Ogdensburg Railroad was established, this place was called Newfane Station. The post office was established in 1876, then the name of the settlement was changed to Burt for Burt Van Horn, the owner of a large farm in the area. [Pool:329; Williams:390]

Bushnell's Basin. Monroe. This place on the Erie Canal was known as Hartwell's Basin for Oliver Hartwell, who had bought the land from a man named Pardee when the canal was surveyed. Then Hartwell sold it to William Bushnell. [French:401; Mc-M:222]

Bushville. Sullivan. In about 1850, Abiel P. Bush built a tannery here with his family. In 1852, the post office was established. [Quinlan:133–4]

Bushwick. Kings. The Dutch named this place Boswijck, meaning "heavy woods," in 1660. [Jackson:171; WPANYC:171]

Buskirk. Rensselaer. John VanBuskirk was an early settler, and Martin VanBuskirk built the first bridge over the Hoosick River. The VanBuskirks first settled here before the Revolutionary War. It was called Buskirk's Bridge in the mid-1880s. [French:556, 680; Gannett:56; Weise:77, 88]

Busti. Chautauqua. The town was named for Paul Busti, general agent of the

Holland Land Company. [D&H:117; French:210; Gannett:56; McMahon:293]

Butler Center, South Butler. Wayne. When the town was formed in 1826, its naming fell to a committee of three men, one of whom thought highly of General William Butler of the Revolutionary War. South Butler was called Harrington's Corners before 1839. When the post office was established, it was named for its location in the town, as was Butler Center. [Cowles:434; Mc-W:78; WPANYS]

Byron, South Byron. Genesee. The town was formed in 1820 and named for Lord Byron, the English poet. South Byron was locally known as Brusselville for Elijah Shumway, an early settler, who had a "brussel head," referring to the wiry hair of a dog. [APN:68; Beers:381–2; French:325; Gannett:57; North:478]

C

Cortland © *2004 by Jon Crispin*

Cadiz. Cattaraugus. First settled in about 1808, it was named for the city in Spain. [APN:70; Ellis:320; Gannett:57]

Cadosia. Delaware. The settlement had been called Cadosia Valley and was named for Cadocia or Cadosia Creek, a Native American word meaning "covered with a blanket." [APN:70; Delaware:213; French:262; WPANYS]

Cadyville. Clinton. In 1833, Cyrus Cady and other members of his family built a forge here. [Hurd-C&F:171]

Cairo, South Cairo. Greene. The town was organized in 1803 as Canton. The name was changed for the Egyptian city at the suggestion of Asabel Stanley, a prominent citizen, in 1808. The hamlet was first called Shingle Kill and then took the name of the town. [APN:70; French:331; Greene:203, 208; Vedder:29–30; WPANYS]

Calcium. Jefferson. This place was previously called Sandfords Corners for an early settler. [French:359; WPANYA]

Caledonia. Livingston. The town was formed as Southampton in 1802, but because many of the early settlers were from Scotland, they had the name changed in 1806 for the ancient name for their former home. The Native American name for the place had been Deonegano or Dynneganooh, "cold water," for the spring that supplied water here. [APN:71; Doty-L:498, 500–502; French:383; Gannett:58; Parker:303]

Callicoon, Callicoon Center. Sullivan. When the town was formed in 1842, it was named for the stream that runs through it. The name of Callicoon Creek comes from the word for turkey, taken by the Dutch from the Native American *kalkoen*. The Dutch name for the creek was Kollikoonkill. The settlement of Callicoon had been Callicoon Depot; it was on Callicoon Creek where it enters the Delaware River. Callicoon Center had been called Thurmanville. [APN:72; Child:118, 133; French:644; Gannett:58; Quinland:149, 216]

Calverton. Suffolk. The ancient name for this place was Conungam. Then it was called Hulse's Turnout and later Baiting Hollow Station because it was a convenient railroad stop for the community of Baiting Hollow three miles north. In 1860, it was named for an early settler. [Bayles:287; Suffolk/Riverhead:6; WPANYS]

Cambria. Niagara. This place was first called Molineaux's Corners for William Molineaux who ran a tavern here and was the first postmaster of the Molineaux's Corners post office. When the post office moved to just west of the settlement, its name was changed to match that of the town, Cambria, which is the ancient name for Wales. Eventually, the settlement changed its name, too. [APN:73; Gannett:59; Pool:242–3; Williams:375]

Cambria Heights. Queens. Named for the Latin name for Wales. [APN:73; Gannett:59; Jackson:177]

Cambridge, South Cambridge. Washington. In 1788, the town was organized as Cambridge and named for Cambridge, Massachusetts, which was named for the city in England. When the village of Cambridge was incorporated in 1866, it joined the villages of Cambridge, North White Creek, and Dorr's Corners, which had been named for Dr. Jonathan Dorr, one of the first physicians in the town. [APN:73; French:680; Gannett:59; Johnson:252, 262; Stone:449–50; WPANYS]

Camden. Oneida. The town was organized in 1799 and briefly known as Linley. It was later named for Charles Pratt, Lord Camden, who was a supporter of the American colonies before the Revolution. The Native American name for the place was Hestayuntwa, the meaning of which is lost. [APN:73; Gannett:59; Oneida:133; Morgan:473]

Cameron, Cameron Mills. Steuben. The town was formed in 1822 and named for Dugald Cameron, an early settler and agent of the Pulteney Estate.

Cameron Mills was first called Hubbardsville for Daniel Hubbard, who built the first flour mill here. The name was changed when applying for a post office because there already was a Hubbardsville in the state. [French:623; Gannett:59; Roberts:174; Steuben:66, 312]

Camillus. Onondaga. The town was formed in 1799 and named for Marcus Furius Camillus, the Roman dictator, during the classical naming of the Military Tract in 1790. The village, originally called Nine Mile Creek for the stream, was renamed after the town when the post office was established in 1811. [APN:73; Bruce:659, 744; Clark-O:314; Clayton:308–11; Gannett:59]

Campbell, East Campbell. Steuben. When the town was formed, in 1831, it was named for Reverend Robert Campbell, an early landowner. [French:623; Gannett:59; Roberts:186; WPANYS]

Campbell Hall. Orange. Captain Lachlin Campbell came here from Scotland in the 1730s and built a house. [R&C:654]

Campville. Tioga. Colonel Asa Camp, a Revolutionary War hero, settled here in about 1792. The place was then called East Owego and had a post office established in 1827. In about 1833, Congressman Stephen B. Leonard had the name changed to honor the veteran. [Gay:400–401; P&H-Ti:146]

Canaan. Columbia. The town was formed in 1772 as Kings District. The name was changed in 1788 for the former home of some of the residents, South Canaan, Connecticut, which was named for the biblical promised land. [APN:73; Ellis-C:319; French:243; Gannett:60; WPANYS]

Canada Lake. Fulton. The lake was once called Stink Lake for the smell of dead fish. There is no record for the current name origin of the lake. The settlement is named for the lake and was a summer resort. [Fulton:220; WPANY:491]

Canadice. Ontario. The name of the town, settlement, and lake comes from a Native American word, Skaneatice, meaning "long lake." [APN:74; Milliken:104; Parker:312]

Canajoharie. Montgomery. The town was formed in 1788 and takes its name from the nearby creek Ganajohie. The creek's name is an Indian word meaning "washing the basin," referring to a deep pothole at the foot of a waterfall on the creek. [APN:74; French:412; Frothingham:242; Gannett:60; Montgomery:95; WPANY:480]

Canandaigua. Ontario. There are different interpretations of the origin of this Native American word used as the name of a lake and city. The original word might have been *canandargua,* meaning "a place for settlement, a chosen spot, a town set off"; *genundewahguah,* meaning "great hill people," because of a large hill near the lake; *cahnandahgwah,* meaning "sleeping beauty"; or *ganadarque* (variously spelled *kanandarqua, kennadarqua,* and *ga-*

nundagwa), meaning "a place selected for settlement"—all possible names of a native village on this spot that was destroyed by Sullivan's army in 1779. The first white settlement was ten years later, with incorporation as a city in 1919. [APN:74; French:495; Gannett:60; Milliken:104; Morgan:469; Parker:312]

Canarsie. Kings. Named for the Native Americans who lived here when the Europeans first came. [APN:74; Jackson:178; French:372]

Canaseraga. Allegany. The village was named for the creek, called by the Native Americans Ganosegago or Kanasawaga, which might mean "among milkweeds" or "several strings of beads with a string lying across" or "among the elms." The place was formerly known as Whitney Valley for Ezra Whitney who, in 1818, owned the land here. [Allegany:226–7; APN:74; French:172; Gannett:60; Minard:616]

Canastota. Madison. The Iroquoian word *kniste* or *kanetota* meant "pine tree standing alone" and gave its name to the village in which a cluster of pine trees had united their branches to seem as one. [APN:74; Gannett:61; Morgan:473; Smith-C&M:725]

Caneadea. Allegany. The town was formed in 1808 and named for the Seneca word *gaoyadeo,* "where the heavens rest on the earth." The community built its homes on the site of a Seneca village. [Allegany:230; APN:75; French:172; Gannett:61; Minard:38; WPANY:681]

Canisteo, South Canisteo. Steuben. The town was formed in 1796 and was named for a Native American village that had been here, Kanestio. The name was applied to a creek, meaning "board in or on the water." [APN:75; French:623; Gannett:61; Morgan:469; Parker:313; Steuben:73]

Canoga. Seneca. The place is named for a spring, the Native American name of which, Ganogeh, means "oil floating on water." [APN:75; French:615; Gannett:61; Morgan:470; Seneca:130]

Canton. St. Lawrence. The town was named for the city in China when it was formed in 1805. The post office of the village was first called New Cairo when it was established in 1804. It took the name of the town in 1807. [APN:76; Gannett:62; Harder:34; WPANY:521]

Cape Vincent. Jefferson. The town was formed in 1849 and named for the principal village, which had been named for Vincent LeRay, a son of James LeRay de Chaumont, proprietor of the land here. The village had been named Gravelly Point when it was settled in 1809, for its location on the St. Lawrence River. [D&P:314; French:356; Gannett:62; Hough-J:109; WPANY:640]

Cardiff. Onondaga. John F. Card built a large gristmill here in 1839. Later, he had a store and a distillery, and did much for the improvement of the hamlet. When the time came to decide on a name for the place, the residents wanted to perpetuate his name with something like Cardville or Cardbury. John Spencer, an influential member of the community, who had come from England, suggested the name of the city in Wales. [Bruce:973; Gannett:62; WPANYA]

Carlisle. Schoharie. The town was formed in 1807 and named for Carlisle Pierce, a prominent citizen. The post office was established in 1811. [French:603; Noyes:154; Roscoe:308, 310; Sias:127]

Carlton. Orleans. The town was formed in 1822 as Oak Orchard. The name was changed in 1825. The settlement was locally known as Two Bridges. [French:514; Signor:624]

Carmel, Lake Carmel. Putnam. When the town was formed in 1795, it was named for Mount Carmel in the Bible. The community of Lake Carmel took its name from the lake. [APN:78; Blake:253; Gannett:62]

Caroga Lake. Fulton. The name comes from a Native American word whose meaning is uncertain. The stream is called Garoga, as was the lake, but the town spelled the name with a C. The hamlet had been called Pine Lake. [APN:78; French:317; Fulton:220; WPANYS]

Caroline, Caroline Center. Tompkins. The town was formed in 1811 and its name was an arbitrary choice at the first town meeting. No one could think of a suitable name; John Cantine, Jr., an early settler, had declined the honor of having the town named after him. A dictionary was opened at random with the idea that the first female name that was come upon would be the name of the town. And so it was named Caroline. Cantine and his friend, Dr. Speed, agreed to name their next daughters after the town; Carol Cantine and Diana Caroline Speed were the result. The community of Caroline was initially named Yankee Settlement for the first New England settlers. This name was later changed to Tobeytown for Nathaniel Tobey, an early settler, and then Caroline. Caroline Center was first called Centerville for its location near the middle of the town. [French:655; Norris:17; Selkreg:291–2]

Carrollton. Cattaraugus. G. Carrollton was one of the original proprietors. [Ellis:399; French:188; Gannett:63]

Carthage, West Carthage. Jefferson. The village of Carthage was previously called Long Falls for its location on the Black River. The name was changed for the city in Tunisia when the post office opened. West Carthage was on the opposite bank from Carthage. A blast furnace was erected here in 1834. [APN:79; D&P:316, 337; French:363; Gannett:63; Hough-J:300]

Cascade. Cayuga. This place seemed to have had "remarkable phenomena, attributed by the believers in spiritualism to spirit agency." What this agency was no one says, but the place was popular enough to keep Malcolm Taylor's hotel, the Cascade House, in business. There is a small stream that runs down the bluff to Cayuga Lake, forming a delightful waterfall for which the place was named. [Storke:443]

Cassadaga. Chautauqua. The village took its name from the creek, the name of which is from the Native American word *gusdago*, meaning "under the rocks." [APN:80; D&H:421; Gannett:64; McMahon:294; Morgan:463]

Cassville. Oneida. This settlement in the town of Paris had been known as Frog Hill or Toad Holler until 1830 when it was called Paris Hollow. The name was changed in 1835 either for General Lewis Cass, a prominent politician who was governor of Michigan Territory in 1820, or for a local settler. [APN:80; Gannett:64; Oneida:175; WPANYS]

Castile. Wyoming. When the town was formed in 1821, it was named for the province in Spain. The village, earlier named Wolf Creek and Oak Hill, was incorporated in 1877. [APN:81; Gannett:64; WPANYS; Wyoming:166]

Castle Creek. Broome. The town was named for the creek, which was named for the location of the old Native American "castle" near its mouth. [French:181; Smith-B:441]

Castleton Corners. Richmond. Earlier names for this place were Centerville and then Four Corners. The first mention of the Castleton Corners post office was in 1872. The town of Castleton was first recognized in 1788. [Davis:71; French:565–6; Jackson:189]

Castleton-on-Hudson. Rensselaer. This place was formerly called Morriches Hastie. It was later named for an ancient "Indian castle" nearby. The village was incorporated as Castleton in 1827, and the name was changed to the present one in 1926. [French:559; Gannett:64; Weise:74; WPANYS]

Castorland. Lewis. This name came from the French word *castor*, meaning "beaver." Beavers were numerous in the area when refugees of the French Revolution set up the Castorland Colony here. [APN:81; Bowen:113, 143; Gannett:65; Hough-L:34–70]

Catatonk. Tioga. The settlement was named for the creek, the name of which is Algonquian, meaning "big stream." [APN:82; Gay:194; P&H-Ti:102]

Catharine. Schuyler. The town was named, when it was formed in 1798, for Catharine Montour, a French woman who married a Seneca chief and continued to live in the village after his death. She was considered to be influential by the English colonial government. [French:610; Gannett:65; P&H-S:76; WPANY:655]

Cato. Cayuga. The town was formed in 1802 and named during the Military Tract naming of 1790 for Cato the Younger, a Roman statesman who became the symbol of honesty and high principles. The village was originally known as Jakway's Corners for Dr. John Jakway, who had settled there from Vermont. Later it took its name from the town. [APN; French:201; Storke:296]

Caton. Steuben. When the town was first formed in 1839, it was named Wormley for Samuel Wormley, the first postmaster and tavernkeeper. The name was changed in 1840 to honor Richard Caton, an original landowner. [French:623; Steuben:79, 318]

Catskill. Greene. The Dutch had named the mountains Katsberg and the stream Kats Kill for the mountain lions in the area. The town was formed in 1788 and named for the stream. The village was once known as Catskill Landing for its location on the shore of the Hudson River. [APN:81; French:332; Gannett:65; Greene:123, 126; WPANY:593]

Cattaraugus. Cattaraugus. The name comes from that of the creek, Gadagesgao, a Seneca Indian term meaning "fetid banks" or "bad-smelling shore or beach." Natural gas used to seep from rock crevices along the creek. [APN:82; Gannett:65; Morgan:685; Parker:289; WPANY:685; WPANYS]

Caughdenoy. Oswego. This was a place on the Oneida River where Native Americans fished for eels, pronounced kok-e-noy and sometimes spelled as Coughdenoy. The post office was established in 1858. In the 1930s, there was a large eel-fishing and processing industry here. [APN:82; French:522; Johnson-O:362–3; Churchill:565; WPANY:526]

Cayuga. Cayuga. Settled in 1789, this village was named for Cayuga Lake, on whose eastern shore it sits and which was named for the Native Americans of that name. Their name for the lake was Gweugweh, meaning "the lake at the mucky land." [APN; Morgan:470; Storke:351; WPANY:427]

Cayuga Heights. Tompkins. Named for its location on a hill above Cayuga Lake. [Norris:13]

Cayuta. Schuyler. The town was formed in 1824 and named for the lake, as were the hamlet and the first post office, which was established in 1815. The name of the lake is from a Native American word, *kaniata*, the meaning of which is uncertain. [APN:83; French:610; P&H-S:101; Parker:312]

Caywood. Seneca. Members of the Caywood family were early settlers here. [WPANYA]

Cazenovia. Madison. The place and the lake are named for Theophilus Cazenove, the first general agent of the Holland Land Company. The village was settled in 1793 by John Lincklaen, the local agent of the company, who named it for Cazenove. The Native American name for the lake was Ahwagee, "perch lake." [APN:83; French:390; Gannett:66; Morgan:473; WPANY:422]

Cedar Hill. Albany. Named for the cedar trees here. [Albany:495; APN:83; Gannett:66; Howell:781]

Cedarhurst. Nassau. The South Side Railroad of Long Island made a stop here in 1869 and called it Ocean Point. In 1887, the Cedarhurst Company bought the land here intending to develop it. The train station name was changed to

Cedarhurst in 1890 and the surrounding village became known as such also. [Winsche:24]

Cedarvale. Onondaga. Named for the tree. [APN:83; Bruce:862; Gannett:66]

Cedarville. Herkimer. Named for the tree. [APN:83]

Celoron. Chautauqua. This place on Lake Chautauqua had been called Sammis Point and Sammis Bay for Charles Wheeler Sammis, an early settler. The name was changed for Pierre Joseph de Celoron de Blainville, a French officer who led an expedition through this area in 1749. [APN:83; D&H:161–2; McMahon:294–5]

Cementon. Greene. This settlement on the Hudson River used to be called Smith's Landing. It later took its name from the cement works in the town. [WPANYA; WPANYS]

Centereach. Suffolk. Named for its location between Lake Ronkonkoma, St. James, and Smithtown. [WPANYS]

Centerport. Suffolk. This place was called Little Cow Harbor and Centerport Harbor for its location on the bay. [Bayles:158; French:636; WPANYS]

Center Village. Broome. The post office was established in 1855 near the center of the town of Colesville. [French:181; Smith-B:335]

Centerville. Allegany. Settlement here was first made at "The Center." When the town was formed, in 1819, it took the name of the village with a slight change. Later, the village changed its name to match that of the town. [Allegany:239; French:172; Minard:780; WPANYA]

Central Bridge. Schoharie. A bridge was built here at the mouth of the Cobles Kill in 1823. It was named for its location on the road between Albany and the village of Cobleskill. [French:606; WPANYA]

Central Square. Oswego. Named for its location below the center of the town of Hastings. [Churchill:562; Johnson-O:360]

Central Valley. Orange. Named for its location in the valleys of the Ramapo and Woodbury Creeks. [R&C:794]

Centre Island. Nassau. This is really a long peninsula that was called Hog Island. Sometime between 1820 and 1839, the name was changed for its location in Oyster Bay. [French:550; Winsche:25; WPANYS]

Ceres. Allegany. This village was on both sides of the boundary between New York and Pennsylvania. By 1830, there was quite a settlement on the Pennsylvania side. The Ceres Land Company held about 300,000 acres of land here that it gave to homesteaders. Ceres was the Roman goddess of grain. [Allegany:294; APN:84; Minard:879, 881; WPAPA:367–9]

Chadwicks. Oneida. John Chadwick had built a cotton mill here in 1809. George W. Chadwick converted a tannery into a bleachery to keep up with changing industry. The place had been known as Chadwicks Mills. [Oneida:169; WPANYA]

Chaffee. Erie. In 1879, the post office was established here at the junction of the Sardinia and Springville Railroad with the Buffalo, New York, and Philadelphia Railroad. It was named for the president of the Sardinia and Springville Railroad, Bertrand Chaffee. [Smith-E:623]

Chamberlain Corners. St. Lawrence. Anson Chamberlain built a house here called the Chamberlain House. [Harder:39]

Champion. Jefferson. General Henry Champion of Colchester, Connecticut, owned the land here. He gave the town a bell for the compliment when the place was named for him. [D&P:331; French:357; Gannett:67; Hough-J:119]

Champlain. Clinton. The town was formed in 1788 and lies on Lake Champlain, for which it was named. The lake was named for Samuel de Champlain who explored it in 1609. [APN:86; French:236; Gannett:67; Hurd-C&F:261, 262]

Chapin. Ontario. The settlement sits on the outlet of Canandaigua Lake on which the first gristmill was built by Captain Israel Chapin in 1789. It was first known as Chapinville. [Milliken:104]

Chappaqua. Westchester. The Native American word on which this place's name is based, *shappequa*, has been translated in several different ways: "laurel swamp, " "vegetable root," and "a place where the brush makes a rustling sound when you walk through it." [Bolton(1):565; French:702; Gannett:67; Lederer:28]

Charleston, Charleston Four Corners. Montgomery. The settlement of Charleston was known as Rider's Corners until the post office was established in 1807. The town and settlements were named for Charles, a nephew of John E. Van Epps, an early settler. [Frothingham:349; Montgomery:103]

Charleston. Richmond. In the eighteenth century, this place was called Androvetteville. In the 1890s, Balthazar Kreisher ran a brick factory here, so the place became known as Kreisherville. The factory closed in 1927, and the place took the current name. [Jackson:202]

Charlotte. Monroe. This place is at the mouth of the Genesee River and was named for Charlotte Augusta, the princess of Wales. It had been called Charlottsburg, Charlotte, and then Port Genesee for its location, and "finally and permanently" Charlotte, although there had been a move to call it North Rochester. [Gannett:68; Mc-M:204; Peck:279]

Charlotte Center. Chautauqua. The community in the center of the town of Charlotte was named for the wife of George III of England, Charlotte Sophia. [APN:87]

Charlotteville. Schoharie. Named for the wife of George III of England, Charlotte Sophia. [French:607; Noyes:156; WPANYA]

Charlton. Saratoga. Early settlers had come here from near Freehold, New Jersey, and had called the area New Freehold or Freehold. The town was formed in

1792 and named for a prominent New York City physician, Dr. Charlton. [Syl-S:316]

Chase Mills. St. Lawrence. Alden Chase built a sawmill here. The post office was established in 1853 as Chase's Mills. It was changed to Chase Mills in 1894. [Harder:40–1]

Chasm Falls. Franklin. Named for the waterfall that drops 200 feet. The place had been called Glen Hope and Titusville. [WPANYA]

Chateaugay. Franklin. This name is either from a French word meaning "castle ford" or a French corruption of a Native American word, *chatauqua* or *chateuga*, "place where one was lost." Another story has it that the name comes from land in Quebec, Canada, owned by Charles LeMoyne that he had named for a place in France. The town was organized under this name in 1799. [APN:88; French:310; Gannett:68; WPANYS]

Chatham, Chatham Center, East Chatham, North Chatham, Old Chatham. Columbia. The town was formed in 1795 and named for the English statesman William Pitt, Earl of Chatham. The village of Chatham was known as Groat's Corners for Captain Peter Groat, who settled here in about 1812. Then it was known as Chatham Four Corners and Chatham since 1869. The other settlements were named for their locations in the town. [APN:88; Ellis-C:291; French:244; Gannett:69; WPANYS]

Chaumont. Jefferson. Named for the bay on which it sits, which was named for the proprietor of the land here, James LeRay de Chaumont. [French:359; Gannett:69; WPANY:640]

Chauncey. Westchester. Henry Chauncey was a landowner in the area, whose name was first used for the train station around which the community grew. [Lederer:29]

Chautauqua. Chautauqua. The village is named for the lake, which also gave the county its name. It was spelled Chautauque until 1859. It comes from a Seneca Indian word *tkenchiatakwan*, which meant "where the fish was taken out." According to Seneca tradition, fishermen caught a muskellunge in the lake, put it in their canoe, and carried it to Lake Erie. When they arrived, they were impressed by the fact that the fish was still alive, and so they let it go. However, there have been other meanings attributed to the word: "foggy place," "place of easy death," and "place where one was lost." In the 1870s, a Methodist clergyman developed a more entertaining way of teaching the Bible that involved audience participation. This idea was taken up by a businessman here who started a short school in summer-camp form for Sunday school teachers. Soon these programs, called chautauquas, expanded to include other subjects and were attracting thousands who came here to hear various speakers, from politicians to explorers. [APN:88; D&H:10–11; Gannett:69; McMahon:295, 321–2; Morgan:463; Parker:292; WPANY:393]

Chazy, West Chazy, Chazy Landing. Clinton. The town, formed in 1804, and the settlements were named for the river, which was named for Lieutenant de Chezy, a French officer who was killed nearby in 1666 by the Iroquois. Chezy was part of the regiment, brought to America in 1664, that played a prominent role in the destruction of Iroquois villages by the French. Chazy Landing, on Lake Champlain, used to be called Saxe's Landing for Judge Matthew Saxe, who had come here in 1808. [APN:88; French:237; Hurd-C&F:278; WPANY:552]

Cheektowaga. Erie. Alexander Hitchcock's family had settled here in 1808. He suggested that the town, when it was organized in 1839, be called Chictawauga, a corruption of a Seneca word *jikdowaahgeh,* meaning "the place of the crab apple tree." [APN:89; French:288; Gannett:69; Parker:296; Smith-E:469; WPANYS]

Chelsea. Dutchess. The settlement took its name from the Chelsea Paper Mill that was here for a short while. The settlement had been known as Carthage and Carthage Landing before that. The name Chelsea comes from the district in London and spread after being used as a placename in Massachusetts in 1739. [APN:89; WPANYD:137]

Chemung. Chemung. The name of the county, town, and settlement comes from that of the river, whose Native American name was Gahato, meaning "a log in the water." Other sources indicate that the word means "big horn in the water" from either there having been found a mammoth tusk in the water or for the number of deer antlers in the stream. A log might look like a horn, and the horn would be a better story. The settlement used to be called Buckville. [APN:89; French:218; Gannett:70; Morgan:469; P&H-C:33; Parker:293; WPANY:229]

Chenango Bridge, Chenango Forks, West Chenango. Broome. *Chenango* is a Native American word meaning "bull thistles." Chenango Bridge is named for the Chenango River and the bridge that was built over it at this point. Chenango Forks is located at the junction of the Chenango and Tioughnioga Rivers. And West Chenango is a village in the western part of the town of Chenango. [APN:90; French:181; Gannett:70; Smith-B:458; WPANYS]

Cheningo. Cortland. Named for the creek, which was named with a variant of *chenango,* meaning "bull thistles." [APN:90; French:250; Gannett:70]

Chepachet. Herkimer. The community sits on Unadilla Creek. Its name comes from a Native American term meaning "turning back" or "where the stream divides" or "the place of separation." The word refers to the idea of a boundary being reached and the need to turn back from it. [APN:90, 353; Gannett:70; Herkimer:128]

Cherry Creek. Chautauqua. The town was named for the stream that was named by surveyor Joshua Bentley, who found that the center of the new town was on an island in the stream. He used a cherry tree to mark this center. A village grew up in the area and took its name from the stream, although it had been known as Puckrum for a while. [D&H:136, 139; Gannett:70; McMahon:296]

Cherry Plain. Rensselaer. Named for the cherry trees in the area. [WPANYS]

Cherry Valley. Otsego. The town was named for the trees in the area when it was formed in 1791. [APN:90; French:532; Gannett:70; WPANYS]

Cheshire. Ontario. Named for Cheshire, Connecticut, from which some early settlers had come. [Milliken:104]

Chester. Orange. The place was settled in about 1751 by John Yelverton, who laid out a plat and named it for the town and county in England. [APN:91; R&C:613]

Chestertown. Warren. The first settler was Otis Collins, who moved his family here in 1805. The community was named for the town of Chester, which was probably named for the town in England. [APN:91; Smith-W:541; WPAW:171–2]

Cheviot. Columbia. Named for the hills of the English-Scottish border. [APN:91]

Chichester. Ulster. L. A. Chichester was a furniture manufacturer who built up the industry here, starting in about 1830. The factories failed in 1938, and the settlement and the machinery went up for sale. [Syl-U:308; WPANY:504]

Childs. Orleans. The Childs family moved here in the early 1800s. [Signor(2):24]

Childwold. St. Lawrence. Addison Child came here from Boston in 1878. The place had been called Atherton. He named the place by putting together his name with "wold," which he defined as "high rolling ground." [Harder:42; WPANYS]

Chili, Chili Center, North Chili. Monroe. The town was formed in 1822 and named for the South American country, the name of which is a Peruvian word meaning "land of snow." The communities take their names from their locations in the town. [APN:93; Parker:305; WPARM:280]

Chilson. Essex. This place was earlier called Chilson Hill for a family of early settlers and the hill near which they located. [Gannett:72; Smith-Ex:429]

Chinatown. New York. Many Chinese immigrants settled in this part of Manhattan early in the twentieth century. [Jackson:215; WPANYC:104]

Chippewa Bay. St. Lawrence. This place took its name from the bay on the St. Lawrence River, which is named for the Native American tribe, meaning "he overcomes" or "he surmounts obstacles." [Gannett:72; WPANYS]

Chittenango, Chittenango Falls, North Chittenango. Madison. Chittenango Creek flows through this area, giving its name to the populated places. The

Native American name was Chudenaang, meaning "where the sun shines out." [APN:96; Gannett:72; Morgan:473; Smith-C&M:680]

Choconut Center. Broome. The settlement was named for the creek of the same name, an Iroquoian word for which the meaning has been lost. [APN:96; Smith-B:493]

Churchtown. Columbia. The post office was established here in about 1850 and may have been named for St. Thomas's Lutheran Church that was located here. [Ellis-C:242; French:244]

Churchville. Monroe. Samuel Church settled here in 1808 and owned much of the land on which the village was built. [French:401; Gannett:73; Mc-M:186; Peck:391–2]

Churubusco. Clinton. This place is named for the village just south of Mexico City where U.S. troops defeated the Mexicans in 1847. It was earlier known as Summit Station, on the Ogdensburg and Lake Champlain Railroad. At one time, it was spelled Cherubusco. The post office was established in 1852. [APN:99; French:237; Hurd-C&F:302; WPANYS]

Cicero. Onondaga. The town was formed in 1807, taking the name of the Roman statesman that was bestowed on the place as part of the 1790 naming of the Military Tract. The post office was opened in 1820 as Cicero Corners, eventually shortened to the present name. [APN:99; Bruce:807; Clark-O:176; Clayton:337; French:481; Gannett:73]

Cincinnatus. Cortland. The town was formed in 1804 and named by the land commissioners for the Roman patriot as part of the Military Tract naming of 1790. [APN:99; French:251; Gannett:72; Goodwin:192; Melone:413]

Circleville. Orange. In 1841 Mary Bull suggested this name, taken from Circleville, Ohio (which was in turn named for nearby circular Indian mounds in the area), because she thought it was a pleasant name. [APN:100; Gannett:74; R&C:448]

City Island. Bronx. This island was called Minnewits by the Native Americans here, then Minneford Island by the British. In 1761, Benjamin Parker bought the island as an agent for developers who saw this as a potential rival to New York City and gave it this name. [French:704; Jackson:231; WPA-NYC:550]

Clarence, Clarence Center. Erie. The town was named for the Duke of Clarence, son of Queen Victoria, when it was organized in 1808. The settlement of Clarence had been called Clarence Hollow. Before that, it was called Ransomville for Asa Ransom, the first settler here in 1799. The post office at Clarence Hollow was established between 1808 and 1811 and named Clarence. Clarence Center had been called VanTine's Corners for David Van-Tine, who had settled here in about 1829. The post office was established in

1847 and called Clarence Center, replacing the name VanTine's Corners. [French:289; Smith-E:379–80, 385, 388; WPANYS]

Clarendon. Orleans. Eldrige Farwell settled here with his wife in 1811. The community was called Farwell's Mills until after the town was formed in 1821, when Farwell named it for his wife's hometown of Clarendon, Vermont. [French:514; Orleans:130; Signor:557, 583]

Clarkson. Monroe. General Matthew Clarkson, a large landowner, gave one hundred acres of land to the town, so when it was organized in 1819, it honored his donation. [French:398; Mc-M:167; Peck:254; WPARM:281]

Clarksville. Albany. This place was first called Bethlehem, but in 1822 Adam Clark bought the tavern here from Harmanus Bogarths, and the name was changed for him. [Parker:551, 558; Howell:901; WPANYA; WPANYS]

Clason Point. Bronx. This point of land between the Bronx River and Westchester Creek was first known as Cornell's or Cornhill's Neck for Thomas Cornell or Cornhill, a farmer who settled here in 1654. Later, it was named fo Isaac Clason, a wealthy merchant, sometimes spelled Classons Point. [French:706; Jackson:143, 239; WPANYC:544]

Claverack. Columbia. The town was recognized in 1788 and named for the white clover fields here, in Dutch called *klaver-akker.* [APN:101; Ellis-C:234; French:244; Gannett:75]

Clay. Onondaga. When the town was formed in 1827, it was named for Henry Clay, the American statesman. The first post office here was established in 1815 and named West Cicero for its location. When this town was formed, the name of the post office was changed to Clay. [APN:101; Bruce:828; Clark-O:190–1; Clayton:332; French:481; Gannett:75]

Clayburg. Clinton. The community was settled sometime between 1825 and 1841 and named either for Miles Clay and his family or for the character of the soil here. [Hurd-C&F:240; WPANYS]

Clayton. Jefferson. The town was formed in 1833 and named for John M. Clayton, U.S. senator from Delaware. In 1823, the village and the post office were named Cornelia, but their names were changed in 1831, and the town name followed. The village was also frequently called French Creek. [D&P:316, 344; French:357; Gannett:75; Hough-J:135, 138]

Clayville. Oneida. This village in the town of Paris had been called Paris Furnace for the iron making industry there. Starting in the 1830s, it manufactured hoes, scythes, and other farming implements. In 1849, it changed its name for Henry Clay. [French:466; Oneida:175]

Clear Creek. Chautauqua. Joseph Bentley first settled here on the banks of Clear Creek in 1814. The community took its name from the creek, which was named for the quality of its water. [APN:101; French:212]

Clemons. Washington. Named for George L. Clemons, the first postmaster. His store burned down in the winter of 1875–76. [Johnson:285; WPANYA]

Clermont. Columbia. The town was formed in 1787 and was named either for the French city, for Chancellor Livingston's former home in Livingston Manor, or named by Livingston himself, a friend of Robert Fulton's, for the first American steamboat. The post office was established in 1792. [Ellis-C:277, 283; French:244; Gannett:76; WPANYA; WPANYS]

Cleveland. Oswego. James Cleveland came here with Peter Smith in 1826. He built a hotel and opened the first store with Samuel H. Stevens. In 1827, the post office was opened. Stevens wanted it to be called Stevensville, but others wanted it to be named for John Cleveland. The compromise was that the name of the post office and village would be Cleveland, but the first postmaster would be Samuel Stevens. [APN:101; Churchill:497; French:521; Gannett:76; Johnson-O:290]

Cleverdale. Warren. This town started as a summer resort community with no record of its name origin. [WPANYS; WPAW:212]

Clifford. Oswego. The settlement was formerly known as Denton's Corners for Robert Denton, a hatter, who settled here in 1823. The post office was established in 1882. [Churchill:656]

Clifton. Monroe. Anan Harmon was an extensive landowner here so the place was called Harmonsburg and Harmon's Mills. When the time came for a post office, in 1850, he and Alfred Mudge suggested that it be called Clifton, but there is no record of why they did so. [WPANYA, WPANYS]

Clifton. Richmond. The town was laid out in 1837, then lost some of its area to neighboring towns. There is no record of name origin. [Jackson:245]

Clifton Park. Saratoga. The town was organized in 1828 as Clifton, the name of the original patent of 1708. The name was changed in 1829 to distinguish it from other places in the state with the same name. The name of the settlement had been Stevens Corners for Ephraim Stevens, a popular landlord here. The name was later changed to that of the town. [French:587; Syl-S:348, 475, 477]

Clifton Springs. Ontario. In 1806, a hotel was opened here that developed into an established water cure facility by 1850, the Clifton Mineral Springs. The place was first called Sulphur Springs. [French:497; Milliken:104]

Climax. Greene. Probably named for its geographic location. [APN:102]

Clinton. Oneida. In the nineteenth century, this village was nicknamed Schooltown for the great number of academies, seminaries, institutes, and colleges located there. It was named for George Clinton, governor of New York in 1777. The Native American name of the place was Kadawisdag, "white field." [Gannett:76; Morgan:472; Oneida:153–54; WPANY:597]

Clinton Corners, Clinton Hollow. Dutchess. The town of Clinton was formed in 1786 and named for George Clinton, the first governor of New York State. The settlements took their names from their locations in the town. [French:270; Gannett:76; Smith-D:284–5; WPANYD:151]

Clintondale. Ulster. James Clinton was a surveyor who mapped the area in 1771. Later he served as a general in the Revolutionary War. George Clinton was his brother and DeWitt Clinton was his son. The post office was opened in about 1860 and named for the Clinton family. [Fried:51; Syl-U:175; WPANY:403]

Clintonville. Clinton. The county and the settlement were named for Governor George Clinton. [APN:102; French:232; Gannett:76; Hurd-C&F:213; WPANYS]

Clockville. Madison. John Conrad Klock moved here in 1792 with his family. The community was known as Shippeville at that time for an old tavern called Shippe. When the post office was established, it was named for the Klock family. [French:392; Gannett:76; Smith-C&M:728]

Clyde. Wayne. Early on, this place was called Block House for the blockhouse that had been built by traders. The village that grew up in the area was called Lauraville for Henrietta Laura, Countess of Bath, daughter of Sir William Pulteney. In 1818, Andrew McNabb from Scotland owned land here that he sold in lots. He named the place Clyde for the river in Scotland. [Cowles:264; French:691; Mc-W:84]

Clymer, North Clymer. Chautauqua. The town was organized in 1821 and named for George Clymer, a signer of the Declaration of Independence and a member of the Constitutional Convention. The communities took their names from the town and, in North Clymer's case, its location in it. [D&H:140; French:211; Gannett:76; McMahon:297; WPANYS]

Cobleskill. Schoharie. The town was formed in 1797 and named for a settler named Cobel who built a mill near Central Bridge and gave his name to the stream, Cobles Kill, that the Native Americans had called Otsgatagee. [APN:103; French:604; Gannett:77; Noyes:156; Roscoe:387; Sias:130]

Cochecton, Cochecton Center. Sullivan. The town was formed in 1828 and named with a Native American word, *cushnuntunk*, meaning "low ground." Cochecton Center had been called Stevensburgh for Alfred and Fletcher Stevens, who bought Alfred Nearing's tannery here, expanded it, and erected other buildings. [APN:104; Child:129, 130; French:644; Gannett:77; Quinlan:215]

Coeymans, Coeymans Hollow. Albany. The town was formed in 1791 and was named for Barent Peterse Coeymans, who had come from Holland in 1636 and bought land here in 1673. The settlement of Coeymans had been called Coeymans Landing until the post office was opened as Coeymans. The post office at Coeymans Hollow was opened in 1840. [Albany:472, 479, 482; APN:105; French:163; Gannett:77; Howell:74, 824, 827, 830]

Cohocton, North Cohocton. Steuben. The town was named when it was formed in 1812 for the river, the name of which is a Native American word, *cohocta* or *gahata,* meaning "steam rising in a black alder swamp with overhanging trees" or "trees in water" or "a log in the water." The river's name had been spelled Conhocton, but the n was dropped. The village had been called Liberty for the liberty pole erected for the Fourth of July celebration in 1813. In 1891, when the village was incorporated, its name was changed to Cohocton as its post office had been called for years. North Cohocton was first called Biven's Corners for Joseph Bivens, who built a tavern and started the settlement on the Cohocton River. [French:624; Gannett:78; Morgan:469; Parker:313; Steuben:82, 85, 318]

Cohoes. Albany. The name comes from a Mohawk word, *gahaoose, chahoos, kahoos, cohos,* and other spellings, meaning either "a canoe falling" or "shipwrecked canoe" or "waterfall." One reference says it means "pine trees." [Albany:434; APN:105; Gannett:78; Howell:949]

Coila. Washington. This place was first called Green Settlement for early settlers of that name. Then it was called Stevenson's Corners for William Stevenson, a prominent resident. Later, Coila was chosen as more appropriate, as a reminder of Scotland, the original home of some of the residents. [Johnson:261; Stone:456]

Colchester. Delaware. When the town was formed in 1792, it was named by Joseph Gee for Colchester, Connecticut, his former home. The first settler was Russell Gregory, who came here in 1776, also from Connecticut. The Native American name for the place had been Pawpacton. [Delaware:133, 139; French:260; Murray:310]

Cold Brook. Herkimer. The village is named for the creek, which was named with a descriptive term. [Herkimer:233]

Colden. Erie. When it was organized in 1827, the town was named for Cadwallader D. Colden, who was in the state senate at that time. The settlement was first called Buffum's Mills for Richard Buffum, who had come here from Rhode Island in 1810 and built a sawmill. The name was changed when the post office was opened in 1833. [Gannett:78; French:289; Smith-E:601–4]

Coldenham. Orange. Cadwallader Colden was an early proprietor here. He wrote *History of the Five Nations,* a rebuttal to the French impressions of the Iroquois. [French:508; R&C:387; WPANY:145]

Cold Spring. Putnam. The village was named for a spring of cold water that was later destroyed by development in the village. [Blake:158; Gannett:78; Pelletreau:557; WPANY:576]

Cold Spring Harbor. Suffolk. Named for the spring and its location at the head of the harbor. The Native American name of the place was Nachaquatuck. [Bayles:140; French:636; Suffolk/Huntington:49]

Collabar. Orange. This might be a corruption of Collaburgh, a post office village. [French:506; R&C:419]

Collamer. Onondaga. This place was previously known as Britton Settlement for the Britton family. There is no record of why the name was changed, but the post office was established with this name sometime before 1835. [Bruce:1028–9; French:482]

College Point. Queens. At one time, this place was known as Lawrence's Neck. In 1790, Eliphalet Stratton bought land here, and the place became known as Strattonsport. In 1836, the Reverend William A. Muhlenberg began building St. Paul's College. This project was never completed, but the idea led to the village being incorporated as College Point. In 1854, Conrad Poppenhusen built up this neighborhood for the workers in his rubber factory. [French:546; Jackson:251; WPANYC:570]

Colliersville. Otsego. Isaac Collier kept the first store here in the 1790s. [French:534; Hurd-O:193; WPANYS]

Collins, Collins Center, North Collins. Erie. The town of Collins was named by Turner Aldrich Jr., who named it in 1821 for his wife, Nancy Collins. The town of North Collins was formed from Collins in 1852 and was first called Shirley, but the name was changed because the residents preferred to be associated with Collins. The village of North Collins was first called Rose's Corner for Chester Rose who opened a store here in about 1820. In 1829, John and Alexander Kerr opened a store here and the name was changed to Kerr's Corners. The post office named Collins was established in the village of North Collins in about 1822. [French:292; Smith-E:648, 649, 661, 662; WPANYS]

Collinsville. Lewis. This was formerly known as High Falls village, being west of the waterfall on the Black River. It was renamed for Levi and Homer Collins, residents in the area. [Bowen:523; French:380; Gannett:79; Hough-L:246]

Colonie. Albany. The town of Watervliet changed its name to Colonie in 1896. The name comes from the adjacent village, which was a colony of those employed by Van Rensselaer. The village was incorporated in 1921. [Albany:394–5; Howell:75; WPANYS]

Colosse. Oswego. The settlement was first called Mexico Four Corners, but when the post office was established, it was given this name from its French settlers, a word meaning "giant, colossus." [Churchill:598; French:522; Johnson-O:266]

Colton, South Colton. St. Lawrence. The town was formed in 1843. Jesse Colton Higley was an early settler here, in 1824, who wanted the place named for him. Others did not like him and proposed that the name be Springfield. But Higley agreed to supply the town with gunpowder for the Fourth of July celebration in exchange for the place being named for him. The first post office was called Matildaville, but that was soon changed to the name of the town. [Curtis:695; French:576; Harder:49; Hough-SLF:285]

Columbia, Columbia Center, South Columbia. Herkimer. The town was formed in 1812 and named for a term that had been coined in about 1775 as a name for the United States. It is a Latinized form of Columbus, who was considered a hero for having found a place to which people who did not agree with the old regimes could come and live freely, the goal of the Revolutionary War. Columbia Center was first called Petrie's Corners for Daniel J. Petrie who settled here in 1800. Its name was changed when the post office was established. [APN:107; Herkimer:105]

Columbiaville. Columbia. This manufacturing community took its name from the county, which was named for the popular name first proposed as the name of the country in honor of Christopher Columbus. [APN:105; Ellis-C:352]

Columbus. Chenango. When the town was formed in 1805, Dr. Tracy Robinson suggested that it be named for the explorer. [APN:107; French:225; Smith-C&M:440]

Commack. Suffolk. Named from the Algonquian word *winnecomac,* meaning "beautiful place." [APN:108; Bayles:169; Gannett:79]

Comstock. Washington. Sometime before 1790, Daniel Comstock settled here, and the place became known as Comstock Landing. The post office, called Comstock, was established in 1832, with Peter Comstock as the postmaster. [Johnson:303]

Conesus. Livingston. The town was formed in 1819 as Freeport. Its name was changed to Bowersville in 1825 for Henry Bowers, a land owner and early settler, but a month later, it was changed again for the Native American word, *ganeosos* or *ganyuhsas,* meaning "place of many berries," which was the name of the lake on which the settlement sat. [APN:109; Doty-L:512; French:383; Gannett:80; Parker:303]

Conesville. Schoharie. The town was formed in 1836 and named for Reverend Jonathan Cone of Durham in Greene County. The Conesville post office was opened in the village of Stone Bridge. [French:604; Noyes:154; Roscoe:131; Sias:132]

Conewango. Cattaraugus. The town and settlement were named for the creek, the Native American name of which, Ganowungo, means "in the rapids" or "walking slowly." The village used to be called Rutledge where the Conewango post office was established in 1825. [APN:110; Ellis:214, 221; Gannett:80; Morgan:463; Parker:289; WPANYS]

Conewango Valley. Chautauqua. When the French mapped the stream, they wrote its name CANA8AGAN, using the numeral 8 to represent a Native American sound like the French word for eight, *huit*. The settlement is named for its location and takes its name from the stream. [APN:110; Gannett:80; McMahon:322; Morgan:463; Parker:292]

Coney Island. Kings. This name is either from the Dutch word for wild rabbits, *konijn*, that were numerous here, or from the Conysis family who might have lived here. [APN:110; French:372; Gannett:80; Jackson:272; WPA-NYC:472]

Congers. Rockland. A. B. Congers gave land for the railroad station here, which then took his name, as did the surrounding settlement. [WPANYA; WPA-NYS]

Conifer. St. Lawrence. A committee was organized in 1912 to name this place in order to have a post office. The name came from looking out the window and observing the scenery. [Harder:51]

Conklin. Broome. The town was formed in 1824 and was named for Judge John Conklin, who was an early settler here. The village took its name from the town. [French:182; Gannett:80; WPANYS]

Conklingville. Saratoga. Colonel Gordon or Gurdon Conkling came here in 1848 and built a large tannery, a store, a hotel, and several houses and put the first steam tugboat on the Sacandaga River. [French:589; Syl-S:417]

Conquest. Cayuga. In 1821, the decision was made to separate a section from the town of Cato. The new town was named Conquest to commemorate the success of those favoring the division over those in opposition. [APN; French:201; Storke:36, 281]

Constable. Franklin. The town was organized in 1807 and named for William Constable, a land agent and proprietor of the Macomb Purchase. [French:310; Gannett:81; Hough-SLF:495; Hurd-C&F:472; WPANYS]

Constableville. Lewis. The village was first called Shalersville for the first land agent hired by William Constable, owner of the land here. The village was later named for Constable's son. [Bowen:525–6; French:380; Gannett:81; Hough-L:245; WPANY:641–2]

Constantia, Constantia Center. Oswego. The town was formed in 1808 and named Rotterdam by George Scriba, the original proprietor of the land. Early on, the settlement was sometimes known as New Rotterdam. When the post office was established in 1798, it was called Rotterdam for the settlement, but the names of the town, the settlement, and the post office were changed to Constantia in 1813. Constantia Center was named for its location in the town. [Churchill:488, 491, 505–6, 510; French:521; Johnson-O:288–9]

Cooksburg. Albany. The place was named in 1840 for Thomas B. Cook, a prominent railroad man who had bought land here in anticipation of growth due to the Catskill and Canajoharie Railroad, which ran for two years and then was abandoned. [French:165; Gannett:81; Howell:915; WPANYS]

Cooks Falls. Delaware. John Cook settled here on the Beaver Kill in 1776. [Delaware:133; WPANYA]

Coopers Plains. Steuben. Judge John Cooper and his son, Dr. John Cooper, are each credited with founding this community in the 1820s. [Roberts:317; Steuben:320]

Cooperstown. Otsego. This village was first called Otsego, an Iroquoian word meaning "rock place" or "welcome water" or "place where meetings are held." William Cooper, father of James Fenimore Cooper, came here in 1785 to look over the land that he owned. He brought his family here in 1790 and founded a settlement. The name was changed in 1812 to honor him. [French:536; Gannett:81; Hurd-O:257; WPANY:500]

Coopersville. Clinton. The place was known as Moore's Mills for General Benjamin Moore, who had come here in 1805 and built a sawmill and a gristmill. Ebenezer Cooper later bought these mills and the village came to be named for him. [French:237; Gannett:81; Hurd-C&F:263]

Copake, Copake Falls, West Copake. Columbia. The town was formed in 1824 and named for the lake, the name of which comes from the Native American name and means "snake lake." West Copake was formerly known as Anderson's Corners. [APN:112; Ellis-C:390–1; French:244; WPANY:406]

Copenhagen. Lewis. This village, in the town of Denmark, was first called Mungers Mills for Nathan Munger, an early settler, who built the first gristmill in 1800 and a sawmill a year later. In 1807, the British fleet bombarded the Danish city of Copenhagen in peacetime. This incensed Danish supporters in Mungers Mills, so they changed the name of their village and post office in sympathy. [APN:113; Bowen:127; French:276; Gannett:82; Hough-L:86]

Copiague. Suffolk. Named for a Native American word meaning "a shut-in place." [WPANYS]

Coram. Suffolk. Named for a Native American chief who lived in the area, sometimes spelled Corum. [APN:113; French:634; Gannett:82; Suffolk/Brookhaven:48]

Corbettsville. Broome. The Corbett family were early settlers here, with Robert Corbett leading the way in 1796. Sewell Corbett was the first postmaster in 1845. [Smith-B:482–3]

Coreys. Franklin. The place was first settled by Pliny Miller and others in about 1812. The hamlet was named for Jesse Corey, who owned a rustic lodge on Upper Saranac Lake. [French:310; WPANYS]

Corfu. Genesee. The village had been called Longs Corners for John Long and his father, Dr. David Long, who settled here in 1808. When the post office was opened, it was named for the Greek island, a name that the village took when it was incorporated in 1868. [APN:113; Beers:620–1; French:327; Gannett:82; North:495]

Corinth, South Corinth. Saratoga. The town was formed in 1818. At a meeting called to decide on the name of the place, held at the home of Mr. and Mrs. Washington Chapman in what was then Chapman's Corners and became South Corinth, Mrs. Chapman asked to be allowed to name the new town. When all acquiesced, she opened the Bible at Corinthians and so the place was named for the ancient city. [APN:113; Gannett:82; Syl-S:394]

Corning, East Corning, South Corning. Steuben. The town of Corning was formed as Painted Post in 1796. Its name was changed in 1852. In 1835, the Corning Company was formed in Albany for the purpose of acquiring and developing lands in the state, particularly in Steuben County because the Chemung Canal had been completed there in 1833. The canal and a railroad connected to it, promoted by the Corning Company, were then used to carry coal from Pennsylvania north. By 1836, there was enough of a settlement to need a name, so residents chose that of Erastus Corning, the prime mover of the Corning Company. In 1868, the Flint Glass Company of Brooklyn was looking to move somewhere where the costs of transportation and coal were cheaper. The village of Corning provided just what they needed, and eventually grew into a city. [APN:114; French:624; Gannett:82; Steuben:261; WPANY:389]

Cornwall-on-Hudson. Orange. The town was organized as New Cornwall in 1788, then changed its name to Cornwall in 1797. It was named for Cornwall, England. The village is named for the town and for its geographical location on the Hudson River. [French:505; R&C:763]

Corona. Queens. A group of speculators developed this area in 1854 and named it West Flushing for its location next to Flushing Bay and Flushing Meadows Park. The village changed its name in 1872 to be "the crown of villages on Long Island." [APN:114; Jackson:284; WPANYC:567]

Cortland. Cortland. The county and the city were named for Pierre Van Cortlandt, first lieutenant governor of New York State, who owned Military Tract land here. [APN:115; French:250; Gannett:83]

Cossayuna. Washington. The settlement was named for the lake, which was named by the Native Americans with a word meaning "pine lake." At some time, it had been called Lakeville and Lake. [APN:115; French:683; Gannett:83; Johnson:353]

Cottage. Cattaraugus. The Cottage post office was established sometime after 1850 in the village of West Dalton. [Ellis:232; French:189]

County Line. Niagara. The community is situated on the Niagara-Orleans county line. [French:456; Pool:318; Williams:388]

Coventry, Coventryville. Chenango. The village was named for the former home of early settlers, Coventry, Connecticut, which was named for the English town. When the town was formed in 1806, it took its name from the village. [APN:117; Smith-C&M:180; WPANYS]

Covert. Seneca. This place was first known as Pratt's Corners, for Colonel Pratt, an early settler. Then it was named for E. Covert and his family. [Seneca:163]

Covington. Wyoming. The town was formed in 1817 and named for General Leonard Covington, a hero of the War of 1812. [APN:117; French:713; Gannett:84; WPANY:531; Wyoming:179]

Cowlesville. Wyoming. This place was first known as Clapp's Mills for the sawmill and gristmill built by Quartus Clapp, who bought the land in 1818. In 1832, the name was changed for that of Hiram Cowles. [Wyoming:156]

Coxsackie, West Coxsackie. Greene. The place is named with a Native American word that means "owl hoot." [APN:118; French:332; Gannett:84; Greene:247; Vedder:65; WPANY:591]

Cragsmoor. Ulster. Named for the surrounding landscape. [WPANYA]

Craig(s)ville. Orange. James Craig built a cotton mill and made paper here in 1890. [French:504; R&C:636]

Cranberry Creek. Fulton. The settlement took its name from the creek around which cranberry-like berries grew. [APN:118; French:318; Fulton:227, 235]

Cranberry Lake. St. Lawrence. The community took its name from the lake, which was named for the cranberry bushes growing on its shores. [Harder:55]

Cranesville. Montgomery. David Crane settled here in 1804 and kept a hotel. [French:412; Montgomery:87]

Crary Mills. St. Lawrence. Edward Crary built a gristmill here. When the post office was opened in 1849, it was called Crary's or Crarys Mills. [French:575; Harder:57]

Craryville. Columbia. This was previously known as Baines Corners or Baines Station for the Baines family, who sold the land to Peter Crary in about 1870. The post office was first called North Copake. [Ellis-C:391; WPANYA]

Crescent. Saratoga. Named for the shape of the land between the Hudson and Mohawk Rivers on which the settlement lies. [Syl-S:349; WPANY:561]

Crittenden. Erie. The post office and the train station were both opened in 1852 and named for John J. Crittenden of Kentucky, the attorney general of the United States under President Millard Fillmore. [French:282; Smith-E:450; WPANYS]

Croghan. Lewis. When the town was organized in 1841, both it and the village were named for Colonel George Groghan, a soldier of distinction during the War of 1812. [Bowen:99; French:376; Gannett:85; Hough-L:74]

Crompond. Westchester. The settlement was named for the pond nearby, the name of which is a Dutch word meaning "crooked pond," describing its shape. [Bolton(2):672; French:708; Lederer:35]

Cropseyville. Rensselaer. Jacob Cropsey was an early settler here. The post office was established in 1854. [Weise:106; WPANYS]

Cross River. Westchester. John Cross was one of the first landowners here in 1680. The community took its name from him and the river. [Lederer:36; WPANYS]

Croton Falls, Croton-on-Hudson. Westchester. The Croton River was named for a Native American chief whose name has been recorded as Kenoten, Knoten, Noton, and Cnoten and meant "wind." Croton Falls, at the junction of the east and west branches of the Croton River, changed its name from Owensville in 1846. Croton-on-Hudson, on the Hudson River, was previously called Collabaugh Landing, Cortlandt Town, and then Croton Landing from 1848 to 1891. [APN:121; Bolton(2):259; French:699; Gannett:86; Lederer:36, 37]

Crown Point. Essex. The town was formed in 1786. The name comes either from its French name, Point au Chevalure, said to mean "Crown Point," referring to the scalping parties that the French and Native Americans sent out from here (although the spelling is incorrect and should be *chevelure*), or for the point's prominent position on which there had been a French fort overlooking Lake Champlain. [APN:121; French:300; Gannett:86; Smith-Ex:324–5]

Crugers. Westchester. John Cruger came here from Germany in 1700. His grandson, Colonel John P. Cruger, married Elizabeth, the granddaughter of Staats Morris Dyckman, owner of the Boscobel Estate. [Bolton(1):181; French:699; Gannett:86; Lederer:37; WPANY:579]

Crum Creek. Fulton. The hamlet with a post office was named for the Crum family. [French:319; Fulton:238]

Crystal Dale. Lewis. A descriptive name, sometimes spelled Crystaldale. [Bowen:430]

Cuba, North Cuba. Allegany. The town of Cuba was formed in 1822 as Oil Creek, for the stream. The name was later changed for the island. North Cuba was called Cadyville first. Then in the 1870s, the post office and the settlement were called Seymour for Horatio Seymour, the governor of the state at the time. Later it became North Cuba. [Allegany:246, 249, 251; APN:122; French:173; Minard:813]

Cuddebackville. Orange. Jacob Cuddeback located here in the 1690s and built the first mill. [French:506; R&C:712]

Curriers. Wyoming. Abner Currier came here in 1831 and the place became known as Curriers Corners. Before that, it was called Fox's Corners for Charles Fox, who had settled here in 1819. [French:714; Wyoming:207]

Curry. Sullivan. Stephen Curry and his family settled here in 1795. [Child:191]

Cutchogue. Suffolk. Named for an Algonquian term that means "principal place." [APN:124; Bayles:369; WPANYS]

Cutting. Chautauqua. Named for the Cutting family. [D&H:187]

Cuyler. Cortland. The town was formed in 1858. [French:256]

Cuylerville. Livingston. Named for Colonel Cuyler, who helped lay out this village on the Genesee Valley Canal in 1840 and settled here in 1844. [Doty-L:584; WPANYA]

D

DeRuyter © *2004 by Jon Crispin*

Dairyland. Ulster. A post office with this name was established in the 1870s here in dairy country. [Syl-U:260]

Dale. Wyoming. This place, settled as early as 1825, was named for its geographic location. [Wyoming:222]

Dalton. Livingston. Early settlers came here from Dalton, Massachusetts, in the first decade of the 1800s. [WPANYA; WPANYS]

Dalton Crossing. St. Lawrence. Named for the Dalton family. [Harder:60]

Damascus. Broome. Named for the city in Syria. [APN:127; Gannett:88]

Danby, West Danby. Tompkins. Named for the Earl of Danby, a one-time prime minister of England, who had bought land in New England. The settlers on that land named it after him, then some of them moved to this area and brought the name with them. [Norris:27]

Dannemora. Clinton. The town was named by General St. John B. L. Skinner, when it was formed in 1854, for the iron region in Sweden. The village grew up around the Clinton Prison, built in 1845, with the purpose of using convict labor to mine and manufacture iron, which they did until about 1880. [APN:127; French:237, 238; Hurd-C&F:304; WPANY:513]

Dansville. Livingston. The place was named for Daniel "Captain Dan" P. Faulkner, a prominent pioneer settler who laid out the village. [Doty-L:633; French:385; Gannett:89]

Darien, Darien Center. Genesee. The town was formed in 1832 and named for what was then frequently the name of the isthmus of Panama, although it was really just a province. The village was often called Darien City. Darien Center was formerly called Kings Corners. [APN:128; Beers:405; French:326; North:480-1]

Dashville. Ulster. In about 1833, the Dashville custom—and flouring mill was started here, but there is no record of which name came first or why. [Syl-U:115]

Davenport, Davenport Center, West Davenport. Delaware. John Davenport came from New England and ran the first store. When the town was formed in 1817 and named for him, he was the first supervisor. West Davenport had been called Adaquightinge by the Native Americans. [Delaware:143; French:260; Gannett:90; Murray:335; WPANYS]

Dayton, South Dayton. Cattaraugus. The town was named for Jonathan Dayton, an American statesman. The post office was established in 1852. [Ellis:233; WPANYS]

Deansboro. Oneida. Earlier called Deansville, the community was named for Thomas Dean, an agent of the Brothertown Indians. This was a group of Native Americans organized in 1774 by Reverend Joseph Johnson, a Mohegan and a Baptist preacher, and others, to live together following Christian teachings. Thomas Dean was the son of John Dean, who had been sent by the Society of Friends in 1795 to work among the Brothertons. [French:465; Gannett:91; Oneida:167]

Debruce. Sullivan. Elias Des Brosses bought land here near the junction of Mongaup and Willowenoc Creeks before the Revolutionary War. [Child:196-B; Quinlan:511]

Decatur. Otsego. The town was named, when it was formed in 1808, for Commodore Stephen Decatur, a hero in the war in Tripoli in about 1804. [French:532; Gannett:91; WPANYS]

Deerland. Hamilton. The place had been called Grove until 1903 when the name was changed through the efforts of A. D. Brown, who owned a hotel here. He probably wanted a name that better reflected the surroundings and made the area more attractive for visitors. [A&K:800; WPANYA]

Deer Park. Suffolk. Named for the large number of deer in the area. [WPANYS]

Deer River. Lewis. The place is located on the Deer River, sometimes called Deer Creek, but it was known by a variety of mill owners' names, such as French's Mills for Abel French, then Myers Mills, until the post office was established as Deer River. [Bowen:122; French:376; Hough-L:90]

Deferiet. Jefferson. The Baroness Jenika de Ferriet was a French émigrée in the early 1800s who lived here. [APN:131; WPANY:516]

Defreestville. Rensselaer. This place was sometimes called Blooming Grove, but was named for the DeFreest or DeForest or DeFreist family. The post office was established in 1830. [French:557; Weise:55]

Degrasse. St. Lawrence. This settlement was named for Comte de Francoise Joseph Paul de Grasse, a French officer who played a major role in Cornwallis's surrender at Yorktown in the Revolutionary War. [Harder:64]

De Kalb, De Kalb Junction. St. Lawrence. When the town was formed in 1806, it was named for Baron de Kalb, a German-born officer in the Revolutionary War who was killed at the battle at Camden in 1780. The village was first called either Williamstown or Cooper's Village for Judge William Cooper, who settled there in 1803 or 1805. [APN:131; Curtis:504, 511; French:576; Gannett:91; Harder:64; Hough-SLF:286; Landon:239]

DeLancey. Delaware. James DeLancey Verplanck was an early landowner here. His agent, Charles Hathaway, named the settlement Lansingville for his employer in about 1843. When it was time to apply for a post office, in 1872, there already was a Lansingville in the state, so Hathaway then suggested DeLancey as the name. [Delaware:201; Gannett:91; WPANYS]

Delanson. Schenectady. The village used to be called Quaker Street and boots, shoes, wagons, sashes, and blinds were manufactured here. Quakers are said to have settled here in 1790. The present name comes from the combination of Delaware and Hudson, either the rivers or the railroad. [APN:132; Clark:56; French:596; Munsell:182]

Delevan. Cattaraugus. The village was named in 1892 for Jack Delevan, a boxing trainer and hotelkeeper. This place was a training center for boxers and wrestlers. [WPANY:686]

Delhi. Delaware. The town was formed in 1798. Some of the residents had wanted it to be called Mapleton, but friends of Judge Ebenezer Foote, who was instrumental in the formation of Delaware County and who was responsible for the naming of the town, asked to be allowed to choose the name. The judge's nickname had been "The Great Mogul," the European name for the emperor of Delhi in India, so the name of the town followed. [Delaware:149; French:260; Gannett:92; WPANY:502]

Delmar. Albany. The settlement was first called Adamsville and Adams Station for Nathaniel Adams, who settled here in 1836. The current name was adopted in the 1890s by new families moving in from Albany. The word is Spanish, "of the sea," and was a popular placename for its sound. [Albany:493; APN:132; WPANYA; WPANYS]

Delphi Falls. Onondaga. Named for the Greek town and for the waterfall on Limestone Creek. [APN:133; Clark-O:254; Gannett:92]

Denmark. Lewis. The town was named by the surveyor general in the early 1800s for the European country. [APN:133; Gannett:92; Hough-L:81]

Denning. Ulster. The town was formed in 1849 and named for William H. Denning, a former landowner of a large part of the town. [French:662; Gannett:92; Syl-U:331]

Dennison Corners. Herkimer. This place was first known as Whitmantown for Benjamin Whitman, who first settled here. Then Stanton Dennison bought 640 acres on which the community began to grow, and the town became Dennison's Corners. [Herkimer:183]

Denton. Orange. The place was originally known as the Outlet, but it is named for John Denton, an early settler, and his family. [French:511; R&C:684]

Depauville. Jefferson. Francis Depau built the stone Union Church here in 1834–35. The settlement had been called Catfish Falls. It sits on the Chaumont River, which used to be called Catfish Creek. [D&P:316, 350; French:357; Gannett:92; Hough-J:143; WPANY:641]

Depew. Erie. Most of the village's early growth was due to the establishment of the New York Central train car maintenance shops here in 1893. The place was named for Chauncey M. Depew, a state senator and the president of the New York Central Railroad. [Gannett:92; WPANY:682]

De Peyster. St. Lawrence. The town was formed in 1825 and was going to be named for Smith Stillwell, a prominent citizen. He declined the honor, saying that there was a good chance that one of the major landholders here would probably give money to the town if it was named for him. Frederick De Peyster, a shipping merchant of New York City who owned land here, gave the town three hundred dollars to help build the Union Church. In 1840, his son gave a seven-hundred-pound bell to the town. [Curtis:641; French:576; Gannett:92; Harder:66; Hough-SLF:294; Landon:239]

Deposit. Broome. The native people called this clearing where they planted corn Cokeose, meaning "owl's nest." This word became corrupted into Cookhouse. The village grew up around lumbering, and this location was where the lumber was deposited after being rafted down the Delaware River before being sent on to Philadelphia in the springtime. [French:265; Gannett:93; Murray:357, 364; Smith-B:313]

Derby. Erie. Named for Derby, England. The place was settled in 1814 and the post office was established in 1874. [APN:134; Gannett:93; Smith-E:582; WPANYS]

Dering Harbor. Suffolk. Henry Dering settled here in 1658. The village was incorporated in 1916. [WPANYS]

DeRuyter. Madison. The town was part of the Lincklaen purchase and was named by John Lincklaen, Admiral DeRuyter, of the Dutch Navy when it was formed in 1798. The village had been called Trompville, but took the name of the town when the post office was established in 1810. [French:390; Gannett:93; Smith-C&M:593; WPANYS]

DeWitt. Onondaga. The town was formed in 1835 and named for Moses Dewitt, an early settler and a prominent citizen. The village has been called Youngsville, for John Young who settled here in about 1790, and Hull's Landing before the post office was established in 1814 as Orville. In 1835, the named was changed to DeWitt. [Bruce:1017, 1020–21; Clark-O:232; Clayton:386; French:481]

Dewittville. Chautauqua. The settlement was earlier called Tinkertown, then changed its name in honor of Governor Dewitt Clinton. [APN:136; D&H:237; WPANYS]

Dexter. Jefferson. S. Newton Dexter of Whiteboro was an early proprietor here. The place was formerly known as Fish Island. [D&P:304, 316; French:356; Gannett:94; Hough-J:104]

Dexterville. Oswego. Rodman Dexter settled here in about 1829, then built a steam sawmill in 1851. [Churchill:531; Johnson-O:393]

Diamond Point. Warren. This place was settled in about 1800, at which time it was called High View. It became known as Diamond Point, probably for the quartz crystals found near the Lake George shore. [WPANYS; WPAW:212]

Diana. Lewis. The town was named for the goddess of hunting by Joseph Bonaparte, who owned land here and thought that the hunting was excellent. [Gannett:94; Hough-L:94]

Dickersonville. Niagara. The community was named for Colonel Alexander Dickerson, an early settler and tavernkeeper. [Pool:300; Williams:384]

Dickinson, Dickinson Center. Franklin. The town was organized in 1808 and named by Jonathan Dayton, a landowner, for his friend Philemon Dickinson, who was interested in the Macomb Purchase of which this land was a part. The village of Dickinson Center had been called Thomasville for John Thomas who settled here in 1839. [French:310; Hough-SLF:496; Hurd-C&F:476]

Dix Hills. Suffolk. Named for Dick Pechegan, said to be a Native American who lived here. [APN:138]

Dobbs Ferry. Westchester. Starting in 1698, Jeremiah Dobbs ran a ferry across the Hudson River from here. This name was applied to landings on both sides of the river until 1759, when the service was taken over by the Sneden family of Rockland County and the western end became Sneden's Landing. The Native American name of this place had been Weecquaesguck, meaning "the place of the bark kettle." [Bolton(1):274; French:700; Lederer:41; S&S:611; WPANY:587, 621]

Dolgeville. Herkimer. The village of Brockett's Bridge was on East Canada Creek and had been named for the man who built or maintained the bridge here. In 1875, Alfred Dolge, a businessman, brought in several thousand factory workers to manufacture felt slippers in a new industry that he built here. In 1881, the village took his name. [French:346; WPANY:491]

Dongan Hills. Richmond. Thomas Dongan was the colonial governor in 1682, and he was granted land here as part of his appointment. [Jackson:341; WPANYC:609]

Doraville. Broome. This was a post office and a station on the Delaware and Hudson Canal Company's railroad. [Smith-B:340]

Dorloo. Schoharie. When Germans settled here in 1754, they named the place New Dorlach for the city in Germany. This name became corrupted into the present name. [French:607; Sias:148; WPANYA]

Dormansville. Albany. Daniel Dorman was a former inn—and storekeeper here. He was the first postmaster when the post office opened in 1832. [Albany:532; French:167; Gannett:96; Howell:923]

Douglaston. Queens. George Douglas bought land here in 1835. Before that time, the place was called Little Madman's Neck, then Little Neck. In 1866, his son, William P. Douglas, donated a right of way to the Long Island Railroad. This resulted in a station being named for him. [Jackson:342; WPANYC:572]

Dover Furnace, Dover Plains, South Dover. Dutchess. The town of Dover was formed in 1807; it contained marble quarries, iron ore, and a limestone ridge, which gave the place its name as reminiscent of Dover, England. Dover Furnace was the location of the South Boston Iron Company, established in 1881. Dover Plains was named by Jackson Wing, an early settler, for its location with the hills to its west that contain iron ore and marble. The train depot at South Dover had been called Wing's Station, for Jackson Wing. The post office at Wing's was established in about 1852, but the post office at South Dover, two miles east of the station, was opened in 1828. Eventually they merged. [APN:141; Gannett:96; Smith-D:489; WPANYD:120]

Downsville. Delaware. George Downs built a tannery here in 1848 and later several mills. His name was attached to Downs Creek and soon to the settlement. [Delaware:139; French:260; Gannett:96; Murray:317]

Dresden, Dresden Station. Washington. When the town was formed in March of 1822, it was named South Bay. A month later, it was renamed for the German city, but there is no record of why. [APN:142; French:680; Gannett:96; Johnson:285; Stone:414]

Dresden. Yates. Named for the city in Germany. [APN:142; French:721; Gannett:96]

Dryden. Tompkins. Named after the English poet, John Dryden, part of the classical naming of the Military Tract. [APN:143; French:656; Gannett:97; Norris:21; Selkreg:244]

Duane Center. Franklin. The community is in the town of Duane, both taking their name from James Duane of Schenectady, son-in-law of William Constable who owned land here, some of which was given to Duane at the time of his marriage. He had the land surveyed in 1821 and settled permanently in 1825. [French:310; Gannett:97; Hough-SLF:497; Hurd-C&F:479; WPA-NYS]

Duanesburg. Schenectady. The town was formed in 1788. James Duane was a principal proprietor who took an active part in public affairs during the Revolution and the early years of the state government, and then was a benefactor of the place, settling here in 1765. The settlement was formerly called Jamesville for a wealthy Mr. James, who owned a good deal of land here. Locally, the place was called the Four Corners. [Clark:56; French:596; Gannett:97; Munsell:172, 185; WPANY:417]

Dublin. Seneca. Named for the city in Ireland. [APN:143]

Dundee. Yates. This village was early known as Harpending's Corners for Samuel Harpending who was postmaster in 1825. There was a move to name the village Plainville for the plain on which it sat, but this was not popular. In 1833, James T. Gifford named the place for the town in Scotland. He had come here from Binghamton in 1832 and built a sawmill. In 1835, he left and founded the city of Elgin, Illinois, which he also named. [APN:144; Cleveland:1126, 1130–1; Gannett:97]

Dunkirk. Chautauqua. The bay here had been called Garnsey's Bay, then Chadwick's Bay for Solomon Chadwick, an early settler. The name Dunkirk was given by Elisha Jenkins, who was a proprietor of the village (later a city) and who had spent some time in France. He found a resemblance between Chadwick's Bay and the harbor in Dunkirk, France. The Native American name for the place was Ganadawao, meaning "running through the hemlocks." [D&H:145; French:214; Gannett:98; McMahon:380; Morgan:463]

Dunnsville. Albany. Christopher Dunn was the original owner of the land here. Locally, the place was known as Hardscrabble. [Albany:524; French:164; Gannett:98; Howell:853]

Dunraven. Delaware. The settlement was first called Clark's Factory for the Clark family, who had a large tannery here. The name was later changed for the Earl of Dunraven, W. T. Wyndham-Quinn, a big-game sportsman in the 1870s. [APN:144; French:263; WPANYS]

Dunsbach Ferry. Albany. This place was the location of a ferry across the Mohawk River named for early settlers, early spelled Dunsback. [Howell:935]

Durham, East Durham. Greene. The town was formed in 1790 as Freehold, from the village that was located on a piece of land between two patents and therefore free for settlement. The name was changed in 1805 to Durham, for the Connecticut home of a number of settlers. The village first took the name New Durham, then dropped the New. [French:332; Greene:256, 257; Vedder:74, 75, 78]

Durhamville. Oneida. Eber Durham came here from Manlius in 1826. He leased water from the Erie Canal that he used to run a variety of mills and factories here. [Oneida:204]

Dwaarkill. Ulster. Named for the stream, whose name comes from the Dutch word used for streams that sometimes flowed in one direction, other times in another, a phenomenon that happens at the mouth of a stream during a flood. [APN:145; French:667]

E

Erie Canal © *2004 by Jon Crispin*

Eagle. Wyoming. This former part of the Holland Purchase was named for the presence of the bird. The town was formed in 1823. [Gannett:99; Wyoming:182]

Eagle Bay. Herkimer. The village is on the north shore of the Fourth Lake of the Fulton Chain of Lakes. It was settled in about 1820. Its name is descriptive. [WPANYS]

Eagle Bridge. Rensselaer. There was a bridge built over the Hoosick River here, probably named for the bird. [French:556]

Eagle Harbor. Orleans. Named for a large bird's nest found when the Erie Canal was surveyed that was thought to be that of an eagle. [Signor:454]

Eagle Mills. Rensselaer. The settlement was first known as Milltown, then Millville, for all the mills built to exploit the power of the Poesten Kill. [French:554; Weise:105]

Eagle Valley. Orange. This station on the Erie Railroad was named for its geographic description. [R&C:795]

Earlton. Greene. Named for an early settler. [WPANYA]

Earlville. Madison. The village was known as the Forks for its location between the two branches of the Chenango River. When the Chenango Canal was constructed through here in 1834, the village changed its name to a more dignified Earlville, for the canal commissioner, Jonas Earl. [French:391; Gannett:99; Smith-C&M:565]

East Aurora. Erie. The town of Aurora was formed in 1804 as Willink, for William Willink, the head of the Holland Land Company. Its name was changed in 1818 for the goddess of the dawn. The village of East Aurora was made up of two hamlets, Upper Village and Lower Village. They came together in 1873 to become East Aurora, named for their location in the town. This village lies ninety miles west of the village of Aurora in Cayuga County. [French:283; Smith-E:541, 546, 550; WPANY:442]

East Branch. Delaware. The settlement had been called Beaverkill, but the post office was named East Branch for its location where the Beaver Kill enters the east branch of the Delaware River. The Native American village that had stood on this spot was called Pacatacan. [Delaware:205, 212; Murray:407; WPANYS]

Eastchester. Westchester. The town was recognized as such in 1788. Before that, it had been called Ost Dorp, "East Town," by the Dutch for its location east of New Amsterdam. [Bolton(1):201; Lederer:45]

East Concord. Erie. This place lies in the east part of the town of Concord, which was named from a hymn. The post office was opened in about 1862. [Smith-E:633, 644]

East Glenville. Schenectady. The town of Glenville was formed in 1820. Sanders or Sandir Leednertse Glen was the original patentee with a manor on the site. [Clark:56; French:597; Gannett:121; Munsell:186]

East Greenbush. Rensselaer. The town was formed as Clinton in 1855; its name was changed in 1858. This place was first settled by the Dutch and called Het Groen Bosch, meaning "green bush," for the pine woods that were perpetually green. The post office was established in 1855. [French:554; Gannett:99; Weise:50–1]

East Hills. Nassau. Before 1931, this was informally a part of the village of Roslyn. But when Roslyn was to be incorporated, this section did not want to be annexed to Roslyn, so they set out to be incorporated on their own. Civil engineer Harold Hawxhurst, surveyor of the area to be incorporated, suggested the name East Hills for the pretty landscape east of Roslyn. [Winsche:27; WPANYS]

East Hounsfield. Jefferson. Ezra Houndsfield was an agent for his brothers, who were proprietors here. He came here in about 1800 from Sheffield, England, where his brothers were manufacturers and merchants. When the town was formed, in 1806, it was named for him through the efforts of his friend August Sacket, who used to spend his summers here. The town's name, however, was spelled without the *d*. The settlement was named for its location in the town. [D&P:392; French:358; Gannett:140; Hough-J:172]

East Meadow. Nassau. This was pastureland east of the village of Hempstead in 1644 and has kept the name since. [Winsche:27–8]

East New York. Kings. John Pitkin came here from Connecticut in 1835 and bought land that he developed. He chose this name to make people think that this place was the eastern end of New York City. [French:373; Jackson:357; WPANYC:500]

East Norwich. Nassau. James and George Townsend settled here in the 1670s and named the place Norwich for the city in England that was their father's home. When applying for a post office, there already was a Norwich post office in the state, precluding their use of the name. In 1846, the post office was opened as East Norwich, and the community took the name as well. [French:551; Winsche:28; WPANYS]

Easton, North Easton. Washington. The town was formed in 1789 and was named for its location in the Saratoga patent. [APN:146; French:680; Johnson:290]

East Park. Dutchess. Named for its location east of Hyde Park.

Eastport. Suffolk. The village was first called Seatuck, for the Native American name of the stream on which it was located. A post office was established in 1849, then discontinued in 1857. The village changed its name in 1860 for its location in the eastern part of the town of Brookhaven. The post office was again established in 1873. [Bayles:281; Suffolk/Brookhaven:56]

East Rockaway. Nassau. In the 1670s, this was called Near Rockaway to distinguish it from Far Rockaway, determined by their proximity to Hempstead. The post office was established here as Atlantic in 1868, but there already was one in the state, so the name was changed to East Rockaway in 1869. In New Jersey, Rockaway is derived from the Native American term *rechawackes* or *achewek*, meaning "bushy" or "difficult to cross," or maybe "sandy place." [APN:408; Gannett:224; Winsche:29]

East Winfield, West Winfield. Herkimer. The town of Winfield was formed in 1816 and named by Dr. John J. Prendergast, the member of the state senate responsible for the legislation that created the town. He proposed that the town be named Scott for General Winfield Scott. When told that there already was a town by that name, he decided to use Scott's first name instead.

The settlements take their names from their locations in the town. [French:349; Gannett:275; Herkimer:126]

Eastwood. Onondaga. This is an eastern suburb of Syracuse, named for its geographic location. [Gannett:100]

Eaton, West Eaton. Madison. The town was formed in 1807 and named for General William Eaton, who had served in the war in Tripoli and then returned in 1806 to Brimfield, Massuchusetts, the home of settlers to central New York. The village of Eaton had been called Log City. West Eaton had been called Leeville. [French:390, 391; Gannett:100; Smith-C&M:623, 636]

Ebenezer. Erie. In 1842, a group of German settlers looking for religious freedom bought land here. They were known to others as Ebenezers, a term used to describe dissenting religious denominations, but they called themselves the "Community of True Inspiration." There were three villages in the town: Middle Ebenezer, Lower Ebenezer, and New Ebenezer. Starting in 1855, they moved to Iowa to become the Amana Colonies. By 1864, they were gone from western New York and were replaced by other German immigrants who bought the houses in the villages. The Ebenezer post office was established at Lower Ebenezer. [Amana; APN:147; French:293; Gannett:100; Smith-E:505–7]

Eddyville. Cattaraugus. Before 1848, William and Levi Eddy built the first frame houses and Enos C. Eddy owned land here. [Ellis:459; French:193]

Eddyville. Ulster. John Eddy operated a gristmill here on Rondout Creek. [French:664; Syl-U:336]

Eden, East Eden. Erie. When the town was organized in 1812, John Hill suggested the name because he considered this place to be "the garden of the world." The community of Eden had been called Tubb's Hollow for Samuel Tubbs who had settled here in about 1808. [APN:147; Smith-E:585; WPA-NYS]

Edenville. Orange. The place was first called Postville for Jacobus Post, whose father settled here and owned the lands on which the village is located. It is in the area of Mounts Adam and Eve, so when the post office was established, it took the name of the garden of paradise in which they lived. [R&C:579]

Edgemere. Queens. Frederick J. Lancaster bought the land here in 1892 and formed a development company called the Sea Beach Improvement Company in 1894. The place was first called New Venice. The name was later changed to the Anglo-Saxon words meaning "edge of the sea." [Jackson:363]

Edinburg. Saratoga. The town was formed in 1801 as Northfield. Its name was changed in 1808 for the city in Scotland by people who had come from there. [APN:148; French:588; Gannett:101; Syl-S:372]

Edmeston, South Edmeston, West Edmeston. Otsego. Colonel Edmeston was granted a large tract of land here in 1770 for his service in the British Army. He and Percifer Carr were the first settlers here in the early 1770s. The town was named for him when it was formed in 1808. The settlements took their names from the town and their geographic locations in it. [French:533; Gannett:101; Hurd-O:143]

Edwards. St. Lawrence. In 1814, the village here was called Sheads Mills and Sheads Corners for Orra Shead who built a gristmill here. In 1827, a town was formed; it was named for Edward McCormack, the brother of the proprietor, Daniel McCormack. However, the names of both the village and the town were changed to Edwards when the first post office was established in 1827 or 1828. [Curtis:662; French:576; Harder:75; Hough-SLF:297; Landon:239]

Edwardsville. St. Lawrence. Sitting on the narrowest part of Black Lake, this place had been known as the Narrows and a ferry had been opened here. The first postmaster was Jonathan S. Edwards. On early maps, it was labeled Marysburgh. [French:580; Harder:75]

Egypt. Monroe. The Ramsdell family came here in about 1800 and planted large crops of corn on their large tract of land. This corn fed many others during a time of scarcity, leading to the Ramsdell land being associated with the biblical story of Joseph in Egypt and the seven years of plenty. [APN:149; Gannett:102; Peck:361; WPARM:402]

Elba. Genesee. When the town was formed in 1820, it was named for the Mediterranean island on which Napoleon had been exiled. The post office named Elba was established in the village of Pine Hill, which eventually changed its name to match that of the post office. [APN:149; Beers:433; French:326; Gannett:102; North:482]

Elbridge. Onondaga. Although the town was formed in 1829, a village had been established before that. In 1813, a post office had opened there, named for Elbridge Gerry, a signer of the Declaration of Independence, vice president of the United States, and a governor of Massachusetts. As governor, Gerry was the one responsible for the practice of manipulating political boundaries that we now call gerrymandering. [C&V:1076; Clark-O:320; Clayton:298–9; French:482; Gannett:102]

Eldred. Sullivan. James Eldred was an early settler here. The place had been called Lumberland for the early activity in the area. This soon changed to quarrying. [French:646; Quinlan:167]

Elizabethtown. Essex. The town was formed in 1798 and named for Elizabeth, the wife of William Gilliland, one of the first settlers in the county. The village had been called Pleasant Valley and sometimes just the Valley. [French:301; Smith-Ex:466, 487]

Elizaville. Columbia. In about 1803, a tavern was built here called the Union Corner House. From this, the community was called Union Corners. In 1840, the post office was opened as Elizaville. [Ellis-C:260; French:248]

Elka Park. Greene. This was originally a colony of private residences, admission allowed only by invitation or with letters of introduction. The name origin is not recorded. [WPANY:408]

Elk Creek. Otsego. Named for the stream of that name when it was settled in about 1790. [WPANYS]

Ellenburg, Ellenburg Center, Ellenburg Depot. Clinton. When the town was formed in 1830, it was named for Ellen Murray, the daughter of John R. and Harriet Murray. The Murrays offered ten homesteads to the first settlers, who then named the town for the Murrays' daughter in return. Ellenburg Depot was sometimes known as Carter's Mills. Ellenburg Center received its name when a post office was established here, near the center of the town, in 1856. [French:238; Gannett:103; Hurd-C&F:313, 316, 318]

Ellenville. Ulster. In the 1820s, this place was known as the City or Fairchild City. When the time came for a post office, in 1823, the decision of the name was left to the women of the community. A Miss Ellen Snyder said, "Name it for me; call it Ellenville," and they did. She later married Captain William Tremper. [Syl-U:258]

Ellicott. Erie. This town was named for Joseph Ellicott of the Holland Land Company. The Seneca name for this place was Gadaoyadeh, meaning "level heavens." [Gannett:103; Parker:298; Smith-E:530]

Ellicottville. Cattaraugus. The town was organized in 1820 and named for Joseph Ellicott, an agent for the Holland Land Company. The first post office was opened in 1822. The Native American name for the village was Deashendaqua or Deahendaqua, meaning "the place for holding court." [Ellis:255, 262; French:189; Gannett:103; Morgan:466; Parker:290; WPANY:688]

Ellington. Chautauqua. Named for Ellington, Connecticut, the former home of early settlers. [D&H:170; McMahon:298]

Ellisburg. Jefferson. Marvel Ellis was an early proprietor here and his brother, Lyman Ellis, was an early settler in 1797. The village was called Ellis Village, but the post office was established as Ellisburg, a name the village eventually took. [D&P:354, 361; French:357; Gannett:104; Hough-J:146, 158]

Elma. Erie. When the town was formed in 1857, it was named for the large elm tree, about four feet in diameter, that stood near the community of Elma that was also named for the tree. [APN:152; French:290; Gannett:104; Smith-E:233, 492]

Elmdale. St. Lawrence. Named for the tree and the valley. [Harder:77]

Elmhurst, East Elmhurst. Queens. In 1652, the place was called Newtown and was the administrative center of the town of Newtown. The name was changed in 1896 because, by that time, Newtown Creek was quite foul smelling and the residents did not want to be associated with it. [Jackson:373; WPANYC:580]

Elmira, East Elmira, West Elmira, Elmira Heights. Chemung. Both the village, now city, and the town of Elmira were first called Newtown. The town was formed in 1792 and changed its name to Elmira in 1808. The village changed its name in 1828. Elmira is the name of a woman, either the daughter of Nathan Teall, whose mother called her name so often that is became associated with the place, or that of a lady admired by Matthew Carpenter, a member of the legislature, who thought that Newtown sitting in its beautiful valley should be named for her. The Native American name for the place was Skwedowa, "great plain." [APN:152; French:220; Gannett:104; Morgan:469; P&H-C:78; WPANY:230]

Elmont. Nassau. The place was first called Foster's Meadow for Christopher and Thomas Foster, but the name Elmont was already in use by about 1659, although there is no record of why. The post office was established in 1882. [French:547; Winsche:30–1]

Elmsford. Westchester. A large elm tree at a crossroads here gave the place its name. It was previously called Storm's Bridge and Hall's Corners. [Lederer:47; WPANYS]

Elm Valley. Allegany. This place on Dyke's Creek, named for Nathaniel Dyke who made the first settlement here in 1795, had been called Shoemaker's Corners. When the post office was established, sometime before 1860, it was called Elm Creek, which became the name of the settlement. [Allegany:189; French:171]

Elnora. Saratoga. This place might have been named by a railroad engineer for his wife when the railroad came through. [WPANYA; WPANYS]

Eltingville. Richmond. This was first called South Side and Sea Side, the latter in 1873 for the post office name. Later, it took the name of a family from the early nineteenth century. [Jackson:374]

Elton. Cattaraugus. This place was first called Cole's Settlement for Nathan and Daniel Cole, the first owners and settlers. [Ellis:395]

Endicott. Broome. This place was named for Henry B. Endicott, the chief stockholder of the Endicott-Johnson Company that had shoe factories in the area. [WPANY:387]

Endwell. Broome. The place was first settled by Elisha Hooper in 1807 and was known as Hooper. There is no record for the present name. [WPANYS]

Enfield. Tompkins. Named for Enfield, Connecticut, from which some early settlers had come, which in turn was named for the Enfield in England. [APN:154; French:656; Norris:31; P&H-T:199; Selkreg:353]

Ephratah. Fulton. When the town was formed in 1827, it was named by Anthony Beck, an old resident, for the place in the Bible, meaning "abundance; bearing fruit." Beck was said to have been able to foresee the future. [APN:155; Fulton:221; Gannett:105]

Erieville. Madison. Eri or Erie Richardson was an early merchant and a prominent businessman here. [Smith-C&M:647]

Erin. Chemung. Named by the many Irish settlers here for the ancient name of Ireland. [Gannett:106; P&H-C:220]

Erwin. Steuben. When the town was formed in 1826, it was named for Revolutionary War colonel Arthur Erwin. Erwin, originally from Bucks County, Pennsylvania, bought land here in 1789. [French:625; Gannett:106; Steuben:100]

Escarpment. Niagara. This place is named for its location on the Niagara Escarpment.

Esopus. Ulster. The town was formed in 1811 and named with a Native American word meaning "a place of high banks." [APN:157; French:662; Fried:7; Gannett:106; Syl-U:113]

Esperance. Schoharie. The town was formed in 1846 and named for the village, land owned by General William North, who bought it in 1800, laid it out in lots, and named it for the French word meaning "hope." [French:604; Gannett:106; Noyes:152; Roscoe:321; Sias:133–4; WPANY:418]

Essex. Essex. The town was formed in 1805 and named for the English county, as was the New York county. The settlement had been called Elizabeth, for William Gilliland's daughter who lived here after she married Daniel Ross in 1785, but the name conflicted with that of Elizabethtown and so the settlement name was changed to that of the town. [APN:157; French:301; Gannett:106; Smith-Ex:542; WPANYA]

Etna. Tompkins. Named for the volcano in Sicily, which was brought to mind because some of the local chimneys spewed flames and smoke from the wood they burned. At first it was known as Miller's Settlement for William Miller who settled here in about 1800. Then it was called Columbia until the post office was established. [Norris:23; P&H-T:181; Selkreg:263]

Euclid. Onondaga. The community had been called Clay Corners for its location in the town, but the name was changed, probably when the post office was established in 1827, to honor the Greek mathematician. [Bruce:826, 830; Clark-O:192; Clayton:334; Gannett:107; WPANYA]

Evans Center, North Evans. Erie. These places take their name from the town, which, when it was formed in 1821, was named for David E. Evans, an agent of the Holland Land Company. Evans Center was called Wright's Mills for William Wright who, with Henry Tuttle, built a sawmill and a gristmill in

1815–16. When the town was formed and the post office was established in 1821 as Evans, the settlement became known as Evans Center. North Evans in is the northwest corner of the town and is named for its location. [French:290; Gannett:107; Smith-E:574, 578, 582]

Exeter Center, West Exeter. Otsego. Major John Tunnicliff named this place for the English city when he settled here in 1789. The town was formed as Exeter in 1799. [APN:159; French:533; Gannett:107; WPANYS]

F

Finger Lakes © *2004 by Jon Crispin*

Fabius. Onondaga. The town was formed in 1798 and named, in 1790 as part of the Military Tract, for one of the Roman consuls. The village was previously called Franklinville, then became Fabius Center for its location in the town. [APN:161; Bruce:873; Clark-O:330–2, 382; French:482, 483]

Factory Village. Saratoga. The settlement took its name from the two paper mills that manufactured paper here in the mid-1800s. [French:590; Syl-S:487]

Fairfield. Herkimer. The town was formed in 1796 and named for Fairfield, Connecticut, the former home of some residents. [French:343; Herkimer:158; WPANYS]

Fair Haven. Cayuga. This village sits on a bay of Lake Ontario and takes its name from the shelter that the bay offers sailing ships as well as the beautiful wooded shoreline.[French:205]

Fairmount. Onondaga. Named with a combination of words meaning "beautiful hill." The post office here was established before 1860. [APN:161; French:481]

Fairport. Monroe. The place had been known as Fullam Town or Fullam's for a family that lived here. When the Erie Canal came through, the village benefited greatly from its business, so when the town was incorporated in 1867, it took its name from its location. [Peck:366; WPARM:290; WPANYS]

Fairview. Westchester. In 1914, a developer thought that this place had a good view of the Westchester County Fairgrounds that used to be to the north of the road where he was doing his developing. [Lederer:48]

Falconer. Chautauqua. Robert Falconer and his sons, Patrick and William, came to this area and bought existing mills at Worksburg, named for Edward Work who had built them in 1844. By 1874, the village was called Falconer. The name Falconer was applied to Kennedyville from 1852 to 1861. [D&H:161; French:214; McMahon:299]

Fallsburg, South Fallsburg. Sullivan. This place was first called the Falls of the Neversink for the twenty-three-foot waterfall on the Neversink River. Thomas Lockwood ran a sawmill and gristmill here that were built in 1808 by Herman Ruggles and Henry Reed. By 1816, the place was known as Lockwood's Mills. When the town was organized in 1826, it was proposed that it be named for Lockwood, but he opposed this, saying that it should be named Fallsburg. [Child:136; French:644; Quinlan:257–8]

Fancher. Orleans. Edward Fancher moved here with his family in about 1872. [Singor:182]

Farmers Mills. Putnam. In 1838, a group of farmers bought land that had a number of mills on it and had been called Milltown. The name change reflected the service the mills provided to the farmers. [Blake:332; Pelletreau:683]

Farmersville Station. Cattaraugus. The first settlers came here in the 1810s to establish farms, and the place was called Farmersville. Eventually, a train station was built, adding the "station" to the name. [Ellis:370–1; French:190; WPANYS]

Farmingdale. Nassau. In 1814, this town was called Hardscrabble. It was changed in 1843 through the efforts of land speculator Ambrose George, who thought that the place needed a nicer name. He coined this name from the main occupation of the folks here and the euphonious "dale." [Winsche:31; WPANYS]

Farmington. Ontario. This settlement was named for Farmington, Connecticut, which was in turn named for a place in England. The New York town was first settled by Quakers in 1789. [French:496; Gannett:108; Milliken:105]

Farnham. Erie. This was the name of the post office established at Mill Branch, which was the Saw Mill Station on the B and E Railroad. It was named for

LeRoy Farnham, the first merchant in the area. [French:283; Gannett:108; Smith-E:629]

Far Rockaway, Rockaway Park, Rockaway Point. Queens. The Canarsee Indians had named the peninsula Reckouacky, probably meaning "place of our people." In 1860, the Rockaway post office was in Far Rockaway. [French:547; Jackson:391, 1013; WPANYC:591]

Fayette. Seneca. The town was called Washington when it was organized in 1800. The name was changed in 1808 for the Marquis de Lafayette, a French officer who served under Washington in the Revolutionary War. [APN:163; French:615; Gannett:109; Seneca:131]

Fayetteville. Onondaga. The village was first called the Corners, then Manlius Four Corners, but after the post office was established, it became Fayetteville for the Marquis de Lafayette. [APN:163; Bruce:790; Clark-O:217; Clayton:370; Gannett:109]

Felts Mills. Jefferson. In 1813, John Felt bought land here that had several mills on it. [D&P:499; French:361; Gannett:109; Hough-J:237]

Fenner. Madison. Colonel Arnold Ballou suggested that the new town, organized in 1823, be named for James Fenner, governor of Rhode Island. [French:391; Gannett:109; Smith-C&M:694]

Ferenbaugh. Steuben. Named for early settlers with this name. [Steuben:321]

Fergusonville. Delaware. The Ferguson family was prominent here in the early 1800s. The Reverends Samuel D. and Sanford I. Ferguson opened the Fergusonville Academy here in about 1848. [Delaware:146; French:260; Gannett:109]

Ferndale. Sullivan. A descriptive name for the area. [Child:159; WPANYS]

Fernwood. Oswego. This might have been called Holmesville, for the Holmes family that lived here, before its name was changed for the plants that grew here. [French:527; Johnson-O:209; WPANYA]

Fernwood. Saratoga. Named for the plants in the area. [APN:164; Gannett:110; WPANYS]

Feura Bush. Albany. The name comes from the Dutch for "burning bush," but why it was chosen is not recorded. In 1860, it was spelled Feuribush. The post office had earlier been called Jerusalem. [Albany:552; APN:164; French:164; Howell:902; WPANYS]

Fillmore. Allegany. This canal village at the mouth of Cold Creek was called "the mouth of the creek" for its location. When the post office was established, in 1850, some folks wanted it to be called Fayette City, but this did not catch on, and the town was named instead for President Millard Fillmore (1850–53).[Allegany:312; French:174; Minard:744–45]

Finchville. Orange. James Finch, a soldier in the French and Indian War and a

minuteman in the Revolution, settled here sometime before the Revolutionary War. [French:508; R&C:511]

Findley Lake. Chautauqua. Alexander Findley came to Greenville, Pennsylvania,
from Ireland in about 1790. In 1811, he bought land at the foot of the lake
that was named for him. He built a sawmill in 1815 and a gristmill in 1816.
The settlement grew up around his mills and took the name of the lake. His
name was sometimes spelled as Finley. [D&H:205–6; French:214; McMa-
hon:300]

Fine. St. Lawrence. John Fine, of Ogdensburg, was a principal proprietor here
when the town was formed in 1844. The community had been known as
Scriba. It was renamed Smithville in 1854 when the post office was established with William P. Smith as the first postmaster. Later the name was
changed to Andersonville for Joseph Anderson, the builder of an oar factory
here. The name was then changed to Fine because of the unpleasant association with the Civil War prison of Andersonville, Georgia. [Curtis:698–9;
French:576–7; Gannett:110; Harder:81; Hough-SLF:298]

Fire Island Pines. Suffolk. Named probably for a fire seen by early explorers.
[APN:165]

Firthcliffe. Orange. This settlement was once known as Montana Woolen Mills,
but the origin of the current name is not known. [WPANYS]

Fishers. Ontario. Named for first settlers of that name. [Milliken:105]

Fishers Island. Suffolk. Adrian Block first set foot on this island in 1614 and
named it Vischer's Island. [Bayles:390; French:639]

Fish House. Fulton. The place is named for a house that Sir William Johnson had
built here in 1762 that was used for hunting and fishing, which had always
been called the Fish House. [Fulton:235]

Fishkill, East Fishkill, Fishkill Plains. Dutchess. The town of Fishkill, formed in
1788, was named for a nearby creek, also named Fishkill from the Dutch term
visch-kill, meaning "fish creek." The town of East Fishkill was formed in 1849
and named for its location. [APN:166; French:271; Gannett:110; Smith-
D:505]

Fishs Eddy. Delaware. Named for the eddy in the river at this spot.
[Delaware:205; WPANYS]

Flackville. St. Lawrence. John P. Flack settled here in 1830, built many buildings,
and was the first postmaster. [Curtis:326; Gannett:110; Harder:82; WPA-
NYA]

Flanders. Suffolk. Josiah Goodale and Ellis Squires were the first white settlers
here. It was named for the place in France. [Suffolk/Southampton:30; WPA-
NYS]

Flatbush. Kings. The Dutch called this place Vlackebos, "wooded plain," for the woods that grew on the flat land here. [APN:167; French:372; Gannett:111; Jackson:416; WPANYC:493]

Flat Creek. Montgomery. Named for the creek that is very smooth at this spot. [Frothingham:343; Montgomery:163, 164]

Flatlands. Kings. The Canarsee Indians called this place Keskachauge. The Dutch called it Neue Amserfoort for a place in Holland. The British called it Flatlands for its geographic description. [French:372; Jackson:417; WPANYC:502]

Fleischmanns. Delaware. Members of the Fleishman family had summer homes here. [Murray:510; WPANY:503]

Fleming. Cayuga. The town was first settled in 1790, organized in 1823, and named for General George Fleming, an early settler in the town. The village was settled in 1798. [French:201; Storke:377]

Flemingville. Tioga. Captain David Fleming was an early settler and the first postmaster. He had come here with his family in about 1804. [Gay:396; P&H-Ti:145]

Flint. Ontario. This place was first known as Flint Creek, named for a stream with a flinty bed. [French:498; Milliken:105]

Floral Park. Nassau. A Central Railroad of Long Island depot was established here and called Hinsdale for Elizur B. Hinsdale, a prominent railroad officer. The village took the name Hinsdale, but when applying for a post office, they found that there already was one in the state, so they changed their name to East Hinsdale in 1877. In 1884, the East Hinsdale post office was closed and a new one, named Floral for the flower beds here, was opened at the John Lewis Childs seed store. In 1886, the East Hinsdale railroad station changed its name to Floral, but not everyone was happy with this. Finally, after much discussion, in 1887 agreement was reached with the name Floral Park. [Winsche:33; WPANYS]

Florence. Oneida. When the town was formed in 1805, it was named for the city in Italy. [French:463; Gannett:111; Oneida:141]

Florida. Orange. This village was formerly known as Brookland, but the name was changed for the Latin *floridus,* "covered with flowers," sometime before the Revolutionary War. [R&C:578; WPANYS]

Flower Hill. Nassau. This was a farming neighborhood that had been referred to as Flower Hill since about 1759, probably for the plants in the area. [French:550; Winsche:33–4; WPANYS]

Floyd. Oneida. When it was organized in 1796, the town was named for General William Floyd, a signer of the Declaration of Independence. [French:463; Gannett:111; Oneida:145]

Flushing. Queens. This name comes from the Dutch, Vlissingen, the name of a village in the Netherlands. [APN:168; French:546; Gannett:112; Jackson:419; WPANYC:568]

Fluvanna. Chautauqua. Named for Fluvia and Anna, daughters of Nathaniel and Jacob Fenton, early settlers here. [McMahon:301]

Fly Creek. Otsego. The creek name comes from the Dutch *vallei* corrupted to *vly*. The first settlers here on the stream were Asel and Dr. William Jarvis in 1789. [APN:168; Hurd-O:247; WPANYS]

Folsomdale. Wyoming. The settlement was first called West Bennington, then Scottsville for David Scott, who owned the land on which the village was built. The first postmaster was John B. Folsom, who later owned all of Scott's land. Frances (Frankie) Folsom grew up here, the daughter of President Grover Cleveland's law partner. She married Cleveland in 1886. [WPANY:436; Wyoming:155]

Fonda. Montgomery. The place was first known by its Native American name, Caughnawaga, meaning "on the rapids." In 1851, its name was changed for Douw Fonda, a friend of Sir William Johnson's, who was murdered in 1780. [French:415; Frothingham:263, 270–1; Gannett:112; Montgomery:141; WPANY:460]

Fordham. Bronx. John Archer was granted land here in 1671. He named it for the Saxon words that meant "houses by the wading or fording place." [Jackson:426]

Forest. Clinton. The first settlement here was in the forest and was surrounded by forest, so it took its name from its surroundings. [Hurd-C&F:203]

Forestburg. Sullivan. The town took its name from its surrounding landscape when it was formed in 1826. [Child:146; French:644]

Forest Hills. Queens. When the Cord Meyer Development Company bought this place, it was called Whitepot. The name was changed for its neighbor Forest Park. [Jackson:426; WPANYC:581]

Forest Home. Tompkins. This place was first called Sydney's Mill for Joseph S. Sydney, who built a gristmill here in 1794. Later, the place became known as Free Hollow, possibly because of its new industries, all of which flourished on Fall Creek, which they used for power. It was often referred to as Flea Hollow, and when the post office was to set up an office, residents asked for a new name. Someone suggested Forest Home. [Norris:12; P&H-T:104; Selkreg:204]

Forest Lawn. Monroe. Named for its location in a thickly wooded area. [WPARM:407]

Forestport. Oneida. The town was formed in 1869 and named Forest Port at the suggestion of Robert Crandall, postmaster, for the settlement that had existed prior to the town's organization. This was a major lumbering community. [French:462, 466; Oneida:149, 150]

Forestville. Chautauqua. This village sits on Walnut Creek and was first called

Walnut Falls. The first post office was called Hanover, but the name was changed to Forestville as a descriptive name for this place in what was an unbroken wilderness. [D&H:191, 194; McMahon:302]

Fort Ann. Washington. When the town was formed in 1786, it was named Westfield for the place in Massachusetts that had been the former home of some settlers. In 1808, the name was changed for the fort that had been erected here in 1709 that was named for Queen Anne, then the queen of England. The village was incorporated in 1820. [French:681; Gannett:112; Johnson:303, 306; Stone:457]

Fort Covington, Fort Covington Center. Franklin. The town was formed in 1817 and named for Brigadier General Leonard Covington, who died after battle in 1813. The first name proposed was Covington, but there already was one in the state so the "Fort" was added to distinguish this one from the other. The community was first called French Mills for the French families that had settled here in about 1796. Settlers from Vermont started coming in 1800. [French:311; Gannett:112; Hough-SLF:498–9; Hurd-C&F:483; Landon:123; WPANY:531; WPANYS]

Fort Edward. Washington. In 1818, the town was formed and named for an old fort that had been built at the portage between the Hudson River and Lake Champlain. This was called the Great Carrying Place by the Native Americans, but white settlers named it for Edward, Duke of York, grandson of George II and brother of George III. The village was incorporated in 1849. [French:682; Johnson:318; WPANY:624]

Fort Hunter. Montgomery. The place was named for the fort that had been built here in 1711, which was named for Governor Robert Hunter. The Native American name for this place was Icanderoga or Teondaloga, "two streams coming together." [French:413; Frothingham:302]

Fort Jackson. St. Lawrence. In 1824, Isaac R. Hopkins built a sawmill on the St. Regis River near here and named the place for Andrew Jackson and for a rock formation that resembled a fort. [Harder:84; Hough-SLF:322]

Fort Johnson. Montgomery. In about 1740, Sir William Johnson built a stone mansion that was fortified with a palisade and became known as Fort Johnson. The village grew up around it, called Mount Johnson, then Akin, and finally for the name of the house. [French:412; Frothingham:174, 183; Montgomery:86; WPANY:458]

Fort Miller. Washington. Colonel Miller had a fort built on the Hudson River here during the French and Indian War in about 1755. [French:682; Johnson:322]

Fort Montgomery. Orange. There was an old fort here for which the village was named. That fort was later called Fort Clinton. [R&C:814; WPANY:619]

Fort Plain. Montgomery. The village was named for the fort here, which was named for the level ground surrounding it that afforded a view of the plain. [Frothingham:220; Montgomery:128]

Fort Salonga. Suffolk. A British post of this name was captured and destroyed here by the Continental Army in 1781. [WPANY:698]

Fosterdale. Sullivan. Jesse M. Foster settled here in 1820, ran a hotel, and was the first postmaster when the post office was opened in 1831. [Child:130; Quinlan:215]

Fowler. St. Lawrence. When the town was formed in 1816, it was named for Theodosius Fowler of New York City, who was a captain in the Revolutionary War. [French:577; Gannett:114; Harder:85; Hough-SLF:301; Landon:240]

Fowlerville. Livingston. Wells Fowler first settled here in 1816. [Doty-L:681; French:387; Gannett:114; WPANYA]

Fox Hills. Richmond. In the 1870s, Henry Meyer had an estate here that he called Fox Hills. In the 1890s, the area was known as Park Hill, but later the name reverted back to that of the estate. [Jackson:435]

Frankfort. Herkimer. Lawrence Frank was an early settler here. When the town was formed in 1796, it took his name. In 1843, William Gates started manufacturing wooden matches here, an industry that he built up over the years. After his death in 1877, the plant was sold to the Diamond Match Company and eventually moved to Oswego. [French:344; Gannett:114; Herkimer:136, 139; WPANY:484]

Franklin, North Franklin. Delaware. The town was formed in 1792 and named for Temple Franklin, Benjamin Franklin's son. [Delaware:170; French:261; Gannett:114; WPANYS]

Franklin Falls. Franklin. The settlement was formerly called McClenathans Falls for William McClenathan, an early settler who built a forge and a sawmill here in 1827. The entire place was destroyed by fire in 1852. The county and the town were named for Benjamin Franklin. When the county was formed, the residents wanted it to be called Norfolk, but when the final papers were returned, they found that it had been named Franklin instead. The settlement was named for the falls on the Saranac River on which it was located. [French:307, 311; Hough-SLF:216, 505; Hurd-C&F:375; Landon:143–4]

Franklin Springs. Oneida. The community started out in 1790 as Franklin. It became Franklin Iron Works in 1867 when the blast furnaces in this iron mining area were erected. Mineral springs were discovered in the 1890s and the name was changed to reflect their development. Throughout all this, the name was for Benjamin Franklin. [APN:171; French:464; Gannett:114; Oneida:153]

Franklin Square. Nassau. This was first a square, called Trimming Square, where sheep were driven to be sheared in the late 1700s. A community grew up around it and in 1851 changed its name to Washington Square, for George Washington. But when applying for a post office, in the 1870s, the post office department refused to allow any more Washington names, so the residents changed the name to Franklin Square for Benjamin Franklin. [Winsche:34; WPANYS]

Franklinton. Schoharie. Like many places, this was named for Benjamin Franklin. It was sometimes called the Vly for the marshy land here. [Noyes:156; Roscoe:141]

Franklinville. Cattaraugus. The town was formed in 1812 and named Hebe, then Ischua in 1816, and finally Franklinville in 1824. Or the town was named Ischua from its start and was never called Hebe: the sources disagree. Ischua was probably a misspelling of the Italian island of Ischia. The town was finally named for Benjamin Franklin. [APN:171, 223; Ellis:313; French:190; Gannett:114]

Fraser. Delaware. Andrew Frazer, or Frasier or Fraser, came here from Scotland in 1805. The place was named for him although he was not the first settler. [Delaware:152, 167; Gannett:115; WPANYS]

Fredonia. Chautauqua. The place was first called Canadaway, for the creek. The name was changed to Fredonia, a word coined by Dr. Samuel Latham Mitchell in about 1800, meaning "land of freedom." He had suggested it as a name for the country, but instead it was used for a number of towns. Fredonia is the home of the first natural gas well in the country. In 1821, Fredonia's streets were lighted with natural gas, and by 1860, half the houses were supplied with light from it. [APN:172; D&H:218–20; French:214; Gannett:115; McMahon:303; WPANY:439]

Freedom Plains. Dutchess. The town of LaGrange was formed in 1821 as the town of Freedom. The town's name was changed in 1828, but the settlement kept the name, adding to it its geographic description. [French:272; Smith-D:468; WPANYD:135]

Freehold. Greene. This place in the town of Durham took its name from the original town name, which referred to this piece of land between two patents that was free for settlement. [Greene:256; WPANYA]

Freeport. Nassau. The village was called Washburn's Neck and then Raynor's Neck for Edward Raynor, who settled here in the early 1700s. It was called Raynortown until 1853 when a change of name was contemplated by the residents. The first suggestion was Bayside village, but that lost out to Raynortown. The fishermen were not pleased and forced another vote with Freeport as an option. This won out as a descriptive name for the place. The post office was established as Freeport in 1853. [French:547; Winsche:35; WPANYS]

Freetown Corners, East Freetown. Cortland. The town of Freetown was formed in 1818. General Hathaway had come here from Freetown, Massa-chusetts, in 1805. [French:252; Goodwin:219; WPANYS]

Freeville. Tompkins. When the settlement had grown large enough to need a name, the first suggestion was to name it after Daniel White, who was the first to come here and build a dam and a mill in 1802. He declined the honor but proposed that the place be called Freeville, maybe as a reference to this new country, but really we do not know why. [Norris:21]

Fremont Center. Sullivan. The town was named for explorer John C. Fremont when it was formed in 1851. The settlement and railroad station on the New York and Erie Railroad were first called Hankins Depot, for John Hankins who came here in about 1839. In 1851, the name was changed to match the town. The post office was established in 1852 as Fremont, although local sen-timent was for the name Hankins. [APN:172; Child:148, 149; French:645; Gannett:115; Quinlan:293, 299]

Fresh Meadows. Queens. This housing development took a pleasant name to at-tract residents. [French:546; Jackson:441]

Frewsburg. Chautauqua. John Frew was the first settler here and was responsible, with others, for the first sawmills and gristmills built here in the early 1800s. [D&H:120–1; McMahon:305]

Friendship. Allegany. The settlement was first called Fighting Corners because the residents could never agree on anything. When time came for the town to be formed, in 1815, the discussion was quite intense about a name for it. Fi-nally, an early settler named Davis suggested that the people stop bickering and name the place Friendship. Both the community and the town were so named. [French:173; Minard:699; WPANYS]

Fruit Valley. Oswego. Asa Rice settled here in 1797 and called the place Union Village. It later changed its name for the fruit orchards that abound here. [Churchill:646]

Fullerville Ironworks. St. Lawrence. Sheldon, Stillman, Heman, and Ashbel Fuller came here from Vermont and started the ironworks in 1833. [Cur-tis:603–5; French:577; Harder:88]

Fulton. Oswego. There were several settlements here at the waterfalls on the Os-wego River. An early one was called Phillipsville for Asa Phillips, who built several mills and houses here. Later settlements were Upper Landing and Lower Landing, on either end of the falls. At Upper Landing, the post office was established in 1810 as Oswego Falls and the village, later city, went by that name. The post office at Lower Landing was opened in 1826 as Fulton, for Robert Fulton, the inventor of the steamboat. Eventually, this area be-came consolidated into one under the name of Fulton. [APN:174; Churchill:526, 797, 810; French:528; Gannett:116; Johnson-O:227]

Fultonham, West Fulton. Schoharie. The town was formed in 1828 and named for Robert Fulton, the inventor of the steamboat. There was a fort here during the Revolutionary War. West Fulton was called Byrneville for the owner of the land but was locally named Sapbush Hollow, for the maple trees from which maple sugar was made. When the post office was established, it was called West Fulton. [French:605; Noyes:156; Roscoe:185–6; Sias:137; WPANYS]

Fultonville. Montgomery. During the Revolutionary War, this place was known as Van Epps Swamp for Charles Van Epp and his family, who settled here. Its name was changed to that of Robert Fulton, the American inventor of the steam engine, when the post office was opened in 1832. [APN:174; French:413; Frothingham:228; Montgomery:122; WPANYS]

Furnaceville. Wayne. The Wayne County Iron Company operated a blast furnace here between 1825 and 1887, manufacturing pig iron from local ore. [Cowles:326; French:692]

G

Lake George © *2004 by Jon Crispin*

Gabriels. Franklin. The settlement came into existence after the introduction of the Adirondack and St. Lawrence Railroad in 1892. It is named for Bishop Gabriels of the Catholic diocese of Ogdensburg who helped inaugurate the Gabriels Sanitarium for tubercular patients here in 1897. [WPANY:520; WPANYA; WPANYS]

Gaines. Orleans. The town was formed in 1816 and named by William J. Babbitt for General E. P. Gaines, who held Fort Erie against the British for nine days in the War of 1812. [French:514; Gannett:116; Signor:416; WPANY:650]

Gainesville. Wyoming. The town was formed as Hebe in 1814. Its name was changed in 1816 for General Edmund Pendleton Gaines, a commander in the War of 1812. [APN:175; French:713; Gannett:116; WPANY:650; Wyoming:193]

Galeville. Ulster. In 1860, there was a sawmill, a gristmill, and a post office here in what was then called Galeville Mills. By 1880, it had lost the second word of its name. [French:667; Syl-U:165]

Gallatinville. Columbia. The town of Gallatin and this village were both named for Albert Gallatin, secretary of the treasury under Thomas Jefferson from 1801 to 1814. [APN:175; Ellis-C:412; French:245; Gannett:116; WPA-NYS]

Gallupville. Schoharie. The Gallup family settled here from New England in 1817. The post office was opened in 1825. [Noyes:155; Roscoe:350; Sias:153; WPANYA]

Galway, East Galway. Saratoga. Early settlers had come here from Scotland and had named the place New Galloway. When the town was formed in 1792, its name was misspelled. [French:588; Syl-S:359; WPANYS]

Gang Mills. Steuben. Isaac Gray and others bought 4,000 acres here in 1832 and started sawmill operations for which the place was then named. [Roberts:317; Steuben:322]

Gansevoort. Saratoga. Colonel Peter Gansevoort settled here after the Revolutionary War in which he had served at Fort Stanwix. [French:591; Gannett:117; Syl-S:403, 405; WPANY:487]

Garbutt. Monroe. John Garbutt was one of three sons of Zachariah Garbutt, who had come to the Genesee country in 1800. In 1803, John Garbutt bought land on Allen's Creek and the entire family moved with him, giving the place the name Garbuttsville. This was later shortened. [French:406; Mc-M:190; Pech:77, 435; WPARM:331]

Garden City. Nassau. Alexander Turney Stewart bought 7,000 acres of land here in 1869 to be built up as a model village. To that end, he planted thousands of trees and shrubs and named the place for them. [Winsche:36–7; WPANY:704]

Gardiner. Ulster. The town was formed in 1853 and named for Addison Gardiner, a former lieutenant governor. The post office was established in the village in about 1870. [French:662; Gannett:117; Syl-U:289–90; WPANYA]

Gardnertown. Orange. Silas Gardner was an early settler. [R&C:280]

Garnet Lake. Warren. The settlement is named for the lake, which was named for the mineral that was mined in the area. [WPAW:122]

Garrattsville. Otsego. John Garratt was the first settler here before the Revolutionary War. His brother William ran the first store. [French:535; Hurd-O:219]

Garrison. Putnam. This place on the Hudson River had been called Nelson's Landing for Caleb Nelson who lived here. He sold 125 acres of land to Harry Garrison in 1803. The landing was also called Mead's Dock for Joseph Mead who kept a store here. But soon, the place was known as Garrison's Landing, eventually shortened to Garrison. [Blake:163; Pelletreau:535]

Garwoods. Allegany. James Garwood came here in about 1865 from England. The post office was first known as Whitney's Crossing. [Allegany:228; French:172; Minard:620]

Gasport. Niagara. This village was a port on the Erie Canal. The name comes from a flammable gas that rose from the earth here. This gas was sent through pipes to a store that used it for lighting. The gas springs were later destroyed during the expansion of the canal. [French:456; Gannett:118; Pool:277; Williams:382]

Gates. Monroe. The town was formed as Northampton in 1802. Its name was changed in 1812 for General Horatio Gates, to whom General Burgoyne surrendered at Saratoga in 1777. [APN:177; French:399; Gannett:118; Peck:260; WPARM:282, 318]

Gayville. Oswego. This place had a large sawmill that, after a fire, was converted to a gristmill. It had a post office and a hotel, but no record of its name origin. [Churchill:509]

Geneseo. Livingston. The town took its name, when it was formed in 1789, from Gennisheyo, "pleasant banks" or "beautiful valley," the name applied to the Genesee River. The village had been known as Big Tree for a large oak (but maybe it was an elm) tree at which various treaties were concluded. [APN:178; Doty-L:520; French:383; Gannett:118; Parker:302–3; WPANY:441]

Geneva. Ontario. Probably named for the Swiss city and lake because of its location at the north end of Seneca Lake. In a letter dated 1788, Dr. Caleb Benton first refers to the place as Geneva. It became a city in 1898. The Native American name for the place was Ganundasaga, meaning "new settlement village." [French:498; Milliken:105; Morgan:469]

Genoa. Cayuga. When the town was formed in 1789, it was named Milton for the English poet. The name was changed in 1808, probably for the city in Italy. [French:202; Storke:484]

Georgetown. Madison. When the residents were petitioning for the formation of a town, in 1815, they asked that it be called Washington. The state legislature, knowing that there already was a town by that name in the state, substituted the former president's first name. The community was locally known as Slab City, suggested by Apollos Drake as a parallel to Log City, the name by which Eaton, a neighboring village, was then known. [Smith-C&M:585, 590; WPANYS]

German. Chenango. When the town was organized in 1806, it was called Brakel Town. Later its name was changed for General Obadiah German, who owned land here and was a prominent resident. [French:226; Gannett:119; Smith-C&M:378; WPANYS]

Germantown. Columbia. The town was recognized in 1788. Earlier, it had been called East Camp and German Camp. In about 1710, 1,200 German Palatines had been brought here by Governor Hunter to make tar and other naval supplies. [Ellis-C:264; French:245; WPANY:609]

Gerritsen. Kings. Wolfert Gerrittsen built a house and a mill on Gerrittsen Creek in the early 1600s here. [Jackson:465]

Gerry. Chautauqua. In 1818, the place was known as Vermont, the former home of many early settlers. In 1820, James Bucklin opened a hotel here and the place became known as Bucklin's Corners. The post office name was changed to Gerry in 1876 and the railroad station in 1881 for Elbridge Gerry, a signer of the Declaration of Independence and a vice president under James Madison in 1812. His name is the root for the term "gerrymandering." [D&H:187–8; French:213; Gannett:119; McMahon:306]

Getzville. Erie. Joseph Getz was an early settler here. [Smith-E:406]

Ghent. Columbia. The town was formed in 1818 and named for the city in Belgium. The Native American name of the place had been Squampamock or Scompamuck. [APN:179; Ellis-C:331; French:245; WPANYA]

Gibson, Gibson Landing. Steuben. George Gibson bought 100 acres and settled here in 1825. He developed the land agriculturally, and in 1865 he became part of the Keuka Lake Wine Company. [WPANYS]

Gilbertsville. Otsego. Abijah Gilbert came here from Warwickshire, England, in about 1787. He bought 1,000 acres. John T. Gilbert ran the first tavern. James T. Gilbert ran a store, as did Samuel C. Gilbert. The place was first known as Butternuts for the town, but soon took the name of the residents. [French:532; Hurd-O:109–11; WPANYS]

Gilboa. Schoharie. The settlement was named for the biblical mountain where the Philistines defeated Saul. When the town was formed, in 1848, it took its name from the settlement. [APN:180; French:605; Gannett:119; Noyes:156; Roscoe:119; Sias:137]

Glasco. Ulster. This place was settled by Dutch, French, and Scots. It became a shipping point for the Woodstock Glass Company. The words "Glass Co." were painted on the warehouse and became the name associated with the place. [Syl-U:42; WPANYA]

Glen. Montgomery. Jacob Saunders Glen owned about 10,000 acres and ran a large store. The town was formed in 1823. [French:413; Frothingham:280; Montgomery:117]

Glen, The. Warren. This name might be a play on words. The place is situated on the west bank of the Hudson River, which forms a valley (a glen), but it was first owned in 1761 by John Glen, an early patentee of the land, for whom Glens Falls is named. [APN:181; French:675; Smith-W:702; WPANYS]

Glen Aubrey. Broome. The Councilman family were the first to live here, giving the name Councilman Settlement to the place. [Smith-B:419, 422]

Glen Castle. Broome. This was a settlement about two miles above the mouth of Castle Creek and was named for the stream. [French:181; Smith-B:458]

Glencoe Mills. Columbia. The place was formerly known as Sober, but it was named Glenco or Glencoe Mills in 1830 for the narrow valley in Scotland where the MacDonalds were massacred in 1692 and for the sawmills here. [APN:181; Ellis-C:259; French:248]

Glen Cove. Nassau. This place on Long Island Sound was first called Mosquito Cove, not for the insect but from a Native American word, spelled in various ways, meaning "meadow" or "place of rushes." The first post office was opened in 1818 as Musquito Cove. In 1833, it was changed to Moscheto Cove to move away from the pesky name. The name Glencoe, for the place in Scotland, was suggested but was misunderstood as Glen Cove, which everyone liked because it kept the Cove in the name. The name was adopted in the 1830s. [French:550; Winsche:38–9]

Glendale. Queens. In 1869, John C. Schooley, a real estate agent, developed the farmland here and named it for his birthplace in Ohio. [Jackson:470]

Glenfield. Lewis. In 1868, the Utica and Black River Railroad came through along the Black River, bypassing the settlement of Glen(s)dale. A station was established and the community moved its operations to be near the depot. In 1899, the post office and community name was changed to avoid confusion with the many other Glendales in the United States. [Bowen:403, 404, 406; French:378; Hough-L:186]

Glenham. Dutchess. This place was early known as Red Rock for the color of the stone in the area. Its name was changed for its location in a pleasant gorge cut by Fishkill Creek. [Smith-D:530; WPANYD:130]

Glen Haven. Cayuga. This place was first settled in 1794, located near the head of Skaneateles Lake in a beautiful location. It was supplied with clean, soft spring water, which led to the establishment of Glen Haven Water Cure and Summer Resort in 1845. [French:204; Storke:484]

Glenmont. Albany. This was a station and a post office on the West Shore Railroad, named for Cornelius Glen. [Albany:496; WPANYA; WPANYS]

Glen Oaks. Queens. The area here was bought by the Glen Oaks Golf Club in 1923. A garden apartment complex was built, called Glen Oaks Village, in 1944. [Jackson:470–1]

Glens Falls, West Glens Falls. Warren; **South Glens Falls.** Saratoga. The city of Glens Falls started out as a village called Four Corners. Some of the residents wanted to call it Pearlville or Pearl Village, but the name did not stick. For a while it was called Wing's Falls for Abraham Wing, who built a sawmill on the falls in the 1760s and who continued to improve the settlement with a second sawmill in 1770. It became known as Glenville, then in 1788 Glens Falls, for Colonel John Glen from Schenectady who bought land in the area and for the sixty-foot falls on the Hudson River on which the village grew. [French:675; Gannett:121; Smith-W:421; WPANY:559; WPAW:141, 144–5]

Glen Spey. Sullivan. Named for the river in Scotland. [Child:168; WPANYS]

Glenville. Westchester. The location of this settlement, in a glen, gave it its name. [Lederer:56]

Glen Wild. Sullivan. This place was named for its geographic location at a glen with a waterfall. [Quinlan:617; WPANYS]

Glenwood. Erie. This place was settled in about 1810 and a post office established in the 1840s. The name is descriptive of the place. [Smith-E:606; WPANYS]

Glenwood Landing. Nassau. When Isaac Doughty bought the land here in 1681, it was called Newark. After 1753, it was called Littleworth, and then finally Glenwood by 1873 for its proximity to Glen Cove. When the post office was established in 1892, the word Landing was added, for the steamboat landing, to avoid confusion with other Glen names. [Winsche:40; WPANYS]

Gloversville. Fulton. Sir William Johnson, back in the 1760s, brought over from Scotland a group of settlers who were glovers. They made gloves for local sale. This industry expanded and the city grew around the glove factories here. [French:317; Fulton:201; Gannett:121; WPANY:490]

Godeffroy. Orange. S. N. Godfroy or Godeffroy was an early settler here in 1695. [WPANYS]

Goldens Bridge. Westchester. In the early 1700s, Abraham Golding built a bridge over the Croton River here. It was called Golding's Bridge, then Goldensbridge. [Bolton(1):460; Lederer:57]

Gorham. Ontario. This town, organized in 1789, was originally known as Easton. Its name was changed to Lincoln in 1806 and changed again in 1807, this time to honor Nathaniel Gorham, a pioneer settler and the son of Nathaniel Gorham, Sr., a statesman during the Revolution and a member of the Constitutional Convention. The village of Gorham within the town was originally called Bethel. [French:496; Milliken:105]

Goshen. Orange. Named for the place in the Bible that was considered to be the best land in Egypt, transferring the perception of fertility to this location. [APN:185; Gannett:122; R&C:527; WPANY:398]

Gouverneur. St. Lawrence. When this town was formed in 1810, it was named for Gouverneur Morris, an American statesman who owned a large tract of land here. [Curtis:541; French:577; Gannett:122; Harder:93; Hough-SLF:307; Landon:240; WPANY:522]

Gowanda. Cattaraugus. The village was first known as Aldrich's Mills for Turner Aldrich, who settled here and built mills. The post office was established as Aldrich's Mills in 1820. In 1822, the name of the village was changed to Lodi, but there already was a Lodi with a post office in the state, so this post office was discontinued. In about 1830, the post office was reopened, this time as West Lodi. After 1835, the post office was called Persia for the town, but since 1848, the post office and the village have been called Gowanda. This name is from the Native American *dyogowandeh,* meaning "below the cliffs" or "almost surrounded by hills." [APN:185; Ellis:377, 379; French:194; Gannett:122; Parker:289]

Grafton. Rensselaer. The town, settled by New Englanders, was formed in 1807. The name was suggested by Nathaniel Dumbleton, the first town supervisor, for his hometown of Grafton, Vermont. The second (Charles Fitz-Roy [1683–1722]) and third (Henry Fitz-Roy [1735–1811]) dukes of Grafton were the inspiration for the name of a number of places in New England. The village was often called Grafton Center and was previously called Patroons Mills. [APN:185; French:555; Gannett:122; Weise:111, 112, 115]

Grahamsville. Sullivan. Lieutenant John Graham was killed near here in a skirmish with Native Americans just after the Revolutionary War. [Child:76, 190; French:647; Gannett:122; Quinlan:460]

Granby Center. Oswego. When the town was established in 1818, as Granby, a petition went to the legislature asking to name the place DeWitt for Simeon DeWitt. This was rejected and the town continued to be called Granby. Granby Center had been called Williams Corners for Seth Williams, who settled here in 1818. The name was changed to that of the town, which might have been named for a town in Canada. [Churchill:512, 515, 521, 531; French:521; Johnson-O:392–3]

Grand Gorge. Delaware. The settlement was first called Moresville for the first settler, John More, who came here in 1786. When the railroad came through, it named its station for the mountain gorge through which it came. The name of the post office was changed to Grand Gorge in 1875 to match that of the rail station. [Delaware:278; French:264; Murray:521; WPANYA]

Grand Island. Erie. This name reflects the fact that this is the largest island in the Niagara River. It was organized as a town in 1852. The Seneca name for it was Gawanogeh, "on the island," or Gawenodowanneh, "great island." [French:290; Parker:298; Smith-E:230]

Grand View-on-Hudson. Rockland. This village was first settled in about 1736. It was previously called Snedens for an early family. When it was incorporated in 1918, it changed its name for its location overlooking the Hudson River. [WPANYS]

Graniteville. Richmond. From the 1840s to about 1896, there were quarries here for which the place was named. Before that, it was known as Bennett's Corners, then Fayetteville. [French:566; Jackson:499]

Grant. Herkimer. The place was first settled by Isaac Woodlin in 1816 but was called Potter's Bush. Then John Post moved in and became the first postmaster, and the name was changed to Postville. Later the post office and settlement changed their name to honor a leading citizen named Booth. But when Lincoln was assassinated by a Booth, the name was changed to that of Ulysses S. Grant. [Herkimer:231–2; WPANYS]

Grant Hollow. Rensselaer. Named for the Grant family that had a number of manufacturing interests in the area. [Weise:68]

Granville, Middle Granville, North Granville, South Granville. Washington. The town was formed in 1786 and might have been named for the Granville in Massachusetts. The village of Granville was incorporated in 1849, but had been called Bishops Corners before that. The other settlements were named for their locations in the town. [French:682; Johnson:203; WPANY:541]

Graphite. Warren. This was once a graphite mining center. [WPAW:169]

Gravesend. Kings. Named for the city on the Thames River in England. [French:372; Gannett:124; Jackson:501]

Gravesville. Herkimer. William Graves settled here in 1800 and was instrumental in the development of the place. [Herkimer:232; WPANYS]

Gray. Herkimer. Latham Gray bought land here in 1820 and started to improve it. The settlement had been called Graysville or Grayville, which eventually was shortened. [French:347; Herkimer:235]

Great Bend. Jefferson. The Black River changes its course from north to west near here. [D&P:336; Hough-J:131; WPANYA]

Great Kills. Richmond. On the shore, the area had been called Clarendon while the interior was called Newtown. These settlements were combined under the name Gifford's for Daniel Gifford, a local commissioner and surveyor of roads. In 1865, the name was changed to Great Kills, the name of a nearby bay. [French:566; Jackson:503]

Great Neck, Great Neck Estates, Great Neck Plaza. Nassau. The village of Great Neck was named for the peninsula on which it sits, which has been called Great Neck since 1672. The village of Great Neck Estates was also on the peninsula and added the Estates when it was incorporated in 1911. Great Neck Plaza was first known as Great Neck when the North Shore Railroad built a station here in 1866. In 1869, its name was changed to Brookdale, which was kept until 1872 when it went back to Great Neck. William R.

Grace acquired the land here through a lawsuit he had filed against the railroad after he tried to use the train washroom while traveling but found it locked. This caused him "considerable discomfort and embarrassment." He sued and won $2,400, but the railroad was broke so he got the land here instead. A plaza was built around the station, so in 1930 the place became Great Neck Plaza. [Winsche:40–2; WPANYS]

Great River. Suffolk. There was a river flowing through this area when it was named. [WPANYS]

Great Valley. Cattaraugus. Named for the broad valley in which Great Valley Creek flows. The post office was established in the 1870s. The Native American name of the creek was Odasquasa, meaning "around the stone." [Ellis:461; French:190; Morgan:466; Parker:291; WPANYS]

Greene. Chenango. The town was formed in 1798 and named for General Nathaniel Greene of the Revolutionary War. The village was first named Hornby when it was laid out in 1806 by Elisha Smith, the agent of the Hornby estate. The post office was called Greene and the name Hornby was not used. [APN:189; French:226; Gannett:125; Smith-C&M:192, 202]

Greenfield Center, North Greenfield. Saratoga. The town was formed as Greenfield in 1793 and named for Greenfield, Connecticut, the former home of some early settlers. The settlements took their names from their geographic locations in the town. [Syl-S:439]

Green Haven. Dutchess. Named for its surroundings. [Smith-D:545]

Green Island. Albany. This island in the Hudson River was named for being covered in vegetation. The village here was incorporated in 1853 and named for the island. [Albany:430; French:166; Gannett:125; Howell:993]

Greenlawn. Suffolk. The name describes the location of this village. [WPANYS]

Greenpoint. Kings. The Dutch named this place for the grassy plain that ran down to the East River. It was earlier spelled Green Point. [French:367; Jackson:505; WPANYC:459]

Greenport. Suffolk. The village was first called Stirling or Sterling for the earl who was the first proprietor of Long Island. The port was called Winter Harbor because it never froze. Across from the port was an area called Green Hill. The name of the village was changed in 1834, combining the hill and the port. [Bayles:25, 379; French:639]

Green River. Columbia. Named for the river. It was formerly called Green River Hollow. [Ellis-C:371; French:246]

Greenville. Greene. The town was formed in 1803 and called Greenfield. It changed its name to Freehold in 1808, then in 1809 to Greenville. It is a descriptive name. The community was once known as the Hemlocks, also descriptive. [French:332; Greene:290; Vedder:86]

Greenville. Orange. The village of Greenville used to be called Minisink before the town of Greenville separated from the town of Minisink in 1853. This reorganization left the village of Minisink in the town of Greenville, so the village changed its name to Greenville, although the post office was called Minisink for a while longer. [French:507; R&C:694]

Greenville. Westchester. In 1842, the Reformed Protestant Dutch Church of Greenville gave the place this name to avoid confusion with the Reformed Church of Greenburg in Elmsford in the town of Greenburg. [Lederer:60]

Greenwich, East Greenwich. Washington. The town was named for Greenwich, Rhode Island, when it was organized in 1803. The village of Greenwich was made up of two villages: Whipple's City, named for the improvements made here by Job Whipple and his family, and Union Village, which straddled the town boundary between Greenwich and Easton. The village took the name of the town in 1867 because most of the village's growth had been on the Greenwich side. [French:683; Johnson:334, 340; Stone:428]

Greenwich Village. New York. Captain Peter Warren named this place for the English city. The Canarsee Indians had called it Sapokanican. [APN:189; French:419; Jackson:506]

Greenwood. Steuben. The town was formed in 1827 and named by Alexander H. Stephens, an early settler, for the landscape. [French:625; Steuben:109]

Greenwood Lake. Orange. This village grew up around the lake that made the area a summer resort destination. The post office was established in 1876. [R&C:794]

Greig. Lewis. The town was named for John Greig of Canandaigua, a lawyer and owner of large amounts of land here. The town was first organized in 1828 as Brantingham for Thomas Brantingham of Philadelphia, who owned what was called the Brantingham Tract. The name was changed to honor Greig in 1832. [Bowen:202; French:375, 376; Gannett:125; Hough-L:101–2]

Griffin. Hamilton. This place was first called Moon's Mills for the sawmills owned by James Moon. The name was changed in about 1880 for Stephen Griffin whose businesses, a tannery and others, helped the community grow. [A&K:928, 930]

Griffins Mills. Erie. The settlement had been called Smith's Mills for Humphrey Smith, who built a gristmill here in 1809. The Griffins moved here in about 1812 and bought the mills, and the place became known as Griffin's Mills or Griffinshire. The post office was established in about 1831. [Smith-E:538, 540–1, 556]

Groom Corners. Saratoga. James Groom was an early settler here. [French:587; Syl-S:477; WPANYA]

Groton, West Groton. Tompkins. When the town was first formed in 1817, it was called Division. Its name was changed in 1818 for either Groton, Massachusetts, or Groton, Connecticut, or maybe both (each of which was named for the English town) by settlers from New England. [APN:190; Gannett:126; French:657; Norris:33; P&H-T:202; Selkreg:310]

Groveland. Livingston. The Native Americans would periodically burn the underbrush in this area, creating groves of trees for which the settlers named the town when it was formed in 1789. [Doty-L:556; French:383]

Grymes Hill. Richmond. In 1836, this area became the home of Madame Suzette Grymes, the widow of the first governor of Louisiana. [Jackson:512]

Guilderland, Guilderland Center. Albany. The town was formed in 1803. The village was first called Glass House for the glass factory there. In 1796, it became Hamilton for Alexander Hamilton. Then for a short time, it was called Sloan's for the family of that name here. Finally it became Guilderland, named for the province in the Netherlands, and so did the post office. Guilderland Center had been called Bangalls locally for the unpleasant citizens living there. [Albany:519–20; APN:192; French:164; Howell:76, 851–2; WPANYS]

Guilford. Chenango. The town was formed in 1813 as Eastern, but the name was changed in 1817 for Guilford, Connecticut. Many settlers in Chenango County had come from Connecticut. The settlement was first called Fayette, but the post office was called Guilford because there already was a Fayette post office in the state. [APN:192; French:227; Smith-C&M:224, 236; WPANYS]

Gulf Summit. Broome. This was a station on the Erie Railroad and a post office. [French:183; Smith-B:324]

Hamburg © *2004 by Jon Crispin*

Hadley. Saratoga. When the town was formed in 1801, it was named for the former home of its early settlers, Hadley, Massachusetts, which was named for a parish in Essex, England. [APN:194; Gannett:127; Syl-S:415]

Hagaman. Montgomery. Joseph Hagaman settled here in 1777 and built a sawmill and a gristmill on the Chuctenunda Creek. The place was first known as Hagaman's Mills. [French:412; Frothingham:180; Montgomery:87]

Hague. Warren. When the town was first formed in 1807, it was called Rochester. Its name was changed in 1808, probably for the city in the Netherlands. [APN:194; French:674; WPAW:169–70]

Hailesboro. St. Lawrence. Brigadier General James Haile, of the Revolutionary War, bought a one-square-mile tract of land here in 1807 and built a sawmill and a gristmill. [Curtis:602; Harder:100; Hough-SLF:302; WPANYA]

Haines Falls. Greene. Aaron Haines and his family settled here near the waterfalls of the West Branch of the Kaaterskill sometime before 1865. [Greene:323; Vedder:96]

Halcott Center. Greene. This is a settlement in the town named for George W. Halcott, a sheriff and politician here. The town was formed in 1851. [Greene:318; Vedder:89; WPANYA]

Halcottsville. Delaware. Matthew Halcott opened the first store here in 1814 and was the first postmaster of the Halcottsville post office. [Delaware:261, 265; French:263; Murray:509; WPANYS]

Hale Eddy. Delaware. Oliver Hale and his family came here in 1790 and settled on the Delaware River. [Delaware:311; French:265]

Halfmoon. Saratoga. The area between the Hudson and Mohawk Rivers was sometimes called the Triangle, for its shape, but more often it was named for the crescent shape formed by the rivers. When the town was formed, in 1788, it took the name of the curve. Its name was changed to Orange in 1816, then back again to Half Moon in 1820. [French:589; Gannett:128; Syl-S:345]

Hall. Ontario. Edward Hall was an early settler here. The community was first called Hall's Corners. It lost the apostrophe, then the Corners to become, simply, Hall. [Milliken:106]

Hallsport. Allegany. Calvin Hall opened the first hotel here in 1838. [Allegany:376; Minard:542]

Halsey Valley. Tioga. This place was first known as Girl's Flat, for the daughter of the first owner, Thomas Nicholson. Thomas died before his daughter was born, and she only lived to the age of eighteen. Her mother married Zephaniah Halsey and the place took their name. [Gay:483; P&H-Ti:209]

Hamburg. Erie. German settlers came here in about 1808 and named the place for the German city. The town was organized in 1812. The village had been called Smith's Mills for Richard and David Smith, who built a gristmill here in about 1808. The post office was established in 1820 at Smithville but was discontinued in 1822. The village then became known as White's Corners for Thomas T. White, who had come here in 1817 and was a leading businessman in the area. Growth was spurred by the building of the railroad. [APN:195; French:291; Gannett:128; Smith-E:511, 517; WPANY:684]

Hamden. Delaware. Early settlers had come here from near Hampden, Massachusetts, and when the town was formed in 1825, it was named Hampden. The p was dropped when the post office was opened so as not to conflict with another Hampden in the state at that time. [Delaware:195; French:261]

Hamilton, East Hamilton. Madison. The town was formed in 1795 and named for Alexander Hamilton. Samuel and Elisha Payne came in 1794 to the place that became the village of Hamilton, but that was then called Paynesville. East Hamilton was originally known as Colchester Settlement. The Native American name for the place was Daudenosagwanose, meaning "round house." [French:391, 392; Morgan:473; Smith-C&M:545, 569; WPANY:421]

Hamlet. Chautauqua. This was the name of the post office at Omar in 1860. The settlement took this name from the post office, for being a small country village. [French:216; WPANYS]

Hamlin. Monroe. When the town was first organized in 1852, it was called Union. Its name was changed in 1861 for Hannibal Hamlin, who was being inaugurated as Lincoln's vice president. [French:405; Gannett:128; Peck:283, 284; WPARM:283]

Hammertown. Dutchess. This was the home of an extensive factory that made scythes and other iron tools. [French:274; Smith-D:228–9]

Hammond. St. Lawrence. Abijah Hammond of New York owned the land here when the town was formed in 1827. He never visited. The village had been known as Hammond Corners. [Curtis:652; French:577; Gannett:128; Harder:103; Hough-SLF:314]

Hammondsport. Steuben. Judge Lazarus Hammond bought land here in 1807 and laid out lots for a village, including a public square. [Roberts:525; Steuben:324]

Hampton. Washington. The town was formed in 1786 and named for a common New England name by early settlers from there. Before organization, the place had been called Greenfield. [French:683; Johnson:363; Stone:444]

Hampton Bays, Hampton Park, Bridgehampton, East Hampton, Southampton, Westhampton, Westhampton Beach, Beach Hampton. Suffolk. All of the Hamptons took their names from Hampton in Middlesex, England, or from Southampton, Virginia, which was named in about 1610 for the Earl of Southampton, who was interested in colonization. East Hampton was first called Maidstone when settled in 1648. Bridgehampton was named for the bridge that was built over Sagg Pond. It was sometimes called Bullhead or Bull's Head. The area around here had been called Mecox. Southampton was named for the town in England. The Native Americans called this place Agwam, "a place abounding in fish." [APN:196; Bayles:333; French:638; Fannett:129; Suffolk/Southampton:30; WPANY:713]

Hancock. Delaware. The village was formerly called Shohakin or Chehocton, meaning "the union of streams." The village is located about a mile above the confluence of both branches of the Delaware River. When the town was formed in 1806, it took the name of John Hancock, president of the Continental Congress. [APN:196; Delaware:205, 214; French:261; Gannett:129]

Hankins. Sullivan. This was a station on the New York and Erie Railroad that was named for John Hankins, who actually settled up on Hankins Creek at Hankins Depot, later called Fremont Center. Hankins Creek enters the Delaware River here. Before 1839, it was known as Pierce's Brook. [Child:148; French:645; Quinlan:293]

Hannacroix. Greene. There is a story that early Dutch settlers here saw a rooster come floating down their creek on a block of ice, so the creek became known as Hannekraai, meaning "cock-crowing creek." The settlement took its name from the stream. [Gannett:129]

Hannawa Falls. St. Lawrence. This place had been called Cox's or Coxe's Mills for Gardener Cox(e), who built mills here in about 1822. Then it was called East Pierrepont, for its location in the town. Finally, it was named for its location on the Raquette River with a Native American word, from *nihanawater,* meaning "noisy water." [APN:196; Curtis:611; French:581; Harder:104; WPANYS]

Hannibal, Hannibal Center, South Hannibal. Oswego. The town was formed in 1806 and named for the general who crossed the Alps with elephants to invade Italy. The village of Hannibal and its post office, which was opened in 1816, were called Hannibalville. The South Hannibal post office was established in the hamlet of Hull's Corners, which later took the name of the post office, which referred to its location in the town. [APN:196; Churchill:533, 545, 547; French:522; Gannett:129; Johnson-O:307, 309]

Harford, Harford Mills. Cortland. The town was formed in 1845 and named for the post office, which was established in about 1825 as Worthington, then changed its name to Harford in 1835. [French:252; Goodwin:260]

Harlem. New York. The Dutch named this Nieuw Haarlem, for the city in the Netherlands. [APN:197; Gannett:130; Jackson:523; WPANYC:254]

Harlemville. Columbia. Named for the town in the Netherlands. [APN:197; Ellis-C:371; Gannett:180]

Harmon. Westchester. Clifford B. Harmon was a World War I pilot who then became a developer in the area. [Lederer:63]

Harpersfield, North Harpersfield. Delaware. The town was named, in 1788, for John Harper, who settled here with his family in 1784. [Delaware:218; French:262; Gannett:130; Murray:415]

Harpursville. Broome. Robert Harpur (also spelled Harper) settled in the town of Colesville in the late 1780s. He owned about 60,000 acres. [Smith-B:325; WPANYS]

Harrietstown. Franklin. Named for the wife of James Duane (see Duane Center) and the daughter of William Constable (see Constable). [French:311; Gannett:130; Hough-SLF:506; Hurd-C&F:499]

Harriman. Orange. Named for E. H. Harriman, who owned 20,000 acres here at the beginning of the twentieth century. [WPANY:385]

Harris. Sullivan. Named for an early settler. [WPANYS]

Harrisburg. Lewis. When the town was formed in 1803, it was named for Richard Harrison, a lawyer in New York and one of the early proprietors of land here. [Bowen:220; French:377; Gannett:130; Hough-L:113]

Harrisburg. Warren. The settlement was name for the Harris family, early settlers. [WPAW:233]

Harris Hill. Erie. Named for Asa Harris, who bought a large piece of land and settled here in 1807. The post office was established in 1843.

Harrison. Westchester. John Harrison bought land here in 1695. The town was formed in 1788. [French:700; Gannett:131]

Hartfield. Chautauqua. This was a post village on the Lake Chautauqua inlet in 1860. [French:211]

Hartford, South Hartford. Washington. The town was formed in 1793 and named for Hartford, Connecticut, by settlers from there. [French:683; Johnson:372]

Hartland. Niagara. Samuel B. Morehouse built a hotel here in 1813 and was postmaster in 1816. At that time, the place was called Morehouse's. The town was called Hartland when it was formed in 1812 for Hartland, Vermont, by settlers from Vermont. Eventually, Morehouse's became Hartland Corners and the post office became Hartland, for the town. Eventually the village name conformed to that of the town and the post office. [French:453; Pool:250, 252; Williams:376]

Hart Lot. Onondaga. The hamlet was called Skaneateles Junction when the Syracuse and Auburn Railroad opened in 1838. Joseph Hart owned land here, and when the post office was established, it was named for him. [Bruce:703; French:482; WPANYA]

Hartsdale. Westchester. Hart's Corners, formerly called Barne's Corners, was named for Robert Hart of Rye who purchased lands here in 1784. In 1843, Eleazar Hart donated land for the railroad station. In 1907, the place was developed further and was given this new name. [Bolton(1):356; Lederer:64; WPANYS]

Hartsville. Steuben. Charles N. Hart was a prominent citizen here. The post office was located in his house in the 1850s. [Steuben:112, 330]

Hartwick, Hartwick Seminary, South Hartwick. Otsego. John Christopher Hartwick, from Thuringia, Germany, was granted a patent here in the 1760s. He died in 1796 and left land to be used to fund a Lutheran Theological Seminary, which was soon established there. [French:533; Hurd-O:156–8, 162]

Hartwood. Sullivan. Reverend Hart was the father-in-law of one of the early settlers in this very forested area. [Child:145; French:645]

Harvard. Delaware. Named for Harvard College. [APN:198; WPANYS]

Hasbrouck. Sullivan. Anthony Hasbrouck was a wealthy and prominent resident here who had settled sometime in the 1830s. He was murdered in his house by Cornelius W. Hardenburgh. [Quinlan:237, 253]

Haskinville. Steuben. William Haskins built a tavern here in 1836. [Roberts:325; Steuben:330]

Hastings. Oswego. The town was formed in 1825. George Scriba's patent included this section, which he called Breda. However, this name did not stick and the town was called Hastings for Hastings Curtiss, who was an enterprising citizen of the county. [Churchill:550; French:522; Johnson-O:359]

Hastings-on-Hudson. Westchester. This village was named for Hastings in England, the birthplace of William Saunders, a local manufacturer. When the post office opened in 1849, it was called Hastings-upon-Hudson. The village was incorporated with this name in 1879, then in 1935, the "upon" became "on." [Bolton(2):160; Lederer:65; WPANY:588]

Hauppauge. Suffolk. This was first called Wheeler Settlement for Thomas and Timothy Wheeler, who came here from East Hampton. It later took the Native American word for "sweet water" or "overflowed land" as its name. [APN:199; Bayles:194; French:637; Gannett:139; Suffolk/Smithtown:19]

Haven. Sullivan. This town used to be called Brownville and was a hamlet on the Delaware and Hudson Canal. [Child:177]

Haverstraw, West Haverstraw. Rockland. Dutch settlers originally named this place on the west bank of the Hudson River Averstroo or Haverstroo, meaning "oat straw," for the vegetation growing on its shore. The town was formed in 1788 with this name. The village was incorporated in 1854 as Warren, but that name was never used so it was officially changed in 1874. West Haverstraw used to be called Samsondale, named by Elisha Peck for the ship, the *Samson*, that brought him from England. [APN:199; Bedell:264, 328, 334; Cole:137; French:569; Gannett:132; Green:370, 381, 387]

Haviland. Putnam. This settlement has been called Haviland's Corner and Haviland Hollow for Jacob Haviland, an early settler, and his descendants, including Benjamin Haviland. [Blake:342; Pelletreau:632]

Hawkeye. Clinton. This place is named for its elevation. [Hurd-C&F:247; WPA-NYS]

Hawkinsville. Oneida. Sterry Hawkins had built a sawmill here in the mid-1800s. [Oneida:128]

Hawleyton. Broome. Major Martin Hawley owned land here starting in about 1829. [Smith-B:194]

Hawthorne. Westchester. In 1901, the place was named by its residents for the father of Mother Alphonsa (Rose Hawthorne Lathrop), who had taken over the Tecumseh Hotel and made it into the Servants of Relief for Incurable Cancer Rosary Hill Home. The hamlet had previously been called Hammonds Mills, Neperan, and Unionville. [Lederer:65; WPANYA]

Haynersville. Rensselaer. This was previously called Cooksborough for Michael Vandercook, who settled here in about 1772. When the post office was established, it was called Haynerville for the family that lived in the area. [French:558; Weise:91, 105]

Hayt Corners. Seneca. S. and N. Hayt settled here in the early 1800s. The post office was established here as Hayt's Corners in 1874. [Seneca:151–2]

Head of the Harbor. Suffolk. Named for its location at the head of Stony Brook Harbor. [WPANYS]

Hebron, East Hebron, North Hebron, West Hebron. Washington. The town was formed in 1796 and was named by settlers for their former home of Hebron, Connecticut, which had been named for an ancient city in Palestine. Before its organization, during the Revolutionary War, the place was called Black Creek. North Hebron had been known as Munro's Meadows, for the Reverend Harry Munro who was an Episcopal minister and a chaplain in one of the Highland Scottish regiments. As such, he drew 2,000 acres of land in 1764 in the northern part of what became the town of Hebron. He moved there with other Scottish families in 1774. It later became known as North Hebron. West Hebron might have been known as Bedlam earlier. [APN:201; French:684; Gannett:133; Johnson:389, 391–2; Stone:466]

Hector. Schuyler. When it was surveyed as part of the Military Tract, the town was named by the land commissioners in 1790 for the leader and hero of the Trojan War who was killed by Achilles. The town was organized in 1802. [APN:202; French:611; Gannett:133; P&H-S:150]

Hedgesville. Steuben. Thomas Hedges came here from Milo in Yates County in about 1826. [Roberts:583; Steuben:182]

Helena. St. Lawrence. Helen was the daughter of Joseph Pitcairn of New York City, who owned a large part of the town in which this village developed. [Curtis:635; French:575; Harder:107; Hough-SLF:269; WPANYS]

Hemlock. Livingston. The settlement was named for the lake, the name of which is a translation of the Seneca *onehdah* or *noehnta*. [French:384; Gannett:384; Parker:304]

Hempstead, West Hempstead. Nassau. This town was called Heemstede by the Dutch since the 1640s. When the town of North Hempstead was erected in 1784, Heemstede changed its name to South Hempstead. In 1796, the name was changed back to Hempstead. The word is derived from the Dutch word for homestead, but when the English took over, their version was from the place in England. West Hempstead began as a station on the Long Island Railroad in 1893. The post office here was established in 1962 as separate from the Hempstead one. [APN:203; French:547; Gannett:134; Winsche:43–4, 102–3]

Henderson, Henderson Harbor. Jefferson. The town of Henderson was formed in 1806 and named for William Henderson, the proprietor here. The community of Henderson was previously called Salisbury Mills for Lodowyck Salisbury, an early merchant and mill owner. Henderson Harbor sits on what William Henderson had called the Bay of Naples; Naples was briefly the name of that settlement. [D&P:379, 381–4; French:358; Hough-J:165, 168]

Henrietta, West Henrietta. Monroe. Henrietta Laura, the Countess of Bath, was the daughter of Sir William Pultney, who was a major landowner in the area. The town was formed in 1818 and took her name. [French:399; Gannett:134; WPARM:284]

Hensonville. Greene. John Henson came here from Colorado in 1860 and was known as "the pioneer of Hensonville" when he died in 1881. [Vedder:123; WPANYA]

Herkimer. Herkimer. The county and city were named for General Nicholas Herkimer, a German who held the land patent. His name was originally Erghemar, but it had been spelled in a variety of ways: Herchkeimar, Hareniger, Harkemeir, Herchamer, Harchamer, Harkemar. There was confusion when it came time to record the names Herkimer and German Flats for two towns along the Mohawk River, one on the north bank, the other on the south. On both sides of the Mohawk was a large community of German settlers, hence the name German Flats. But when the place was mapped in Albany, there was confusion as to which side of the river the surveyor meant as left or right, so the name German Flats ended up on the south side while Herkimer was on the north. And Fort Herkimer ended up in the town of German Flats. The village was originally called Stone Ridge. [French:340, 345; Gannett:135; Herkimer:155]

Hermitage. Wyoming. This place was named for Andrew Jackson's home in Tennessee. The post office was established in 1837. [APN:204; Wyoming:299]

Hermon. St. Lawrence. The town was named Depau, for Francis Depau, a large landowner here, when it was organized in 1830. The name was changed in 1834 because there was already a Depauville in the state. The new name comes from a biblical mountain. [APN:204; Curtis:678; French:578; Gannett:135; Harder:108; Hough-SLF:317]

Herricks. Nassau. The Herricks family settled here in the 1650s. [Winsche:44]

Heuvelton. St. Lawrence. Nathan Ford had a village platted at this place, which had been called East Branch for its location on the Oswegatchie River, and named it Fordsburgh. People started to settle here in about 1806. In 1820, Jacob A. Vanden Heuvel (whose name was later changed to Van Heuvel) settled here, bought the unsold village plat and other land, and built a gristmill and a church. In 1832, the name of the village was changed to honor him. [Curtis:340; French:581; Harder:109; Hough-SLF:416–7; Landon:234]

Hewlett, Hewlett Bay Park, Hewlett Harbor. Nassau. The Hewlett or Heulitte family were early settlers here. The village of Hewlett was called Cedar Grove in 1869 when the South Side Railroad opened a station here. The station was renamed Hewletts later in 1869 because Samuel M. Hewlett, who had deeded land to the station here, stipulated that it perpetuate the family name.

In 1890, the train station name was again changed by the railroad, this time to Fenhurst, but the village had established a post office in 1889 and refused to change the name. Finally, in 1896, the station name reverted to Hewlett. Hewlett Bay Park was first the name of a steeplechase course here. A village grew up around it, and the name was in regular use by 1914. Hewlett Harbor was named for its location on the water. [Winsche:44–6; WPANYS]

Hibernia. Dutchess. Early settlers from Ireland, a family named Everson, named the place with the Latin and poetic name for their former home. [APN:205; Gannett:135; Smith-D:286]

Hicksville. Nassau. According to one source, the place was named for either Charles Hicks, a Quaker reformer, or Elias Hicks, also a Quaker reformer. According to another source, it was definitely not named for Elias but was instead named, in 1836, for Valentine Hicks, the president of the Long Island Railroad Company. This last is most likely the case. [French:550; Gannett:135; Winsche:47]

Higgins. Allegany. Russell Higgins and Packard Bruce built a gristmill here in 1817. The place was then known as Higgins Mills. [Allegany:239; Minard:782]

Higgins Bay. Hamilton. This was previously known as Lower Rudeston for the Rudes family home that was here. [A&K:320]

Higginsville. Oneida. This was a stop on the original Erie Canal, probably named for an early settler. [Oneida:201]

High Falls. Ulster. Named for the fifty-foot falls on Rondout Creek. [French:664; Syl-U:193; WPANYA]

Highland. Ulster. Philip Elting was an early settler who had grand schemes for a village to be founded here. For this, the place was known as Philip's Folly. Eventually, the place took the name of its geographic surroundings. [Syl-U:128; WPANYA]

Highland Falls. Orange. This place was named for its location at the falls on Bog Meadow Brook. The post office was established in 1849 as Buttermilk Falls. The name was changed sometime between 1860 and 1880. [French:505; R&C:814]

Highland Lake. Sullivan. The settlement was named for the lake, which had been called Hogan's Pond but which took the name of the nearby town, named for its geographic characteristics. [Child:150; French:645]

Highland Mills. Orange. This village was formerly called Orange and had a post office established under that name in about 1829. Its name was later changed for the mills in the Highland Mountains here. [R&C:794]

Highmount. Ulster. Named for its elevation. It was first called Grand Hotel. [WPANYA]

High View. Sullivan. Named with a descriptive term of its location in the Shawangunk Mountains. [Child:170]

Hillburn. Rockland. This village was originally called Woodburn for its proximity to water and woods. In 1882, when residents applied for a post office and found out that there already was a Woodburn in the state, the name was changed to Hillburn, another descriptive term for the area. [Cole:277; Gannett:136; Green:399]

Hillsdale, North Hillsdale. Columbia. The town of Hillsdale was recognized in 1788 and named for the hills and dales of the area. [Ellis-C:370; French:246]

Hillside. Queens. The railroad opened a station here in 1911 and named it for its location at the foot of a terminal moraine. Previously, the place had been called East Jamaica and Rockaway Junction. [Jackson:544]

Hilton. Monroe. The village was first known as Unionville, then as North Parma, for its location in that town, until 1895 when the name was changed to honor Reverend Charles A. Hilton of the Freewill Baptist Church. [WPANYS]

Himrod. Yates. Wilhemus M. Himrod opened the first store here in 1831. The post office was established in 1832 as Himrod's Corners. Its name was changed to Milo, then, sometime before 1873, it was changed to Himrods. Later it lost the s. [Cleveland:726; French:720]

Hinckley. Oneida. The place was first called Gang Mills because the sawmills erected there by Gardner Hinckley and Theodore Ballou in 1849 had gang saws. The name was changed in 1891. [Gannett:136; Oneida:192; WPANYS]

Hinmansville. Oswego. The stream here was called Six-Mile Creek, and so was the place, at first. John Hinman, whose wife owned land here, wanted to established a village here, so he built several buildings, including a church and a school. [Churchill:753–4; Johnson-O:331]

Hinsdale. Cattaraugus. The town was named by Elial T. Foote, a member of the state assembly from Jamestown who was on the standing committee on the erection of towns and counties. When the town was formed in 1820, he named it for his mother's birthplace, Hinsdale, New Hampshire, which was named for Colonel Ebenezer Hinsdale, a prominent resident. [Ellis:426; French:191; Gannett:136]

Hoag Corners. Rensselaer. William Hoag kept a hotel here in the 1810s. The post office was opened in 1832. [French:557; Weise:126]

Hobart. Delaware. Waterfalls providing water power gave this village its first name, Waterville. Then it was called Tinkertown for a fellow who had set himself up for business as a tinker by stealing his tools from another man. Eventually, the place was large enough to want a post office and so needed a name. The Reverend Philander Chase of the Episcopal church suggested the name for Bishop Hobart of New Jersey. [Delaware:301; Gannett:137; Murray:549, 559]

Hoffmans. Schenectady. In 1790, Harmanus Vedder established a ferry here across the Mohawk River. It was called Vedders Ferry until John Hoffman bought it in 1835 and it became known as Hoffmans Ferry. Eventually, the place became a stop on the New York Central Railroad and "Ferry" was dropped. [Clark:57; French:597; Gannett:137; Munsell:186]

Hoffmeister. Hamilton. The Hoffmeister brothers ran a hotel here. [A&K:796; Donaldson(1):80]

Hogansburg. Franklin. The community was formerly called Gray's Mills for an early settler. Michael Hogan was born in Ireland in 1765 and spent many years as a ship captain, traveling the seas. He married "a princess of India" in Bombay and brought her to New York in 1804 (see Bombay). In 1818, he built a gristmill here and the place was named for him. [French:309; Hough-SLF:483; Hurd-C&F:446; Landon:250]

Holbrook. Suffolk. Richard Holbrook was one of the original owners of the land here in the 1650s. [Suffolk/Huntington:11]

Holland. Erie. This town was organized in 1818 and took its name from the Holland Land Company of which it had been a part. [Smith-E:607]

Holland Patent. Oneida. In 1769 King George III of England granted 20,000 acres of land here to Henry Fox, Lord Holland, of England. The village was first called Public Square for the large central square on which settlers' livestock grazed to be protected from predators. In 1845, the villagers changed the name for Holland's land patent. [French:467; Gannett:138; Oneida:195]

Holley. Orleans. The village was named for Myron Holley, who was one of the first canal commissioners in the state. [French:515; Gannett:138]

Hollis. Queens. Frederick W. Denton established this place in 1885. He planned to name it Woodhull for a Revolutionary War general. But, to avoid confusion with an upstate place of that name, he changed it to that of his birthplace in New Hampshire, which had been named for Thomas Hollis, a benefactor of Harvard College. [Gannett:138; Jackson:551; WPANYC:585]

Hollowville. Columbia. This place was previously called Smoky Hollow for its surroundings. The post office was established as Smoky Hollow in 1837. The name was changed in 1867. [Ellis-C:241; WPANYA]

Holmesville. Chenango. Jedediah Holmes was the first settler here in 1804. The settlement was named for his son, Abraham, who had opened a store here in 1844. [Smith-C&M:401; WPANYS]

Holtsville. Suffolk. The Long Island Railroad called this stop Waverly Station, but the post office was called Holtsville. Eventually, the station name was changed to match the post office. [Bayles:267; Suffolk/Brookhaven:48]

Homer, East Homer. Cortland. The town was formed in 1794 and named for the Greek poet as part of the Military Tract naming of 1790. [APN:209; French:252; Gannett:138; Goodwin:166]

Honeoye. Ontario. Named for the lake from a Native American word, *hanyahyeh* or *hayeayeh,* meaning "a finger lying." Honeoye Lake is one of the lesser Finger Lakes. However, there is an alternative story about a Native American who cut off his finger at this location after having been bitten by a snake. [APN:209; Gannett:138; Milliken:106; Morgan:469; Parker:312]

Honeoye Falls. Monroe. The village was first known as Norton's Mills, for the mills built here by Zebulon Norton. In 1838, the name was changed to that of the creek, which is the same as for Honeoye Lake and its falls. The Native American name for the falls was Skosaisto, "falls rebounding from an obstruction." [French:400, Mc-M:261; Morgan:468; Peck:309–10; WPARM:362]

Hoosick, Hoosick Falls, North Hoosick. Rensselaer. The town and the villages took their names from that of the river, which is named for a Native American word meaning "stony place." However, there might have been an early settler named Alexander Hosack from whom the name was derived. The town was formed in 1788. The village of Hoosick Falls was named for the forty-foot waterfall on the Hoosick River used to power mills. North Hoosick had once been called McNamarasville for an early settler. The village of Hoosick had been called Hoosick Corner until the post office was established there in 1785. [APN:210; French:555–6; Gannett:139; Weise:86, 88; WPANY:447]

Hope Falls, Hope Valley. Hamilton. The town of Hope was formed in 1818, reflecting the sentiments of the residents. Hope Falls was named for the waterfalls on the Sacandaga River, while Hope Valley was named for the Sacandaga River valley. [A&K:390; French:338]

Hopewell Junction. Dutchess. This hamlet, at the junction of the Duchess and Connecticut Railroad and the New England road, was named in 1869 for nearby Hopewell Church, which dated back to 1757. [Smith-D:537; WPA-NYD:115]

Hopkinton. St. Lawrence. Roswell Hopkins was the first settler here in about 1802. [French:578; Harder:113; Hough-SLF:319; Landon:241]

Hornby. Steuben. When the town was formed in 1826, it was named for John Hornby, a landowner here. [French:626; Gannett:139; Roberts:344]

Hornell, North Hornell. Steuben. The town of Hornellsville was formed in 1820 and named for Judge George Hornell, an early settler who had come here in about 1793, built a gristmill and a tavern, and was a prominent citizen of the place. [French:626; Gannett:139; Roberts:355; Steuben:120, 280; WPANY:662]

Horseheads. Chemung. In 1779, General Sullivan and his troops camped here and killed a number of horses either for food, or because they were superfluous, or because they were worn out—the stories vary on this point. At any rate, the horses' heads were piled up and left for future settlers to find, and the place became known as Horseheads. The village here, however, was first called Fairport, but in 1845 it officially became Horseheads. [APN:211; French:221; Gannett:140; P&H-C:225, 234; WPANY:655]

Horton. Delaware. Named for first settler and town supervisor William Horton, who came here in 1790. [Murray:318; WPANYS]

Hortonville. Sullivan. This place, near the junction of the North Branch of Callicoon Creek and the East Branch of Callicoon Creek, was named for an early settler. [Child:134]

Houghton. Allegany. The village was early known as Jockey Street for the horse racing that went on at this location on the Genesee Canal. Luther Houghton settled in the area in about 1817, and by 1860, Houghton Creek village had formed. In 1883, Reverend Willard J. Houghton started Houghton College here. [Allegany:232; French:172; Minard:663, 665; WPANY:681]

Howard Beach. Queens. William J. Howard owned land here in the 1890s on which he raised goats to supply his glove factory with goatskins. He bought more and more land, and, in 1909, formed the Howard Estates Development Company. A railroad station opened in 1913 and a post office, which was first called Rambersville. This name was changed to Howard Beach in 1916. [Jackson:569]

Howells. Orange. Samuel C. Howell was the first postmaster here when the post office was opened in 1846. It had been called Howells Depot, a station on the Erie Railroad. [French:510; R&C:449]

Howes Cave. Schoharie. In 1842, Lester Howe discovered this cave, which has a number of remarkable rooms and became a popular tourist attraction. [French:604; Noyes:155; Roscoe:407; WPANY:449]

Hubbardsville. Madison. Calvin Hubbard came here in about 1813 and was a prominent citizen. The post office was moved here from East Hamilton in 1846, by which name it continued to be known. About ten years later, the name was changed to Hubbard's Corners, then to Hubbardsville. [French:392; Smith-C&M:568, 569]

Hudson. Columbia. This village was first called Claverack Landing. Governor George Clinton wanted it to be named Clinton for him, but the proprietors named it in 1784 for Henry Hudson, who was supposed to have landed here. [APN:213; Ellis-C:157; French:247; Gannett:141]

Hudson Falls. Washington. This village sits at the point on the Hudson River where it changes course from east to south, and where there are falls. [WPANY:624]

Hughsonville. Dutchess. Before the Revolutionary War, a family named Hughson, sometimes spelled Houston or Hewson, settled here. The post office was established in about 1847. [Smith-D:502]

Huguenot. Orange. Named for the early Huguenot settlers. [R&C:713]

Huguenot. Richmond. Huguenots settled here in the seventeenth and eighteenth centuries. The place was called Bloomingview in the nineteenth century, but the name was changed when the railroad put a station at the intersection of Amboy Road and Huguenot Avenue. [Jackson:573]

Hulberton. Orleans. Isaac Hulbert settled here in 1825 and was the first postmaster when the post office opened in 1835. [Gannett:141; Signor:406]

Huletts Landing. Washington. A man named Hulett settled here on the shore of Lake George in about 1804. [WPANYS]

Hume. Allegany. The town was formed in 1822 and probably named for the Scottish historian and philosopher David Hume. The post office named Hume was opened in the village of Cold Creek and named for the stream on which it sits, before 1860. The village eventually took the name of the post office. [Allegany:311; French:174; Minard:736]

Humphrey, Humphrey Center. Cattaraugus. The town was named for Charles Humphrey, who was speaker of the assembly when the town was formed in 1836. Humphrey Center had the nickname Tickletown, given by Abraham Wright for a time when the residents were jubilant over some triumph at a town meeting. [Ellis:417; French:191; Gannett:141]

Hunt. Livingston. Sanford Hunt came here from Connecticut in 1818. The place had been called Hunts Hollow and Hunts Station. [Doty-L:653–4; French:386; WPANYA]

Hunter. Greene. The town was formed in 1813 as Greenland, then changed its name in 1814 for John Hunter, an early proprietor of a part of the Hardenburgh patent. The village was first called Edwardsville for Colonel Edwards, who was a prominent citizen here. [French:333; Gannett:141; Vedder:93]

Huntington, Huntington Bay, Huntington Station, South Huntington. Suffolk. The town was incorporated by patent in 1666 and was recognized as a town in 1788. It was named either for Oliver Cromwell's birthplace in England by supporters or for the fruitful hunting ground here. [Suffolk/Huntington:49]

Hunts Corners. Cortland. Asa Hunt was an early settler here, in 1822, who ran a tavern. [WPANYA]

Hunts Point. Bronx. Thomas Hunt owned a large estate here, called the Grange, on which he built a stone mansion in 1688. The Native American name for the place was Quinnahung, "a long, high place." [Jackson:577; WPA-NYC:543]

Hurley, West Hurley. Ulster. The town of Hurley was granted by patent in 1708 and named for George Lovelace's family who were Barons Hurley in Ireland. The settlement of Hurley had earlier been called New Village. It was renamed for Francis Lovelace, Baron Hurley of Ireland, in 1669. His brother had been sent here from Ulster County to settle some differences. [French:663; Fried:129, 181; Gannett:142; Syl-U:146, 149; WPANY:404]

Hurleyville. Sullivan. William Hurley was an early settler. When a station was established here on the New York and Midland Railroad in 1872, it was named for him. [Child:138; Quinlan:268]

Hyde Park. Dutchess. The village was founded in 1741 as Stoutenburgh for Judge Jacob Stoutenburgh, an early settler. Later the name was changed to Hyde Park, either for Hyde Park in London or for Edward Hyde, Lord Cornbury, who was governor of the province of New York from 1702 to 1708. When the town was formed in 1821, it took its name from the village at the urging of Dr. John Bard, a prominent citizen here. [APN:215; French:272; Gannett:142; Smith-D:303; WPANYD:89]

Hyndsville. Schoharie. Henry Hynds was an early settler, and William Hynds built the first sawmill. [French:607; WPANYA]

Ithaca © *2004 by Jon Crispin*

Ilion. Herkimer. By 1843, this village, known as the Corners, had grown enough to want a post office. About thirty names were proposed for the post office name, two of which were most popular: Vulcan and Fountain. The residents voted and Fountain won, nine to one. But no one was really satisfied with this result, so a suggestion was made to name the place Remington, for the firearms factory here. The residents adopted the name, but Eliphalet Remington refused to use the name and had his mail sent to the German Flats post office nine miles away. Meanwhile, letters to the Remington post office were coming addressed to Bennington, Vermont; Perrinton, New Jersey; Bennington, New York; and a place in Pennsylvania. This was annoying, so a new name was needed. A Mr. Devoe had been suggesting that the place be named for the ancient city of Troy, and it was. [APN:218; Gannett:143; Herkimer:161–2; WPANY:483]

Independence. Allegany. The town was formed in 1821. The village was first called Green's Corners for the Green family, early settlers; Josiah Green had the first store in 1822. The post office, named Independence, was opened in the village of Green's Corners. The village eventually took the name of the post office. [Allegany:321; French:174, 175; Minard:598, 601]

Indian Falls. Genesee. This place, at the falls on Tonawanda Creek, was once to be a city named Tonawanda Falls. Instead, it took its name from its location just south of the Tonawanda Indian Reservation. [Beers:122, 624; French:324; North:460, 496; Parker:301]

Indian Lake. Hamilton. The town was formed in 1858 and named for the lake, which had been named for Sabael Benedict, a Native American who settled here in about 1775. [A&K:427]

Indian River. Lewis. The settlement was named for the river. [French:376]

Ingleside. Steuben. The place was early known as Riker's Hollow for an old family. Its name was later changed to a more pleasant-sounding word. [APN:220; Roberts:477; Steuben:331]

Ingraham. Clinton. This settlement had been called Samson's Brick Tavern and Monty's Bay. When the post office was established, it was named for Captain Ingraham, who was commander of the U.S. warship to which Martin Koszta, a Hungarian refugee, was delivered in 1853. Koszta had been captured by the Austrians but had been trying to get U.S. citizenship. Ingraham was awarded a sword by Congress for his part in the matter. [Hurd-C&F:288]

Inlet. Hamilton. When the town was formed in 1901, it was named Inlet after one of its settlements, located at the head of Fourth Lake. [A&K:564, 567; WPANY:498]

Interlaken. Seneca. Named for the city in Switzerland, also located on a ridge between two lakes. [APN:221]

Inwood. Nassau. This was called Northwest Point until 1871 when it was called Westville. In 1888, when time came for a post office, it was found that there already was a Westville in the state. William L. Kavanaugh suggested the name Inwood because the place reminded him of an area in Manhattan called Inwood. The name was adopted and a post office was opened in 1889. It closed in about 1920, then opened again in 1949. [Winsche:48; WPANYA]

Inwood. New York. The parklike, wooded setting and varied topography of this place at the northern tip of Manhattan suggested its name. [APN:221; Jackson:597; WPANYC:302]

Ionia. Ontario. Miller's Corners changed its name to Ionia, a district in Greece, in 1898 because of confusion between post offices with similar names. [APN:222; Gannett:143; Milliken:106]

Ira. Cayuga. The hamlet, called Ira Center, was first settled in 1805. In 1821, this section of Cato Town broke off to become the town of Ira. [French:202; Storke:276]

Ireland Corners. Ulster. This hamlet was named for the early settlers here who came from Ireland. [Syl-U:290]

Irona. Clinton. Named for the iron mines and forge in the area. [APN:222; Hurd-C&F:203]

Irondequoit. Monroe. The town was formed in 1839 and named for the bay, which was called Neodaondaquat or Onyuhdaondagwat, meaning "the place where the waves gasp and die." [APN:222; French:400; Gannett:144; Mc-M:209; Morgan:468; Parker:306; Peck:299; WPARM:284]

Ironville. Essex. This settlement was first called Penfield, then Irondale. Both names refer to the iron mining that was done here by people named Penfield and Harwood. The company was called the Irondale Iron Works, which later became Ironville, and so did the settlement. [French:301; Smith-Ex:342]

Irving. Chautauqua. At the mouth of Cattaraugus Creek grew a settlement that took the name of the creek, as did the harbor built by the government. However, the first post office was called Acasto. In 1836, the post office name was changed for the Irving Company, a developer. The Seneca name for this place was Dyohgeyjaiey, "green flats," for the meadows at the mouth of the creek. [D&H:192; McMahon:94; Parker:293]

Irvington, East Irvington. Westchester. Washington Irving, the writer, lived nearby at his estate, Sunnyside. The village had been called Dearmans or Dearman's Landing for Justus Dearman whose land was auctioned off in lots in 1850. In 1854, the name was changed, then in 1872, the village was incorporated. [APN:223; French:700, Gannett:144; Lederer:39, 73; WPANY:586]

Ischua. Cattaraugus. The town was formed as Rice in 1846. The village was also first called Rice. The name was changed to Ischua in 1855. This might be a misspelling of Ischia, an Italian island. Or it might come from nearby Ischua Creek, the Native American name of which was Hesoh, "floating nettles." [APN:223; Ellis:500; French:191; Morgan:466]

Island Park. Nassau. This village was originally called Hog Island until 1874 when the island came up for sale and was bought by Sarah A. Barnum, the wife of Peter C. Barnum, a New York clothier. She was a philanthropist and offered the island, at the same price that she had bought it, to the county for use as a poor farm. In the 1880s, it was called Barnum Island. In 1881, the name was changed to Jeckyl Island. The poor farm was never established, and, by the 1920s, after the Island Park-Long Beach Corportation had bought the island for development, it finally started growing and took the descriptive name. [Winsche:50; WPANYS]

Islip, Islip Terrace, Central Islip, East Islip, West Islip. Suffolk. Named for Islipe, Oxfordshire, England, this was recognized as a town in 1788. The settlements took their names from their locations in the town. [Bayles:197; French:636; Gannett:144; Suffolk/Islip:5]

Italy, Italy Hill. Yates. This town was formed from the town of Naples in 1815. [Cleveland:375; French:719]

Ithaca, East Ithaca. Tompkins. The name is attributed to Simeon DeWitt, who owned much of the land in the area. The village had been named the Flats for its location on the shore of Cayuga Lake. The surrounding area, however, is hilly and rugged. The village, later city, went through several other names, including Markle's Flats, Sodom, Cayuga City, and The City. DeWitt is said to have called the place Ithaca as it was the center of the town of Ulysses at the time, just as the Greek Ithaca was the royal seat of Ulysses. Another interpretation, however, is that the place resembled Odysseus's description of his home as being rugged and only good for goats, and so the name fit in with the classical naming of the surrounding Military Tract. [APN:224; French:657; Gannett:145; Norris:5; P&H-T:72, 93; Selkreg:106]

J

Jockeys at Saratoga © *2004 by Jon Crispin*

Jackson Heights. Queens. Named for Jackson Avenue, a street that ran through the neighborhood as it was being developed in the 1910s. [Jackson:607]

Jacksonville. Tompkins. The settlement had been called Harlow's Corners for William Harlow, a local innkeeper. Later it was referred to as VanCortlandt for Colonel Philip VanCortlandt, a Revolutionary War soldier who had visited the area soon after its settlement. After the Battle of New Orleans in 1815, the name was changed to honor President Andrew Jackson, who was popular at the time. [Norris:49–50; P&H-T:281; Selkreg:244]

Jacks Reef. Onondaga. The settlement of Peru, when it got a post office, became known as Jack's Reef. The original name should have been Jack's Rift for the name of a black man, Darky Jack, who lived here and the rifts in the river. The postal authorities rewrote rifts to reef. [Bruce:702; Clark-O:328]

Jamaica. Queens. The Dutch had named this place Rustdorp, "a place to rest."

Later, some residents wanted to call it Canorasset; others preferred Crawford. The final name comes from the Jameco or Yamecah Indians who used to live here. The word means either "beaver" or "a country abounding in water." [APN:225; French:547; Gannett:145; Jackson:610; WPANYC:583]

Jamesport, South Jamesport. Suffolk. Old or Lower Aquebogue (so named to differentiate it from Upper Aquebogue) received a post office named for James, Duke of York, and changed its name to match. [Bayles:301; French:637; Suffolk/Riverhead:7; WPANYS]

Jamestown. Chautauqua. Named for James Prendergast, who bought ten thousand acres from his brother who had bought the land from the Holland Land Company. James settled here in about 1810. [D&H:162; Gannett:146; McMahon:265; WPANY:392]

Jamesville. Onondaga. James DeWitt started a forge here in what used to be the village of Sinai. The name was changed when the Jamesville Iron and Woolen Factory was incorporated in 1809. [Bruce:1027; Clark-O:233–4; Clayton:388; French:482; Gannett:146]

Jasper. Steuben. The town was formed in 1827 and named for William Jasper, a sergeant and hero in the Revolutionary War. [APN:226; French:626; Gannett:146; Steuben:130]

Java Center, Java Village, North Java. Wyoming. The town of Java, formed in 1832, was named for the island in Indonesia. The villages were named for the town. Java Village had been called Gurney's Mills when the post office was established there in 1826. [APN:226; Gannett:146; Wyoming:206]

Jay, Upper Jay. Essex. The town of Jay was formed in 1798 and named for John Jay, then governor of New York. The community of Jay had been known as Mallory's Bush for Nathaniel Mallory, who settled here in about 1796. Upper Jay is upriver of Jay on the Ausable River. [French:302; Gannett:146; Smith-Ex:454–5]

Jeddo. Orleans. The place was first known as Batesville. When the time came for a post office, in 1848, several names were suggested, but no one could agree on any of them. Finally, a young boy named Warren proposed this name, a variant spelling of Tokyo's old name, Edo or Yeddo. The community laughingly adopted the name, not thinking that it would be official. But then, when Zechariah Haskins received his commmission as postmaster, it was for the post at Jeddo, and that was that. [APN:226; Gannett:146; Orleans:250; Signor:340]

Jefferson. Schoharie. The town was formed in 1803 and named for Thomas Jefferson. [APN:226; French:605; Gannett:146; Noyes:156; Roscoe:142; Sias:139; WPANYS]

Jefferson Heights. Greene. The place was first known as the Flats, then as Jefferson Flats, and finally as Jefferson Heights, as though risen from the plains. [Greene:143; Vedder:51]

Jefferson Valley. Westchester. Dr. James Fountain, a local resident, named this place for Thomas Jefferson in 1850. [Lederer:74]

Jeffersonville. Sullivan. Charles K. Langhorn named this village for Thomas Jefferson. It is located only eighteen miles from the city of Monticello. [APN:226; Child:120]

Jericho. Clinton. The settlement was named for the biblical city. [APN:227; Hurd-C&F:203]

Jericho. Nassau. Robert Williams bought the land in 1648 and named it for the biblical city. It had been called Lusum, which was thought to be a Native American term but was probably a contraction of Lewisham, taken from a place in England. [APN:227; French:551; Winsche:51]

Jewell. Oneida. This was known as West Vienna for its location in the town of Vienna. In 1921 it changed it name to honor its first settler, Eliphalet Jewell, who had come to the area before 1817, by which time he had built a sawmill. Silas Jewell was the first postmaster in 1839. [Oneida:206; WPANYA]

Jewett, East Jewett. Greene. The town was formed in 1849 and named for Freeborn G. Jewett, justice of the supreme court. The community was formerly called Lexington Heights. East Jewett had been called East Kill after the stream. [French:333; Gannett:147; Greene:345, 346; Vedder:101; WPANYA]

Johnsburg. Warren. The town, when organized in 1805, was named for John Thurman, who had cleared land here and built a sawmill and a gristmill in 1790. In 1794, he opened a store and a rye distillery. He established the first calico printing works in the United States in 1797. In 1807, he was killed by a bull at Bolton Landing. [French:674–5; Smith-W:549; WPANYS; WPAW:108, 176–8]

Johnson. Orange. Benjamin Smith was the first settler here in 1769 and the place was known as Smith's Village. It was later renamed for William Johnson, who gave land for the railroad through here. [R&C:666; WPANYA]

Johnsonburg. Wyoming. George Johnson had the first post office established here. [Wyoming:268]

Johnson City. Broome. George F. Johnson got himself a position, in 1881, in a shoe factory in Binghamton. A few years later, he was able to persuade the owner to build a new factory outside the city on the belief that industry should not be in congested urban areas. [WPANY:387]

Johnson Creek. Niagara. The creek was named for the Johnson family who had settled on its banks early in the county's history. The settlement that grew up in the area then took the name of the creek. [French:453; Pool:252; Williams:376]

Johnsonville. Rensselaer. At the place called the Lick, William Johnson built a gristmill in about 1800. One day, the neighbors were surprised to see that he had erected a sign on the front of his mill that said "Johnsonville." The name stuck. [Weise:95; WPANYS]

Johnstown. Fulton. Sir William Johnson built a mansion here in 1763, and the town grew around it, taking his name. [French:317; Fulton:188; Johnstown:33]

Jones Point. Rockland. This used to be called Caldwell's Landing, but then the name was changed. Both names were for local residents. [Bedell:84, 200]

Jonesville. Saratoga. The first town officer of the town of Half Moon, serving in 1799, was named Jones. The settlement took his name. [Syl-S:477]

Jordan. Onondaga. Named for the biblical river. [APN:229; Clayton:304; Gannett:148]

Jordanville. Herkimer. The Jordan family were early settlers here. [Herkimer:113; WPANYS]

K

Cliffs on the Hudson River © *2004 by Jon Crispin*

Kanona. Steuben. The community was first called Kennedyville for Colonel
Henry Kennedy, who had come here in about 1795. In 1852, the name of the
post office, and therefore that of the community, was changed for the name of
the creek, a Native American word meaning "rusty water" or "bottom of the
water." [French:622; Roberts:167; Steuben:332–3; WPANYA]

Kasoag. Oswego. The Oneida Indians had had a meeting place here before the
village and station on the Watertown and Rome Railroad were established.
The meaning of the name is uncertain. [APN:234; Churchill:842;
French:529; Johnson-O:354]

Katonah. Westchester. Named for a Native American chief who lived here in
about 1680. His name was Ketatonah, meaning "great mountain."
[APN:234; Gannett:150; Lederer:75; S&S:183]

Kattellville. Broome. The creek and the settlement on it were named for the Kat-
tell family who settled here. [French:181; Smith-B:441]

Kauneonga Lake. Sullivan. This place was named for the fictional name of White Lake, Kaunaongga, in a popular poem by Alfred B. Street. It is a Native American word that might mean "two wings," which describes the shape of the lake. [APN:234; Child:106, 110; French:643; Quinlan:117, 136]

Keeseville. Essex. John W. Anderson came here with Richard and Oliver Keese to build a woolen factory and ironworks in 1813. At that time, the village was known as Andersons Falls, but later it became known for the Keeses, many of whom had settled here, including John Keese, a Quaker, who came here in 1806. [French:300; Gannett:150; Smith-Ex:510; WPANY:555]

Kelloggsville. Cayuga. Judge Charles Kellogg was the first merchant to open a store here in 1804. [Storke:446]

Kelly Corners. Delaware. Hiram B. Kelly settled here in 1812. The post office was established in 1873, and Limburger cheese was manufactured here in the 1890s. [Delaware:261, 266; Murray:509; WPANYS]

Kelsey. Delaware. James Kelsey came here in 1794 from New Hampshire. [Delaware:308; WPANYS]

Kendall, West Kendall. Orleans. The settlement was first called North Murray for its location in that town before the town of Kendall separated from it in 1837. The name of the settlement was changed when it got a post office in 1835 and named for Amos Kendall, who was then postmaster general. The name had been suggested by Webster and Pearsley, merchants here. Locally the town was called Kendall Corners. In West Kendall, the post office was established in 1848. [French:515; Gannett:150; Orleans:182; Signor:659, 679, 681]

Kennedy. Chautauqua. The settlement was named for Dr. Thomas Ruston Kennedy who owned and ran mills in the area. He built the first sawmill in 1805. The place was called Kennedy's Mills, Kennedyville, Falconer (from 1852 to 1861), and finally Kennedy. [D&H:209–10, 214; McMahon:299, 307–8]

Kenoza Lake. Sullivan. The lake on which this hamlet sits was called Pike Pond, a translation of its Native American name, meaning "pike, pickerel." The lake and the village went back to the original name. [APN:237; Child:133–4; Gannett:150]

Kensington. Kings. Named for the village in England that is now a part of London. [APN:237]

Kent. Orleans. The community was previously called East Carlton for its location in that town. [Orleans:99]

Kent Cliffs. Putnam. The town of Kent was first organized as Frederickstown in 1795. Its name was shortened to Frederick later in 1795 and changed to Kent in 1817 for the Kent family of early settlers. Kent Cliffs had been called

Boyd's Corners for Ebenezer Boyd, who was a captain in the Revolutionary War and who settled here in about 1780. [French:541; Pelletreau:679, 681]

Kenyonville. Orleans. Barber Kenyon was the first settler to build a gristmill and a sawmill here. [Signor:654]

Kerhonkson. Ulster. This was a place on the Delaware and Hudson Canal called Middleport. Its name was later changed to a Native American word meaning "place of wild geese." [French:608; Fried:75; Syl-U:260; WPANY:405]

Keuka. Steuben. This name comes from the Native American name of the place, meaning "landing place" or "boats drawn out," referring to a portage area. [APN:238; Parker:313; WPANYS]

Keuka Park. Yates. This community, the home of Keuka College, was named with a Native American word meaning either "bended elbow" or "landing place." [APN:238; Cleveland:450; WPANY:656]

Kew Gardens. Queens. The sons of Albon P. Man, who bought the land here in 1863, named this place for the botanical gardens in England in 1909. [Jackson:635; WPANYC:582]

Kiamesha Lake. Sullivan. The lake from which the community took its name was called Pleasant Pond or Pleasant Lake occasionally. Its Native American name means "clear water." [APN:239; Child:196-E; French:647; WPANYS]

Kiantone. Chautauqua. The town was the home of a spiritualist movement in the 1860s. The name comes from an Iroquoian word, *gentaieton,* meaning "planted fields." [D&H:204; McMahon:214; Parker:292]

Kidders. Seneca. James Kidder was an early settler here. It had been called Kidders Ferry for the ferry run across Cayuga Lake in the mid-1880s. [French:616; Seneca:100]

Killawog. Broome. This place was first settled in about 1795 and was called Union Village, but there was confusion with a village called Union that was not too far away, so they needed a new name. The present name was suggested by John Thompson for an incident in which a child was killed by being run over by some reckless drivers. [Smith-B:396]

Kill Buck. Cattaraugus. Named for a prominent Delaware chief who served in the Revolutionary War. [Ellis:462; Parker:289; WPANYS]

Kinderhook. Columbia. The town was organized in 1788. The name is Dutch for "children's point," either for the number of Native American children that Henry Hudson saw here or for a family with many children who lived here. The post office in the village was established in 1792. [APN:240; Ellis-C:219, 224; French:247; Gannett:152; WPANY:565]

King Ferry. Cayuga. This place was named for the King family, one of whom, John King II, started the first ferry across Cayuga Lake in the southwest corner of the Town of Genoa. This was a very successful enterprise, as were the family farms of the numerous Kings. It was first called Northville, but the post office was named for the family and ferry. [Storke:487]

Kings Bridge. Bronx. Frederick Philipse built and named the first bridge connecting Manhattan with the mainland here over Spyuten Devil Creek in 1693. [French:708; Jackson:637; WPANYC:273]

Kingsbury. Washington. In 1762, a patent was granted here to James Bradshaw and others and was named in honor of King George III. The town was organized in 1786 and retained the name. [French:684; Johnson:421; Stone:378; WPANYS]

Kingston, East Kingston. Ulster. The Dutch named this place Esopus in 1615. Peter Stuyvesant called it Wiltwyck, Dutch for "wild retreat," in 1661. In 1669, English governor Francis Lovelace named it Kingston L'isle for his family seat in England. Briefly, during Dutch reoccupation in 1673–74, it was called Swanenburgh. The town of Kingston was recognized as such in 1702. The Native Americans called the area Atkarkaten, meaning "smooth land." [French:663; Fried:129, 181; WPANY:595]

Kirkland. Oneida. The town, when it was formed in 1827, was named for the Reverend Samuel Kirkland, who was an early missionary among the Oneida Indians. He settled in the county in 1792 and was the principal founder of an academy that merged with Hamilton College. He died in 1808. The settlement was first called Manchester, but the post office was established as Kirkland in 1815. [French:464; Gannett:153; Oneida:153; WPANY:466]

Kirkville. Onondaga. Edward Kirkland settled here and, in 1824, became the first postmaster of the office named for him. [Bruce:795; Clark-O:219; Clayton:374; WPANYA]

Kirkwood. Broome. The town was named for the community, which may have been named for Kirkwood, Delaware, the former home of some of the early settlers. [Smith-B:485; WPANYS]

Kirschnerville. Lewis. This place was named by German settlers. [Bowen:428]

Knapp Creek. Cattaraugus. The place took its name from the creek that was named for early settlers. [Ellis:442]

Knowlesville. Orleans. William Knowles came here in 1815 from Sanderfield, Massachusetts. The post office was established in 1826 as Portville, but the name was soon changed to Knowlesville. [French:515; Orleans:250; Signor:316, 339–40]

Knox. Albany. The town was formed in 1822 and named either for John Knox, "The Reformer" of Scotland, or for Colonel Knox of the Revolutionary War. The settlement had been called Knoxville, but the post office was called Knox. [Albany:537, 542; French:164; Gannett:153; Howell:77, 870]

Knoxboro. Oneida. This place was called Cook's Corners, for Josiah Cook who settled here in 1799, before it became Knox Corners. It was named for James C. Knox, the postmaster when the post office was opened in 1850. [French:462; Gannett:153; Oneida:119; WPANYA]

Kortright, South Kortright. Delaware. Lawrence Kortright held a patent on 22,000 acres here. In 1785, the patent was surveyed into 150-acre lots and offered to settlers free of rent for the first five years and for sixpence an acre per year "forever thereafter." [Delaware:238; French:262–3; Gannett:154; Murray:461]

Kossuth. Allegany. Louis Kossuth was a Hungarian revolutionary hero who visited the United States in 1851–52 to much acclaim. [APN:244; C&V:1497; Gannett:154]

Kripplebush. Ulster. The name comes from the Dutch word *kreupel bosch*, meaning "thicket, underbrush." [APN:244; Syl-U:193]

Krumville. Ulster. William Krum was an early settler here who built a sawmill. An earlier spelling of the place was Kromville. [Syl-U:298; WPANYA]

Kuckville. Orleans. Reverend George Kuck settled here in 1815. [Signor:643, 653]

L

Lake Placid © *2004 by Jon Crispin*

Lackawack. Ulster. Named for the Native American word meaning "at the forks" or "stream that forks." [APN:246; WPANYA]

Lackawanna. Erie. This place had been known as Limestone Hill until the Lackawanna Steel Company moved its operations here from Scranton, Pennsylvania, in 1899. The steel company name came from a Native American word meaning "stream that forks" or "at the forks," and was applied to several features in Pennsylvania. [APN:246; Gannett:154; WPANY:474]

Ladentown. Rockland. Michael Leyden or Laden kept a tavern and a store here. The place was settled in about 1816. [Cole:269, 284; Green:401]

LaFargeville. Jefferson. This place was first called Rixford's Corners for Sabin Rixford, who settled here in 1817. Then it was called Log Mills for the mill built in 1819 by Dr. Reuben Andrus, who came here from Vermont. In 1823, the name was changed for John LaFarge, who was the proprietor of the land here and who came to live here about then. [D&P:456; French:360; Hough-J:212–3; WPANY:535]

LaFayette. Onondaga. The town was formed in 1825 and named for the Marquis de Lafayette. The community had been called LaFayette Square for a clearing made by early residents around which the settlement grew. [APN:163; Bruce:966; Clark-O:282; Clayton:359; French:483; Gannett:155]

Lafayetteville. Dutchess. Early on, the settlement was called simply Lafayette, named for the Marquis de Lafayette, who had served in the American Army during the Revolutionary War and then visited the United States in 1824 to great popular acclaim. [APN:163; Gannett:155; Smith-D:216; WPA-NYD:96]

Lagrange. Wyoming. This place was named for Lafayette's home near Paris. [APN:186–7; Gannett:155]

Lagrangeville. Dutchess. The town of LaGrange was formed in 1821 as Freedom. In 1828, the name was changed for Lafayette's house in France. The change of name probably occurred when the post office was established in the town, but because there already was a post office with the name Freedom, this one took the name of the popular Lafayette's home and the town followed suit. The village of Freedom, however, kept its name. [APN:186–7; French:272; Gannett:155; Smith-D:467]

Lake Bluff. Wayne. Named for its location on the Lake Ontario shore. [Cowles:425]

Lake Bonaparte. Lewis. The lake was named for Joseph Bonaparte, who had bought land here in about 1828. He built a log house on the banks of the lake that he used for hunting and fishing excursions during his summer stays at his residence in Natural Bridge. The village that grew up here took its name from the lake. [Bowen:178; French:376; Hough-L:98; WPANY:516, 523]

Lake Clear Junction. Franklin. The lake was named for its clear water. The settlement came into existence after the railroad came through in 1892 and is named for the lake. [WPANYA; WPANYS]

Lake George. Warren. This place, situated on the southern tip of Lake George, was first called Caldwell for General James Caldwell, a merchant from Albany who was granted a land patent here in 1787. Fort William Henry from the 1750s and Fort George, first built in 1759 and captured by American forces in 1775, were located here. The post office was called Lake George, and the village changed its name to match when it was incorporated in 1903. The lake was named for King George III. [French:673; Smith-W:565–6; WPAW:101–2, 156–9]

Lake Grove. Suffolk. This village took its name from its location on Lake Ronkonkoma, which meant "white sand." It had been called Lakeland, Lakeville, and Lake Ronkonkoma. [Bayles:265–6; Suffolk/Brookhaven:48]

Lake Hill. Ulster. This was the post office name for Cooper's Hotel. [French:668; Syl-U:320]

Lake Huntington. Sullivan. The community was named for the lake, which may have been named for an early settler. [Child:129; French:644]

Lake Katrine. Ulster. Named for the lake in Sir Walter Scott's "Lady of the Lake." [WPANYA]

Lake Luzerne. Warren. This settlement in the town of Luzerne is named for the lake, all named for the Chevalier de la Luzerne, a French nobleman and minister from France to the United States. He was sent to aid the Americans after the Battle of Saratoga. When the town was first organized, in 1792, it was called Fairfield. Its name was changed in 1808. [APN:267; French:675; Gannett:165; Smith-W:507; WPAW:207]

Lake Minnewaska. Ulster. Named for a Native American word meaning either "floating waters," referring to its location on top of a mountain, or "good water." [APN:298; WPANY:403]

Lakemont. Yates. Named for its location overlooking Seneca Lake. [WPANYS]

Lake Placid. Essex. Although this village sits on Mirror Lake, it is named for a nearby lake, known for its calm. [French:303; Smith-Ex:661; WPANY:506]

Lake Pleasant. Hamilton. The town was formed in 1812 and named the lake. [A&K:616; French:338]

Lakeport. Madison. This place takes its name from being on the shore of Oneida Lake. It was the place where Reuben Spencer, in a sawmill, turned on a lathe the small wooden wheels on which the salt vat covers ran at the salt works in Syracuse in the early nineteenth century. [Smith-C&M:758]

Lake View. Erie. This is a descriptive name for the community's location on the Lake Erie shore. [Smith-E:523]

Lakeview. Nassau. This was a depot on the South Side Railroad of Long Island called Woodfield. In 1903, its name was changed to Lake View until 1926 when it became one word. The name comes from overlooking the lake made by the Brooklyn Water Supply Company as a reservoir in the 1870s. [Winsche:54]

Lakeville. Livingston. Named for its location at the outlet of Conesus Lake. [Doty-L:610; French:384]

Lakewood. Chautauqua. The village is on the shores of Lake Chautauqua and was a popular resort. It was formerly called Cowings. [D&H:161; McMahon:308]

Lamont. Wyoming. This name might be from the French, "the mountain." [APN:249]

Lamson. Onondaga. This was a railroad station named for the family that were early settlers here. [Bruce:760; French:484]

Lancaster. Erie. The town was organized in 1833 and named for the county in

England. At the same time, the name of the post office in the village of Cayuga Creek was changed to match that of the town, as was the village name to match that of the post office. [APN:249; Gannett:156; Smith-E:455]

Langdon Corners. St. Lawrence. Frank Langdon came here from Dorset, Vermont, and opened the first store nearby in 1807. [Harder:132]

Langford. Erie. The settlement was first called Sippel's Corners for G. Paul Sippel, who was a merchant and hotelkeeper in the 1840s. The post office was established in about 1850 as Langford, possibly for the name of the first postmaster. [Smith-E:665]

Lansing, North Lansing. Tompkins. Named for John Lansing, a jurist, a Supreme Court judge, and state chancellor. North Lansing was first known as Beardsley's Corners for Roswell Beardsley, an early merchant and settler. [APN:250; Norris:37, 39; P&H-T:241; Selkreg:337, 348]

Laphams Mills. Clinton. The settlement was first called Travis Forge for the fellow who built the first forge here. Then Caleb D. Barton either built another forge or took over the existing one and the place became known as Bartonville in the early 1800s. Later, Nathan Lapham built a gristmill to supplement the sawmills that he already had on the Ausable River. He then built more mills, and the place took his name. [French:238; Hurd-C&F:346, 350]

Larchmont. Westchester. Peter Jay Munro bought land here in 1798 and the place became known as Munro's Neck. In 1845, Edward K. Collins bought it and named it Larchmont for the large planting of Scotch larch that Munro's gardener had planted to conceal the mansion from the road. Later, a Mr. Flint bought the land and laid out the village, keeping the estate's name. [Bolton(1):502; Lederer:80; S&S:502]

Lassellsville. Fulton. The Lassell family were early settlers here. [Fulton:222, 224]

Latham. Albany. James Latham settled here in 1768 and ran a hotel. The place was called Town House Corner, then Van Vranken's Corners, and finally Latham's Corners. [Albany:405; Howell:935; WPANYA; WPANYS]

Lattingtown. Nassau. The Latting family settled here in the 1660s. [Winsche:54; WPANYS]

Laurel. Suffolk. Named for the tree growing in the area, for which neighboring Laurel Lake was also named. [WPANY:701; WPANYS]

Laurelton. Queens. William P. Reynolds bought this land in 1906 and incorporated the Laurelton Land Company to develop it. [Jackson:637]

Laurens, West Laurens. Otsego. The town was organized in 1810, but there is no record of name origin. [French:534; Hurd-O:167; WPANYS]

Lawrence. Nassau. Newbold, Alfred, and George Lawrence were brothers who came in to develop this area after the South Side Railroad of Long Island built a branch line here in 1869. [Winsche:56; WPANYS]

Lawrenceville. St. Lawrence. This village was named for the town, which was named for William Lawrence, a proprietor from New York, when the town was formed in 1828. [French:578; Harder:133; Hough-SLF:325]

Lawtons. Erie. Named for John Lawton, an early settler, this settlement was called Lawton Station and was a stop on the Buffalo and Southwestern Railroad. [Smith-E:664]

Lawyersville. Schoharie. Lawrence Lawyer was an early settler here who came in about 1780. At one time, this place was called New Boston because many of the early settlers were from New England. [French:604; Noyes:155; Roscoe:397, 413; WPANYA]

Lebanon. Madison. The name for the town, when it was formed in 1807, was suggested by General Erastus Cleveland of Madison County for the place in Connecticut, the former home of many settlers, which was named for the biblical mountain. The settlement was known locally as Toad Hollow. [APN:253; Smith-C&M:574, 579; WPANYS]

Lebanon Springs, New Lebanon, New Lebanon Center, West Lebanon. Columbia. The town of New Lebanon was formed in 1818 and named for Lebanon, Connecticut, which was named for the biblical mountain. Lebanon Springs, once called Montepoale, contained thermal springs and was named for the town, as were all the other settlements. [APN:253; Ellis-C:305; French:248; Gannett:158; WPANYA]

Ledyard. Cayuga. The town was named for General Benjamin Ledyard, an early settler, when it was formed in 1823. He had been a clerk and agent for the apportionment of Military Tract lands. The hamlet was first known as Capins Corners, then Tallcots Corners for the early merchants who settled there. [French:202; Storke:390, 415]

Lee, Lee Center. Oneida. The town was formed in 1811 and named for Lee, Massachusetts, which was named for General Charles Lee of the Revolutionary War. [APN:253; French:465; Gannett:159; Oneida:159]

Leeds. Greene. This place was called Pasqoecq when still inhabited by Native Americans. White settlers first called it Madison, then Mill Village. In 1827, the post office was established as Leeds, in honor of Richard Hardwick, a prominent resident, who had come from Leeds, England. The community took the post office name. [Greene:143; Vedder:49; WPANYA]

Leicester. Livingston. The town was formed in 1802 as Leister. Its name was changed in 1805 for Leicester Phelps, the son of Oliver Phelps, one of the owners of the Phelps and Gorham Purchase. The pronounciation was the same for both names. The village had been known as Moscow, but the name was changed in 1917 as a reaction to the Russian Revolution. [Doty-L:573; French:384; Gannett:159; WPANYS]

Lenox. Madison. The settlement took its name from the Lenox Iron Works, which were organized in 1815, and was called Lenox Furnace. The Native American name was Skawaisla, meaning "a point made by bushes." [Morgan:473; Smith-C&M:733]

Leon, East Leon. Cattaraugus. The town was named by James Waterhouse, the first town supervisor in 1833, for the ancient kingdom in Spain as a complement to Castile where he and other settlers had previously lived. The East Leon post office was established in about 1830 as Pleasant Grove. [Ellis:484, 486, 489; WPANYS]

Leonardsville. Madison. Reuben Leonard started trading here in 1801, became the postmaster, and was a prominent businessman. [Smith-C&M:536]

LeRoy. Genesee. When the town was formed, in 1812, it was named Bellona, for the goddess of war. Its name was changed in 1813 for Herman LeRoy, an original proprietor of the land here. [Beers:475, 478; French:326; Gannett:160; North:484]

Levanna. Cayuga. This place may have been named from Levant, "east," because it sits on the eastern shore of Cayuga Lake. It was a steamboat landing two miles north of Aurora. The Cayuga Lake Tomato Catsup Manufactory was established here in 1874, although most of the village's business came from commerce on the lake. [French:202; Storke:414]

Levant. Chautauqua. This post office village was located at the junction of Cassadaga Creek and the Lake Chautauqua outlet, east of Jamestown, and took its name from the word for "east." [French:212]

Levittown. Nassau. From about 1747, this was called Island Trees, as a description of the area. In 1947, William Levitt built a large housing development here. In 1948, he announced his plan to change the community's name to Levittown. There was some disagreement, but his wishes prevailed. [Winsche:57–8]

Lewbeach. Sullivan. This place used to be called Shin Creek, but there is no record of the origin of this name. [French:647; WPANYS]

Lewis. Essex. The town was formed in 1805 and named for Morgan Lewis, then governor of New York. [French:302; Smith-Ex:560]

Lewiston. Niagara. At the suggestion of Judge Silas Hopkins, who settled in the town early and had been a colonel in the American army in 1812, the town and the village were named for Morgan Lewis, who was governor of New York in 1804. Lewis had served on the Canadian frontier here during the War of 1812 as a general, and it was thought that his name was appropriate. [French:453; Gannett:161; Pool:284; Williams:383; WPANY:651]

Lexington. Greene. The town was formed in 1813 as New Goshen, for Goshen, Connecticut, the home of early settlers. The name was changed a few months later in commemoration of the Revolutionary War battle. [French:334; Greene:351; Vedder:105]

Liberty. Sullivan. The town was formed in 1807 and named for the reason that the Revolutionary War was fought. [Quinlan:354; WPANYS]

Libertyville. Ulster. This place was previously known as Nescotack, but the name was changed when the post office was opened. [French:663; Fried:92]

Lido Beach. Nassau. Named for Lido, Italy. [Winsche:60]

Lily Dale. Chautauqua. This is a community of spiritualists that grew up around what used to be called the Cassadaga Lake Free Association, a spiritualist center in the 1870s. The name of the center was changed to the Lily Dale Assembly and the post office took its name from this. [D&H:421; McMahon:294; WPANY:130, 439]

Lima, South Lima. Livingston. The town was formed in 1780 as Charleston. Its name was changed in 1808 either for the Peruvian city, an exotic name popular at the time, or as a variation of Old Lyme, Connecticut, by settlers from Connecticut. The village of Lima had been known as Brick School House Corner, a descriptive name. [APN:257; Doty-L:601; French:384; WPANYS]

Lime Lake. Cattaraugus. The village was named for the lake, which contains deposits of shell lime on its bottom. The Native American name for the lake was Tecarnowundo, which means "lime lake." [Ellis:356; French:192; Gannett:161; Morgan:466; Parker:291; WPANYS]

Limerick. Jefferson. Named for the place in Ireland. [APN:258; Gannett:161; WPANYA]

Limestone. Cattaraugus. Early in the settlement of this area by white people, some skeletons were found buried in nearby mounds. When the bones were exposed to air, they crumbled into a white dust that resembled lime. This led to the stream near the mounds to be called Limestone Creek, and then the hamlet took the name of the creek. [Ellis:403]

Lincklaen. Chenango. The town, formed in 1823, and the settlement were named for Colonel John Lincklaen, agent for the Holland Land Company and early proprietor of the town. [French:227; Gannett:161; Smith-C&M:482]

Lincoln. Wayne. This place used to be called Lincklaen, but the name became corrupted sometime between 1877 and 1895. [Cowles:400; Mc-W:186]

Lincolndale. Westchester. In 1909, the hundredth anniversary of Abraham Lincoln's birth, this place changed its name from Somers Center. Before that, it had been called Teed's Corners. [Lederer:82]

Linden. Genesee. The settlement had been called Gad-Pouch for the supposed prominence here of gadding women. The clerk at the store suggested that the place be called Linden, for the tree, and the first sign with that name was put up over the mill. [Beers:357; North:475–6]

Lindenhurst. Suffolk. This village was settled by Germans and called Breslau, for the city in Germany, until 1900 when its named was changed for an early settler. It was incorporated in 1923. [WPANY:707; WPANYS]

Lindley. Steuben. Colonel Eleazar Lindsley bought land here in 1790. The town was named for him when it was formed in 1837, but the name was spelled without the s by mistake. [French:626; Steuben:134–8]

Linlithgo. Columbia. Robert Livingston, an early proprietor of land here, came from Linlithgow, Scotland. [APN:258; Ellis-C:260; French:248; WPANYA]

Lisbon. St. Lawrence. The town was named for the city in Portugal when it was formed in 1801. [APN:259; French:578; Harder:136]

Lisle, Center Lisle, Upper Lisle. Broome. The town was named for Lisle, France, at the suggestion of General Lafayette, so it is said. The village of Center Lisle used to be called Yorkshire, but the post office was established as Center Lisle, so the village became that, too. [APN:259; French:182; Gannett:162; Smith-B:411–2, 418]

Lithgow. Dutchess. Named with a variant for Linlithgow, Scotland. [APN:259]

Little America. Oswego. Named in contrast to Little France, located nearby.

Little Britain. Orange. Peter Mullinder, an Englishman, settled here in 1729 and named his farm, and by extension the settlement that grew up around it, for his former home. [R&C:222]

Little Falls. Herkimer. When people first settled here, the name they used was descriptive of the waterfall on the Mohawk River and used in contradistinction to the falls at the mouth of the river where the settlement named Cohoes was located. The village was incorporated in 1811 as Little Falls, but by 1850, it had grown enough that a group thought that it deserved a better name. The name was changed to Rockton in 1850, but the old residents were not happy about this and petitioned that the original name be restored. It was in 1851, and the city was incorporated as such in 1895. [French:346; Herkimer:187, 190; WPANYS]

Little France. Oswego. Named for the colony of French Canadians who settled here. [Churchill:567]

Little Genesee. Allegany. Little Genesee is a stream that runs through the town. The post office here was established in 1831 and named for the stream. [Allegany:293; French:173; Minard:878–9]

Little Neck. Queens. Named for its location on Little Neck Bay. [Jackson:686; WPANYC:572]

Little Valley. Cattaraugus. Not far from Great Valley is this smaller valley for which the town was named. The Native American name for the valley was Odasquawateh, meaning "small stone beside a large one." [Ellis:266; French:192; Morgan:466]

Little York. Cortland. This was a post village in 1860. [French:253]

Liverpool. Onondaga. This was first called Little Ireland, but when it was laid out as a village by the surveyor general, it was named for the prosperous English port by the commissioners of the land office. [APN:260; Bruce:953; Clark-O:148; Clayton:262; Gannett:163]

Livingston. Columbia. Robert Livingston held title to the land here in 1683. The name was first applied to a manor, in 1686, then to the town in 1788. [Ellis-C:273; French:247; WPANY:607–9]

Livingston Manor. Sullivan. This place was named for Chancellor John Livingston. [WPANYS]

Livingstonville. Schoharie. The Livingston family owned a large tract of land here. [Noyes:155; Roscoe:138]

Livonia, Livonia Center, South Livonia. Livingston. The name, derived from a Russian province, was suggested by Colonel George Smith in the petition for the formation of the town in 1808. [APN:260; Doty-L:607; Gannett:163]

Lloyd. Ulster. The town was formed in 1845, with no record of name origin. The Lloyd post office was opened in the community of Centerville, which later took the name of the post office and the town. [French:664; Syl-U:127]

Lloyd Harbor. Suffolk. James Lloyd of Boston owned the neck of land here in 1679, which at one time was called Horse Neck. The village was incorporated in 1926. [Bayles:144; French:636]

Loch Muller. Essex. This was first called Muller Pond for an early settler and the pond on which he settled. Then the name was changed to something that the residents thought was more poetic. [WPANYA]

Loch Sheldrake. Sullivan. Named for the lake, which was named for the wild ducks that lived on it. [Child:136]

Locke. Cayuga. The town was formed in 1802 and named for the English philosopher John Locke. The post office and train station were then named for the town. The main settlement in the town was named Milan, but later the name was changed to conform with the post office and station name. [French:202–3; Storke:509]

Lockport, South Lockport. Niagara. This city owes its existence to the series of locks needed to carry the Erie Canal over the Niagara escarpment at this point. When the course of the canal had been finalized in 1821, and proposals were to be received by the canal commissioners for the building of the locks here, of which there are more in this one area than anywhere else on the canal, the landowners planned a village and sold lots. Jesse P. Haines suggested that the new village be called Locksborough, but Dr. Isaac W. Smith proposed the name Lockport, which was adopted. [French:454; Pool:105; Williams:394]

Lockwood. Tioga. The post office was established here in 1869 as Bingham's Mills, with G. W. Bingham as postmaster. The name was changed some time later, but there is no record of why. [Gay:106; WPANYS]

Locust Grove, Locust Valley. Nassau. This area was called Chechagon or Chechagon Swamp in the 1680s. In the early 1700s, the name was Old Kaintuck Mill for the mill that manufactured fabric called buckram. By the 1740s, the place was being referred to by the fabric name. In 1857, the residents requested that the name be changed to Locust Valley because it was nicer than Buckram and more descriptive of the place. [French:551; Winsche:58]

Lodi. Seneca. When it was formed in 1826, the town was named for the city in Italy and Napoleon's victory there in 1796. [APN:262; French:615; Gannett:163]

Long Beach. Nassau. This was called Long Neck or Long Neck Beach until about 1722, after which it became known as Long Beach for its geography. [Winsche:59; WPANYS]

Long Eddy. Sullivan. This place was located just up the river from Basket, which had been referred to as Long Eddy by the riverboatmen on the Delaware River. When Basket took that name, it allowed this place, at the north end of the long eddy in the river, to be called by this descriptive term. [French:645; WPANYS]

Long Island City. Queens. In 1870, the villages of Hunter's Point, Blissville, Dutch Kills, and Middletown were consolidated and named for their location. [Jackson:691; WPANYC:575]

Long Lake. Hamilton. The town was formed in 1837 and named for the main lake within its borders, which was named for its shape. The community was previously called Gougeville and named by an itinerant peddler for his perception of the residents of the place. [A&K:750; French:338; Donaldson(1):75–6]

Loomis. Sullivan. Dr. Epaphras Loomis, who settled here in the 1820s, ran a tuberculosis sanatorium here that was called the Loomis House. The community took its name from him. [WPANYS]

Loon Lake. Franklin. The settlement and the lake may be named for the Van Loon family, who were early settlers. [WPANYA; WPANYS]

Loon Lake. Warren. Named for the bird. [APN:264; WPAW:189]

Lordville. Delaware. Named for John Lord, an early settler. [Delaware:211; WPANYS]

Lorraine. Jefferson. The town was formed in 1804 as Malta. This was changed for the French province in 1808 because there was another Malta in the state. The hamlet was called Lorraine Huddle or just the Huddle. [APN:264; D&P:438; French:359; Hough-J:195; WPANYA]

Loudonville. Albany. Elias H. Ireland bought land here in 1832 and the place became known as Ireland's Corners. The post office was established in 1850. The name of the place was changed in 1871 for Lord Loudon of London. [Albany:406; Howell:936; WPANYA]

Louisville. St. Lawrence. The town was formed in 1810 and named for King Louis XVI of France for his aid during the American Revolutionary War. The settlement was known locally as Millersville for Reverend Levi Miller, who came here in 1823. [French:579; Harder:142]

Lowville. Lewis. The town was named for Nicholas Low, an early proprietor, when it was formed in 1800. It was the home of Franklin B. Hough, who wrote many county histories in the late nineteenth century. [Bowen:273; French:378; Gannett:165; WPANY:641]

Ludingtonville. Putnam. Colonel Henry Ludington (or Luddington or Luddinton) settled here in about 1760. He was active during the Revolutionary War, as was his daughter, Sybil, "the female Paul Revere," who took a nighttime ride to warn her sleeping neighbors of the approach of the British just before the Battle of Danbury in 1778. [Blake:328; Pelletreau:691–2; WPANY:546]

Ludlowville. Tompkins. Named for Silas, Henry, and Thomas Ludlow, who moved into the area in 1791 and built the first gristmill in 1795. The settlement was called Ludlow's Mills, then Ludlowtown, Ludlowvillage, and finally just Ludlowville. [Norris:37; P&H-T:235; Selkreg:346]

Lycoming. Oswego. The post office with this name was opened at Scriba Station on the Rome, Watertown, and Oswego Railroad. The name comes from Pennsylvania where it is a Native American word meaning "sandy," regarding to a river. [APN:268; Gannett:165; Johnson-O:412]

Lykers. Montgomery. Henry Lyker built a gristmill at Brown's Hollow. Then Cornelius Lyker kept a store here. Sometime after 1860, the settlement changed its name. [Frothingham:343; Montgomery:165]

Lynbrook. Nassau. By the 1850s, this place was called Pearsall's Corners for the Pearsall family, who were early settlers and ran a store here. In 1870, the name was changed to Pearsallville, then shortened to Pearsall's in 1873, when the first post office was opened. Starting in 1891, there was dissatisfaction with the name, and a move to change it resulted in several votes. In 1894, the name Lynbrook was approved by the residents, and the Long Island Railroad changed the station name as did the post office. The name had been suggested by Thomas P. Brennan, a local railroad agent. He transposed the two syllables of Brooklyn to arrive at Lynbrook. [Winsche:60–1; WPANYS]

Lyndonville. Orleans. Named for Lyndon, Vermont. The suffix *ville* was added when the post office was established to distinguish it from another Lyndon in the state at the time. [Signor:616]

Lyon Mountain. Clinton. The settlement is named for the mountain, which was named for Nathaniel Lyon, an uncle of General Nathaniel Lyon, who served in the Mexican War before dying in the Civil War. The village developed from the iron mining done in the mountain. [Hurd-C&F:305–12, 353, 355; WPANY:513]

Lyons. Wayne. The town was formed in 1811 and named for the village, which had been named by its landowner, Captain Charles Williamson, for the city in France. The village was first known as the Forks, for its location where Mud Creek meets the Canandaigua Lake outlet and forms the Clyde River. [Cowles:238; Mc-W:97; WPANY:671; WPANYS]

Lyonsdale. Lewis. Caleb R. Lyon settled here in 1819. He died in 1835, just before his project of a canal to the Black River was authorized to be built. His son, Caleb Lyon, had built a large house here. [Bowen:356; French:377; Gannett:166; Hough-L:109]

Lyons Falls. Lewis. The village was originally called High Falls for the sixty-three-foot falls. It is at the junction of the Moose and Black Rivers and was the place where the Black River Canal met the Black River. The canal was 35 miles long, begun in 1838 and finished in 1855, went from Rome to Lyons Falls. The village and the falls were named for Caleb R. Lyon who was the first resident agent and proprietor of the Brantingham Tract. [Bowen:512, 517; French:379–80; Hough-L:246; WPANY:642]

Lysander. Onondaga. The town was formed in 1794 and named as part of the Military Tract in 1790 for the Spartan commander. The Lysander post office was opened in the village of Betts Corners. In 1817, the Betts family settled in what was known as Vickery's Settlement for the Vickery family, who came here in about 1810. Chauncey Betts was the first postmaster of the Lysander post office at Betts Corners. The name of the settlement was soon changed to that of the post office. [APN:269; Bruch:748–9; Clark-O:161, 168; Clayton:315, 324; French:483, 484; Gannett:166]

M

Manhattan © *2004 by Jon Crispin*

Mabbettsville. Dutchess. Early on, the place was called Finkeltown, in honor of one of the Great Nine Partners, early proprietors of the land. Then James Mabbett bought land here, which he farmed in the 1820s and '30s and around which a settlement grew. [French:277; Gannett:166; Smith-D:325; WPANYD:98]

Macedon, Macedon Center. Wayne. The town was formed in 1823 and named for Macedonia in Greece from its references in the Bible. [APN:270; Gannett:167]

Machias. Cattaraugus. The town was named for Machias, Maine, the previous home of many of the settlers. The word is from the Algonquian, meaning "bad little falls," places that were dangerous to canoes. [APN:270; Ellis:359; WPANYS]

Madison. Madison. The town, like the county earlier, was named for President Madison when it was formed in 1807. [Smith-C&M:605]

Madrid. St. Lawrence. When it was formed in 1802, the town was named for the city in Spain as a complement to nearby Lisbon, which was named for the city in Portugal. The village was first called Robert's Mills for Seth Roberts, who built a gristmill here in 1803. Before the War of 1812, the name was changed to Columbia Village or Columbiaville. Later the village name was changed to match that of the town. [APN:272; Curtis:394; Harder:145]

Mahopac, Mahopac Falls, West Mahopac. Putnam. These communities were all named for Lake Mahopac, a contraction of a Native American word, *achkook-pang,* meaning "snake lake or pond." Mahopac Falls was called Red Mills for the buildings painted red. Earlier, it was called Kirkham's Mills for the early owners. [APN:112, 173; Blake:261; French:540; Pelletreau:345]

Maine. Broome. This town, settled by families from New England, took the name of the state. [Smith-B:493]

Malden Bridge. Columbia. This settlement on both sides of Kinderhook Creek took its name from the bridge, probably built by someone by the name of Malden. [Ellis-C:289]

Malden-on-Hudson. Ulster. Named for Malden, Massachusetts, which was named for the town in England. [APN:274; French:666; Gannett:169; WPANYA]

Mallory. Oswego. In 1810, Edward Smith built a sawmill here, prompting the name Smith's Mills for the place. In the 1830s, Isaac W. Brewster owned the mills, and the place was known as Brewsterville. Later Jared Mallery bought them, naming the place Mallery Mills. Eventually the spelling was changed. [Churchill:565–6; French:522; Johnson-O:361–2; WPANYA]

Malone. Franklin. The town was organized in 1805 as Harrison for Richard Harrison, a member of the Macomb Purchase. In 1808, the name was changed to Ezraville for Ezra L'Hommedieu, a landowner from Suffolk County. Finally, in 1812, it was changed to Malone, the name suggested by Richard Harrison for his friend Edmund Malone, the Irish Shakespearean scholar. [APN:275; French:311; Hurd-C&F:416; Landon:227; WPANYS]

Malta, Malta Ridge, Maltaville. Saratoga. The town was named for the island in the Mediterranean when it was formed in 1802. [APN:275; French:590; Gannett:169; Syl-S:384]

Malverne. Nassau. The South Side Railroad of Long Island named this station on a branch line Norwood Station in 1870. When it came time for a post office in 1911, after much confusion of mail being sent to other Norwoods in the state, the residents suggested Lynmouth as a new name. The Long Island Railroad Company rejected this as being too similar to Lynbrook. Ernest Child, an official of a company whose shipments had regularly gone to Norwood in St. Lawrence County, suggested that the place be named for

Malvern, England. This was acceptable all around, but when the railroad timetables were published, the name came with an extra e. The post office was opened in 1919 as Malverne. [APN:275; Gannett:169; Winsche:61–2; WPA-NYS]

Mamaroneck. Westchester. The town was recognized as such in 1788. The story is that it was named for a Native American chief who lived here in the 1640s, but it might also come from a Native American word, spelled in a variety of ways, meaning "the place where the fresh water falls into the salt water." [APN:275; Bolton(1):84, 463; French:701; Gannett:169; Lederer:87; WPANY:380]

Manchester. Ontario. The town was first called Burt when it was set up in 1821. In 1822, the name was changed to Manchester. The village of Manchester was named for Manchester, New Hampshire, and Manchester, England, because of its location on a stream that gave it potential as a manufacturing center. [French:497; Gannett:170; Milliken:107]

Mandana. Onondaga. There was a post office here by this name before 1849, but there is no record of name origin. [Clark-O:312; French:487]

Manhasset. Nassau. The settlement was formerly called Head of Cow Neck. This was changed to Robinia in 1837, which was thought to be the botanical name of the abundant locust tree. This turned out to be false, so the name was again changed, this time to Manhasset, the Native American name of Shelter Island (which is not near here) and of the Native Americans who lived on the island. The word means "little island" or "an island sheltered by islands." [APN:277; French:550; Gannett:170; Winsche:62–3; WPANYS]

Manhattan. New York. The origin of this name is uncertain; it might come from the Munsee *manhactanienk,* "place of general inebriation" (refering to the time that Verrazano gave liquor to the Native Americans), or *manahatouh,* "place where timber for bows and arrows is found," or *menatay,* "island." It is the earliest known Munsee placename, found as Manahatta on a 1610 map made by a Spanish spy in the English court where Henry Hudson was jailed before he returned to the Netherlands. [APN:277; Gannett:170; Jackson:718]

Manhattan Beach. Kings. The Manhattan Beach Improvement Company developed this area as a summer resort in 1877. [Jackson:719]

Manitou. Putnam; **Manitou Beach.** Monroe. Named for the Native American term for "great spirit." [APN:277; Gannett:170]

Manlius. Onondaga. The town was formed in 1794 and named during the classical naming of the Military Tract in 1790 for one of the many Roman generals of this name. Charles Mulholland, one of the earliest settlers here, called the village Liberty Square in about 1801. The name was changed to Manlius

Square, then to Manlius. [APN:177; Bruce:768, 775; Clark-O:207, 218; Clayton:363, 365; French:484; Gannett:170]

Mannsville. Jefferson. When the post office was established here, it took the name of Colonel H. B. Mann, who had built a factory here that burned down in 1827. [D&P:367; French:357; Gannett:170; Hough-J:161]

Manorhaven. Nassau. This was first known as Dodge's Island for the Dodge family. By 1873, it became known as Sunny Side, but then Richard Gorman bought the land and it became known as O'Gorman's Island. In 1926, after being sold several times, the name was changed to Manhasset Isle. In 1930, the communities of Manhasset Isle, Beach Haven, and Orchard Beach voted to incorporate as one village called Manorhaven, a name chosen for its pleasant sound. [Winsche:63–4; WPANYS]

Manor Kill. Schoharie. Named for the stream that runs through the town of Conesville. [French:604; Noyes:159]

Manorville. Suffolk. This was once part of the St. George's Manor patent. Parts of it had been called Brookfield and Halsey's Manor. [Bayles:254; French:634; Suffolk/Brookhaven:51; WPANYS]

Maple View. Oswego. Named for the trees in the area. [WPANYA]

Marathon. Cortland. The town was formed in 1818 as Harrison and named for William Henry Harrison, a victorious American general in the War of 1812 who later became the ninth president of the United States. The name was changed in 1827 for the battlefield in Greece because there already was a Harrison in the state. [APN:279; French:253; Gannett:171; Goodwin:226]

Marbletown. Ulster. The town was recognized in 1788 and named for the limestone deposits here from which many of the old houses were built. The name was first spelled Marbleton. [APN:279; French:664; Fried:130; WPANY:404]

Marcellus. Onondaga. The town was formed in 1794 and named as part of the classical naming of the Military Tract in 1790 for the Roman general and stateman M. Claudius Marcellus. The post office in the village was established in 1799. [APN:279; Bruce:631; Clark-O:289; Clayton:283, 285; French:484; Gannett:171]

Marcy. Oneida. The town was named for William Marcy, then governor of the state, when it was formed in 1832. [French:465; Gannett:171; Oneida:163; WPANYA]

Margaretville. Delaware. Margaret, the daughter of Governor and Mrs. Morgan Lewis, inherited the land here through her mother's side of the family. She was the daughter of Chancellor Livingston, whose family was granted the land by Queen Anne in 1708. The post office was established in 1848. [Delaware:258, 261; Gannett:171; Murray:510; WPANYS]

Mariaville. Schenectady. Named for one of James Duane's daughters. [Clark:57; French:596; Gannett:171; Munsell:185]

Marietta. Onondaga. Named for Queen Marie Antoinette of France. [APN:280; Gannett:171]

Marilla. Erie. The town was named for the wife of John Rogers, an early settler, when it was formed in 1823. The hamlet had been called Shanty Town until the formation of the town when it took the same name. [French:292; Gannett:172; Smith-E:480]

Mariners Harbor. Richmond. Named for the primarily maritime business conducted here on Newark Bay. [French:566; Jackson:728; WPANYC:622]

Marion. Wayne. When the town was formed in 1825, it was named Winchester, but then its name was changed a year later, probably for General Francis Marion, a popular Revolutionary War hero whose biography was published in 1809 by Parson Weems. [APN:280; French:692; Gannett:172]

Markhams. Cattaraugus. Named for Joshua Markham, who settled here in 1834 and ran a tavern for thirty years. It was then called Markham's Corners. [Ellis:233]

Marlboro. Ulster. The town was recognized in 1788 and named for the Duke of Marlborough. The post office in the village was established in 1825. [APN:281; French:665; Syl-U:83–4]

Martindale Depot. Columbia. A Mr. Martin was a large landowner here. The post office was established in about 1849. [Ellis-C:242; WPANYA]

Martinsburg, West Martinsburg. Lewis. The town was named, when it was formed in 1803, for George Walter Martin, who built a mill in 1801 and a tavern in 1805. He later served in the War of 1812. [Bowen:372; French:378; Hough-L:172; WPANY:641]

Martville. Cayuga. The first settlers were Chauncy Hickock and Timothy Austin in 1823 who built a mill on the site, and the first store was opened here in 1825. The name may have come from the early meaning of the word "mart" as the coming together of people to buy and sell. By 1860, the town had a post office. [French:205; Storke:258]

Maryland. Otsego. The place was first settled in 1790 by Israel, Elephas, and Phineas Spencer and Elisha Chamberlain. The town was organized in 1808, but there is no record of name origin. [French:534; Hurd-O:175–8; WPA-NYS]

Masonville. Delaware. The town and settlement were named for the Reverend John M. Mason of New York, who, through his wife, owned the Evans patent that became the town in 1811. [Delaware:244; French:263; Gannett:174; Murray:481]

Maspeth. Queens. This place was settled by the English, who often called it English Kills to distinguish it from Dutch Kills nearby. Ultimately it was named for the Mespat Indians who had lived here. [APN:283; French:549; Jackson:733; WPANYC:579]

Massapequa, Massapequa Park. Nassau. Early on, the area was known as Massapequa, meaning "great water land." By 1706, it was known as Oysterbay South until 1842 when it became South Oyster Bay. In 1887, the village of Massapequa was plotted and surveyed. The name Massapequa became official in 1889, named by Thomas H. Brush, the developer of the village. Massapequa South had been called Wurtemberg or Stadt Wurtemberg by the German settlers there in the 1870s. In 1926, more of the land was developed and the place was called Massapequa Park by Michael J. Brady, one of the developers, because it was near Massapequa and he envisioned his development as a park. [Gannett:174; Winsche:64–5]

Massena, Massena Center. St. Lawrence. Andre Massena was a French general in Napoleon's army who had distinguished himself at the Battle of Rivoli against the Austrian army in 1797 and was considered a hero. When the town was formed in 1802, its residents petitioned that it be named for him. [APN:283; Curtis:407; French:579; Gannett:174; Harder:149; WPANY:532]

Mastens Lake. Sullivan. This place was named for the lake, which had been called Masten Pond and was used as a reservoir. There is no record of its name origin. [Child:170; French:646]

Mastic, Mastic Beach. Suffolk. The Algonquian name for the Great River was Mastic or Mystic, meaning "big stream." [APN:284; WPANYS]

Mattituck. Suffolk. The creek that extends into the town was named with an Algonquian word meaning "no timber" or "place without wood." [APN:285; Gannett:175; Suffolk/Southold:29]

Mayfield. Fulton. The town was named for the Mayfield patent that was granted in 1770. [French:318; Fulton:225]

Mayville. Chautauqua. May Busti was the daughter of Paul Busti, general agent of the Holland Land Company who had settled here. [D&H:132; McMahon:310]

McClure. Broome. The McClure family, headed by William Macclure, first came here in about 1787. The name was changed from the Scottish spelling to the Irish. [Smith-B:301]

McConnellsville. Oneida. Joseph McConnell was an early settler here in about 1800. The post office was opened in 1812. [Oneida:206; WPANYS]

McDonough. Chenango. The town was formed in 1816 and named for Commodore Thomas MacDonough of the Revolutionary War. The spelling changed over the years. [French:227; Gannett:167; Smith-C&M:368; WPANY:553]

McGraw. Cortland. Samuel McGraw came here in 1803 and the place was called McGrawville. The post office changed its name to McGraw in 1898. The railroads and the telephone and telegraph soon followed. The village changed its name to match in 1932. [Goodwin:252; Melone:420; WPANYA]

McKownville. Albany. The McKown family was prominent here. In the 1930s, the place was considered a "clambake and midget-auto racing paradise." [Albany:525; Howell:853; WPANY:416]

McLean. Tompkins. This hamlet was originally called Moscow, but when the post office was established in 1824, there already was a post office with that name so this post office was named after the new postmaster, Judge McLean. [Norris:33; P&H-T:207; Selkreg:325]

Meadowdale. Albany. This was a small hamlet and post office in the late 1890s, probably named with a pleasant-sounding name. [Albany:525]

Meads Corners. Putnam. The Mead family were early settlers here. [Pelletreau:684]

Mechanicville. Saratoga. In the mid-1800s, the American Linen Thread Manufacturing Company employed 125 people here. There were many other factories here that also employed mechanics, a term that meant a worker in a factory. [APN:287; French:593; Syl-S:295]

Mecklenburg. Schuyler. When King George III of England married Charlotte Sophia, Duchess of Mecklenburg-Strelitz of Germany, her name was used in a variety of forms as placenames in the early nineteenth century. [APN:287; WPANYS]

Meco. Fulton. The place had been called McEwen's Corners for the family name, the first of whom had built a gristmill here in 1816. It was also called Bennet's Corners for another family. When the time came for a post office, the present name was chosen so as not to offend anyone for whom the place was not named. [Fulton:210; WPANYA]

Medford. Suffolk. This was a railroad station in the middle of the woods and was probably named for the Medford in Massachusetts. [APN:287; Bayles:261]

Medina. Orleans. Ebenezer Mix was a surveyor for Joseph Ellicott. He named this place for the Arabian city. The Native Americans called this place Diegehhoseh, "water over water." [APN:288; Orleans:272; Signor:346]

Medusa. Albany. Uriah Hall and his family settled here in about 1783. The place became known as Halls Mills or Halls Hollow. Then in 1850, the names of the hamlet and post office were changed for the snake-haired Gorgon sister of Greek mythology during the high period of classical naming. [Albany:463; APN:288; C&V:1738; French:165; Howell:915; WPANYA; WPANYS]

Melrose. Rensselaer. The community was early known as the Junction but was later named for the town and abbey in Scotland, popularized by the writings of Walter Scott. [APN:289; Gannett:176; WPANYS]

Melville. Suffolk. This place was formerly called Sweet Hollow, but there is no record of the current name origin. [Bayles:168]

Memphis. Onondaga. The settlement was called Canton, but when the post office was opened, it could not take that name because there already was a Canton in the state, so it was named for the city in Egypt instead. [APN:289; Bruce:726; Clayton:329]

Menands. Albany. Louis Menands established large gardens and greenhouses here in 1842, for which the depot on the Albany and Northern Railroad was called Menand's Station. [Albany:407; Howell:936]

Mendon. Monroe. When the town was formed in 1812, it was named by settlers from Mendon, Massachusetts, which was named for Mendham, England. [APN:290; Gannett:176; WPARM:285]

Meredith, East Meredith. Delaware. The town was named in 1800 for Samuel Meredith of Philadelphia, who owned much of the land here. East Meredith had been called Brier Street from a line in a poem, "And since it goes up so nice and complete / We'll name it the flower of Brier Street," after the first frame house was built. [Delaware:253; French:263; Gannett:177; Murray:493]

Meridale. Delaware. This place was formerly known as Meredith Hollow and had a post office open as such in 1877. Sometime later the new name, meaning "happy valley," was adopted. [Delaware:254; WPANYS]

Meridian. Cayuga. Originally called Cato Four Corners, the name was changed in 1849, possibly for a principal line of longitude nearby. It was incorporated in 1854 under that name. [French:201; Storke:290]

Merrick. Nassau. This name has been variously spelled as Meric, Moroke, and Merikohe since its first use in 1643. It comes from the Native American tribe Merricoke, meaning "bare land" or "plain." The post office was established in 1802, discontinued in 1811, and reopened again in 1843. [APN:291; French:547; Winsche:66]

Messengerville. Cortland. Nathan Messenger was an early settler here in about 1794. Messengerville became the name of the post office for State Bridge and a railroad station. [French:255; WPANYA]

Mettacahonts. Ulster. Possibly named for an early prominent Native American here. [APN:293]

Mexico. Oswego. The town was formed in 1792 and named for the country during a time when there was sympathy for the Mexican struggle for independence. The village was first called Mexicoville. [APN:293; Churchill:570; French:522; Johnson-O:262, 266]

Middleburgh. Schoharie. The town was formed in 1797 as Middletown and named for the village. The names of both were changed in 1801. The village was first settled by Palatine Germans who called it Weisers Dorp for John Conrad Weiser, who founded it in 1712. [French:606; Sias:140–1; WPANY:634]

Middle Falls. Washington. Named for its location on the Battenkill River. [WPANYS]

Middlefield. Otsego. This settlement was early known as Newtown-Martin, but then took its name for its central location in the county. [Hurd-O:184; WPANYS]

Middle Grove. Saratoga. The Middle Grove post office, named for a group of pine trees that separated the eastern and western portions of the village, was opened in the village of Jamesville, which was named for John W. James, who had built a dam here in 1836 and erected a paper mill. In about 1860, he returned to New York City, and the village took the name of the post office. [French:589; Syl-S:441; WPANYA]

Middle Hope. Orange. This place was first called Middletown for its location between Newburgh and Marlborough. But when the time came for a post office, there already was a Middletown in the county, so James P. Brown, a settler here from Hopeton, Scotland, proposed this hybrid name, at one time written as one word. [R&C:279]

Middle Island. Suffolk. The geographical location of this community, in the middle of Long Island, was a natural name for it. [Bayles:261]

Middleport. Niagara. This village was named for its location on the Erie Canal midway between Lockport in Niagara County and Albion in Orlean County. [French:456; Gannett:178; Pool:273; Williams:382; WPANY:674]

Middlesex. Yates. The town was formed as Augusta in 1789, but its name was changed in 1808 for the county in England because there was another town named Augusta in the state. [APN:294; Cleveland:586; French:720; Gannett:178]

Middletown. Orange. Named for its location halfway between Montgomery and Mount Hope. [R&C:443]

Middle Village. Queens. Named for its location at the midpoint of the Williamsburgh and Jamaica Turnpike, now Metropolitan Avenue. [Jackson:759]

Middleville. Herkimer. In about 1807, the residents of this place decided to name it. Several names were suggested and rejected. This one was thrown out as a joke but was the one adopted. [Herkimer:160]

Midland Beach. Richmond. Named for its location. [Jackson:760]

Mileses. Sullivan. The Miles family settled here and ran a tannery. Charles Miles was a supervisor of the town of Fremont from 1853 to 1855. The place had been called Milesville. [Child:149; Quinlan:301]

Milford. Otsego. The town was formed in 1796 as Suffrage, then the name was changed in 1800. It was named either for the town in England or for the many mills along the Susquehanna River here. [APN:295; French:534; WPA-NYS]

Millbrook, South Millbrook. Dutchess. George H. Brown had an estate here in the 1860s that he called Millbrook Farms. The Newburgh, Dutchess, and Connecticut Railroad built a station here in 1869 named Millbrook, through Brown's enterprise. The village that grew up around his estate and the station was incorporated in 1895. [Smith-D:324; WPANYD:99]

Millen Bay. Jefferson. This place was previously called Hubbard's Bay for an earlier settler. It was later called Millens Bay, then dropped the s. [D&P:316, 327; French:356; Hough-J:115]

Miller Place. Suffolk. Andrew Miller, son of John Miller, one of the early settlers in Easthampton, founded this settlement in 1671. [Bayles:252–3; French:633; Suffolk/Brookhaven:47]

Millers. Orleans. The Miller family settled here in 1847. When the post office was opened in 1882, Edgar Miller was the first postmaster. [Signor:617]

Millerton. Dutchess. Sidney G. Miller was a builder of the extension of the New York and Harlem Railroad into this part of the state in 1845. The village that grew up around the station was incorporated in 1875 and was named for him because he had established this as his headquarters. In the 1860s, the post office was called Northeast Station. [French:273; Gannett:179; Smith-D:246; WPANYD:96]

Millport. Chemung. James T. Gifford purchased eighteen acres of the Bentley farm in 1825 on which he built a house and tannery and laid out a village plat, calling it Millvale. (Gifford moved on to Illinois in 1835 and founded the city of Elgin. He died of cholera in 1851.) There was a possibility of a canal being built through this valley, which inspired many people to move to the area. The day in 1829 the canal bill was passed, a meeting to celebrate took place at Erastus Crandall's store. Brandy was drunk. The name of the village was discussed, and it was decided to change the name to Millport now that it was going to be on the Chemung Canal instead of just in an unimportant valley. [P&H-C:264]

Millville. Orleans. Named for the number of gristmills, sawmills, and turning mills here. [Orleans:295; Signor:548]

Millwood. Westchester. This was a railroad station named for the Rockdale Mills located here. [Lederer:93]

Milo, Second Milo. Yates. The town, when it was formed in 1818, was to be called Milan, named by Samuel Lawrence who started the town. There already was a Milan in the state, so he changed the name to Milo, either for the Greek strongman, the Roman tribune, or the Greek island. There is no record of name origin for the intriguing Second Milo. [Cleveland:634; Gannett:179]

Milton. Ulster. Peter McCoon was an early settler who wanted the community to be called Petersburgh. Instead, it was named for the poet John Milton. The post office was established in about 1820. [APN:296; Gannett:179; Syl-U:84; WPANYA]

Minaville. Montgomery. George Smith, a local merchant and politician, named this place in 1818, replacing its previous names of the Street and Yankee Street, but there is no record of why he chose this name. [Frothingham:304; Montgomery:115]

Mineola. Nassau. The place was called Hempstead Plains. After 1839, this was called Hempstead Branch for being at the junction of the main line of the Long Island Railroad and a branch line to the village of Hempstead. In about 1840, the place was often called Haviland for Isaac E. Haviland, a prominent resident who did not want his name used officially. Another proposal was for the name Titusville, for another wealthy resident, who also opposed the use of his name. In 1858, the post office changed its name to Mineola. The railroad changed the name of the station in 1859. The word comes from *meniolagamike,* meaning "a pleasant or palisaded village" or "much water." There is no record of why the name was chosen. [APN:297; Winsche:68; WPANYS]

Minerva. Essex. The town was formed in 1817 and named for the Roman goddess of the arts and handicrafts. [French:302; Gannett:180; Smith-Ex:632; WPANYA]

Minetto. Oswego. Named for the creek. [Churchill:645; French:526]

Mineville. Essex. There was an extensive iron mining industry here. The post office was established in about 1870. [Smith-Ex:607; WPANY:537]

Minisink Ford. Sullivan. Located on the Delaware River, this was a crossing that took its name from the Native American word *minsies,* meaning "lands from which the water had gone" or "islanders." [French:507; Gannett:180]

Minoa. Onondaga. Named for the Minoan civilization, which was named for King Minos of Crete. [APN:298]

Model City. Niagara. This place was planned and named by William T. Love, who in the early 1890s founded "a city on scientific and artistic principles." Love had a scheme to divert Niagara River water to provide power for industry in Model City. The financial panic of 1893 brought an end to Love's plans. His name is linked with Love Canal, the hazardous waste site that was the result of industry and municipal use of his unfinished hydropower canal. The post office here was first called Middletown. [Pool:300; Williams:384]

Modena. Ulster. The post office was established in about 1830 and named for the city in Italy. [APN:300; Gannett:181; Syl-U:175]

Moffitsville. Clinton. J. H. Moffit was an agent and general manager of the Chateaugay Iron Company here. The settlement used to be called Russia. [Hurd-C&F:308, 358; WPANYS]

Mohawk. Herkimer. This place took its name from the river on which it sits. The name comes from the Dutch name of the Native Americans in this area. They wrote the name as Maquaas. By the 1770s, the river's name was spelled Mohok on a map of New York. [APN:301; Gannett:181; Herkimer:32, 172]

Mohawk View. Albany. Named for its location overlooking the Mohawk River.

Mohonk Lake. Ulster. The settlement was named for the lake, which has a Native American name, either related to Mohawk or meaning "great hill." [APN:301; WPANYA]

Moira. Franklin. Named for the Earl of Moira in Ireland. [French:312; Gannett:181; WPANYS]

Mombaccus. Ulster. Named for Rochester Creek, which used to be called Mombackus Kill. The name first appeared in 1676 as "the Mumbakers," refering either to a Native American tribe or to a Dutch family. [APN:302; Fried:83]

Mongaup Valley. Sullivan. This place was named for the river valley. Until 1847, it was known as Mongaup Mill for the gristmill built here by the Livingston family. The Native American name has been spelled Mangawping and has been translated as "huckleberry valley" and "dancing feather." [APN:303; Child:62, 108; French:643, 644; Quinlan:134]

Monroe. Orange. When the town was formed in 1799, it was first called Chesecocks, or Chesekook, the name of the original patent. The name was changed to Southfield in 1801 and to Monroe, for the president, in 1808. The village was named for the town. [French:507; R&C:787, 793]

Monsey. Rockland. In 1840, the president of the Erie Railroad, Eleazar Lord, bought about eight acres of land here for the train station. He named it Kakiat, from the Dutch *kijkuit*, meaning "lookout," but when the railroad began operations, it was called Monsey at the suggestion of Judge Sarven. The word comes from the Native Americans, variously written as *muncie* or *minsi* and meaning "wolf." [APN:239, 304; Cole:262, 279; Gannett:182; Green:406]

Montauk, Montauk Beach. Suffolk. The local Native Americans were called the Montauks by the white settlers, although the natives really applied this word to the location where they lived rather than to themselves. The word, a corruption of *minnawtawkit* or *meantaut*, meant "island place" or "in the island country." [APN:304; French:635; Gannett:183; Suffolk/Easthampton:2]

Montebello. Rockland. A descriptive term from the Italian meaning "beautiful mountain." [APN:305]

Monterey. Schuyler. The place was early called Gaylord's for a former resident. The first post office was established in about 1823 as Mead's Creek. The name was later changed for the place in Mexico as a result of the Mexican War in the 1840s, which produced a number of related placenames from the romance of victory in foreign places. [APN:305; P&H-S:198-9]

Montezuma. Cayuga. The town was formed in 1859. It and the village were probably named after the last Aztec emperor of Mexico. The town consists of marshy, wet land, much of which is now part of the Montezuma National Wildlife Refuge. The settlement was an early manufacturer of salt but could not compete with the saltier brine of Syracuse and Salina. The Native American name for this place was Tecarjikhado, meaning "place of salt." [APN:305; French:203; Morgan:470; Storke:302]

Montgomery. Orange. The town was organized in 1788 and named for General Richard Montgomery, a Revolutionary War hero. The village took its name from the town. [APN:305; French:508]

Monticello. Sullivan. Samuel Frisbee Jones and John Paul Jones, brothers, came here in 1804 from Connecticut. They were great admirers of Thomas Jefferson and so named their settlement for his estate, the name of which means "little mountain." [APN:305; Child:196-F; French:647; Gannett:183; Quinlan:548, 551]

Montour Falls. Schuyler. The village had been called Havana when it was laid out in 1829. The name was changed in the 1890s to honor Catharine Montour, a French woman living with the Native Americans here. The Seneca name for the falls was Shequagah, "place of falling or roaring waters." [P&H-S:164, 173-6, 186; WPANY:655]

Montrose. Westchester. John Montrose and his family were early settlers here. [Lederer:94; WPANYS]

Montville. Cayuga. This place is situated in hilly country for which it is probably named from the French word for mountain. Millard Fillmore read law here with Judge Wood. [French:203]

Moody. Franklin. The place was named for Jacob Smith Moody, the first settler in the region. His son, Martin, became a distinguished guide, leading such folks as Presidents Chester A. Arthur and Grover Cleveland, and the members of Boston's Philosophers' Club on hunting and fishing expeditions. [Hurd-C&F:503; WPANY:507, 514]

Mooers, Mooers Forks. Clinton. When the town was organized in 1804, it was named for Major General Benjamin Mooers, an early settler and prominent citizen of the county. The post office in the village of Mooers was established in 1822. The village of Mooers Forks, on the north branch of the Chazy River, was previously called Centerville and was settled in about 1812. The post office was opened as Mooers Forks in about 1840. [French:238; Gannett:183; Hurd-C&F:331, 332; WPANYS]

Moores Mill. Dutchess. Alfred Moore operated a mill here on a tributary of Sprout Creek. [WPANYD:144]

Moravia. Cayuga. The town was formed in 1833 and named for the religious sect that was also called "United Brethren." Members came here from Pennsylvania in the 1750s. St. Matthew's Episcopal Church contains seven impressive wood carvings by Hans Meyer from Germany. This was the church in which Millard Fillmore married Abigail Powers. [French:203; Storke:451; WPANY:426]

Moreland. Schuyler. Named for the Moreland patent. [P&H-S:106–7]

Morganville. Genesee. This place was named for William Morgan, a former Mason, who had written a book that was supposed to reveal the secrets of Masonry. He disappeared in 1826, a possible murder victim. His disappearance sparked the anti-Masonic movement. [Beers:643; French:328; North:498; WPANY:472]

Moriah, Moriah Center. Essex. The town was formed in 1808 and named for the biblical mountain. The post office was established in Moriah Center in 1866. It was moved to Mineville in 1870 and a new one opened here in 1871. [APN:308; French:302; Gannett:184; Smith-Ex:566, 608]

Moriches, Center Moriches, East Moriches. Suffolk. This name is derived from the Native Americans who lived here. [APN:308; Bayles:177; French:634]

Morley. St. Lawrence. This place had been called Long Rapids for its location on the Grass River. Its name was changed to Morley, a name in the W. H. Harrison family, first permanent settler and proprietor here, in 1835. The post office was established in 1839. [Curtis:458–9; French:575; Harder:157; Hough-SLF:280; WPANYA]

Morris. Otsego. General Jacob Morris, the son of Lewis Morris, a signer of the Declaration of Independence, held the Morris patent here. He settled here in the 1770s and had wanted the town to be called New Morrisania, but that name did not catch on. The town was formed in 1849. [French:535; Hurd-O:201; WPANYS]

Morrisania. Bronx. The Morris family owned this property from 1670. The first Lewis Morris died in 1691. The land was inherited by his nephew, Lewis Morris II, who became lord of the manor. Lewis Morris IV was a signer of the Declaration of Independence. The town was formed in 1855 in Westchester County, and the land was later transferred to the Bronx. [French:701; Gannett:185; Jackson:772; WPANYC:529]

Morrisonville. Clinton. This is probably a family name, although there is no record of name origin. There was a large iron business here that ended in

1830 when a flood on the Saranac River took out the forge, the dam, and all the mills. [Hurd-C&F:170; WPANYS]

Morristown. St. Lawrence. The town was named for Gouverneur Morris, a landowner here, when it was formed in 1821. [Curtis:614; French:580; Harder:158; Landon:235]

Morrisville. Madison. Thomas Morris settled here in 1797. Before the village was incorporated in 1819, it was called Morris Flats. The post office had been established in 1808. [French:390; Gannett:185; Smith-C&M:629]

Morton. Monroe. This place was made up of the settlements of Webster Mills, Kendall Mills, and East Kendall and lies on the border with Orleans County. It was named for Levi P. Morton, governor of New York. [Peck:288; WPA-NYS]

Mott Haven. Bronx. Jordan L. Mott developed the area in 1850 for his Mott Iron Works, which he had established in 1828, and as a suburb for those working in Manhattan. He was the inventor of the coal-burning stove. [French:701; Jackson:776; WPANYC:518]

Mottville. Onondaga. This place was previously called Sodom, but became Mottsville for Arthur Mott, son of Lydia P. Mott, who came here in about 1818 and started the Friends' Female Boarding School, known as the Hive. The name Mottsville later lost its s. [Bruce:992; WPANY:425]

Mountain Dale. Sullivan. Named for its surroundings. [WPANYS]

Mountain View. Franklin. A descriptive name of its location. [WPANYS]

Mountainville. Orange. Named for its location. [R&C:764]

Mount Hope. Orange. James Finch Sr. named this place at the raising of house frames for Benjamin Woodward and Dr. Benjamin B. Newkirk in 1807 for the positive future that the name invoked. [R&C:510]

Mount Ivy. Rockland. The community's name had been Gurnee's Corners for W. F. Gurnee and his family who lived here. When the New Jersey and New York Railroad came through, the station was called Mount Ivy, a descriptive term. The place followed suit. [Cole:162; Green:386; WPANYA]

Mount Kisco. Westchester. Stephen Wood, a farmer here in the place that was known as Kisco Plain in 1701, suggested the present name. The word comes from *cisqua,* an Algonquian word meaning "muddy place" or "edge of creek land." [APN:241; French:698; Lederer:30, 96]

Mount Marion. Ulster. Named for General Francis Marion of the Revolutionary War. [APN:280; Gannett:172; WPANYA}

Mount Morris. Livingston. The place had been called Allen's Hill for Ebenezer Allen, an early settler here. In 1792, Robert Morris, a Revolutionary War veteran, bought Allen's farm, and from him came the name of the town and the village. [Doty-L:619; French:385; Gannett:185; WPANYS]

Mount Sinai. Suffolk. In 1718, a grant for a mill was given to Moses Burnet at this place that had been called Old Man's Harbor for a fellow who used to put up travelers in his little inn. Mount Sinai is where Moses received the Ten Commandments from God. [Bayles:251; French:633; Suffolk/Brookhaven:47]

Mount Upton. Chenango. There is no record for the origin of the name, but the settlement is situated in a hilly part of the county and might have been named for its location. [French:227; WPANYS]

Mount Vernon. Westchester. This area was first known as Hutchinson's for Anne Hutchinson, who lived here after leaving Massachusetts. Later, the New York Industrial Home Association #1 bought land just east of the junction of the New York Central and the New Haven Railroads. Soon there were 300 homes and it was time to open a post office. The residents first asked to be named Monticello, but because of the post office already established by that name upstate, they chose the name of the home of another president. George Washington's estate in Virginia had been named by his older brother, Lawrence, for Admiral Edward Vernon under whom he had served. [APN:511; Gannett:186; Lederer:97; WPANY:549]

Mount Vision. Otsego. This was first called Jacksonville, but the post office was established as Mount Vision and eventually the community took the name also. [French:534; WPANYS]

Mumford. Monroe. The settlement was first called McKenzie's Corners for the early settlers. Then it was called Slab City for the material used in the building of the first dwellings. In 1809, Thomas Mumford bought into the place, and in 1817 he built a gristmill, which his son, Elisha H. S. Mumford, took over. The place became known as Mumfordville, but the name was shortened at the suggestion of the post office. [Mc-M:192–3; Peck:440; WPANYA]

Munnsville. Madison. The first storekeeper in the town was Asa Munn, who came here in 1817. The post office was established in 1858. [French:393; Gannett:186; Smith-C&M:710]

Munsey Park. Nassau. This was once a part of Manhasset, but in 1822, Frank A. Munsey, a major newspaper publisher, bought a large estate here to which he added more land. Munsey died in 1925 and bequeathed the estate to the Metropolitan Museum of Art, which decided to build a model village here. By 1930, enough homes were sold to help the Museum expand its art collection and for the residents to vote for incorporation as the Village of Munsey Park. Soon the Museum sold the rest of its holdings but left as its legacy streets named for American artists: Hunt, Peale, Copley, and others. [Winsche:68–9; WPANYS]

Murray. Orleans. The town was formed in 1808 and named for John Murray, a New York City merchant who owned a good deal of land here when the town was formed. [French:515; Orleans:203; Signor:378]

Muttontown. Nassau. In 1781, this was a sheep district. The name was in use until about 1851, by which time there were few sheep and the name seemed inappropriate. The place began to be referred to as being a part of Brookville or East Norwich, neighboring communities. In 1931, the residents decided to become an incorporated village, which they did, and chose again the name Muttontown. [Winsche:71]

Myers. Tompkins. Named for Andrew Myers and his family, who settled here in 1792. The village sits on the shore of Cayuga Lake at the mouth of Salmon Creek and has often been referred to as Myers Point. When Henry H. Plough was appointed postmaster in 1880, the office was called Ploughs, but it was changed to Myers in 1882. [Norris:39; Selkreg:331]

N

Niagara Falls © *2004 by Jon Crispin*

Nanticoke. Broome. The town and settlement were named for the creek that runs through the area. The creek name is a Native American word meaning "tidewater people." The settlement was first called Lamb's Corners for Isaac Lamb, who had settled there in 1804. It was then called Nanticoke Springs and later shortened. [APN:317; French:182; Gannett:187; Smith-B:419; WPANYS]

Nanuet. Rockland. There was a railroad station here that was called Clarkstown, for the town. In 1856, James DeClark proposed that the name be changed for that of a Native American chief. [APN:317; Cole:119; French:569; Green:422]

Napanoch. Ulster. This place, named for a Native American chief, had a post office in 1860, which was spelled Napanock. [APN:317; French:668; Syl-U:260]

Naples. Ontario. The town was formed in 1789 as Middletown. The name was changed in 1808 for the Italian city. The village was first called Watkinstown for one of the founders, William Watkins, who came from Massachusetts in 1790. The Native American name was Nundawao, which meant "great hill." [French:497; Milliken:107; Morgan:469]

Napoli. Cattaraugus. The town was named Cold Spring when it was first organized in 1823. The name was changed for the Italian city in 1828. [Ellis:475; French:193]

Narrowsburg. Sullivan. This place, on a narrow portion of the Delaware River, was first called Homan's Eddy for Benjamin Homan, an early settler. After he died, the rivermen called the place Big Eddy. It was later named for its other geographic description. [Child:196-Q; French:648; Quinlan:640]

Nassau, East Nassau. Rensselaer. The town was formed in 1806 as Philipstown, named for Philip Van Rensselaer. The name was changed in 1808 for the Duchy of Nassau in Germany. Dutch rulers had carried the title of Prince of Orange-Nassau in the seventeenth century and so lent the name to many places in the New World. The village of Nassau was early known as Union Village. The post office was established in 1811. The village of East Nassau used to be known as Schermerhorn's for John Schermerhorn, who kept the first tavern here. The post office here was opened in 1830. [APN:319; French:557; Gannett:188; Weise:123, 125, 126]

Natural Bridge. Jefferson. The Indian River eroded a limestone arch that serves as a bridge over the river. The settlement was named for this natural phenomenon that had brought tourists to the area for years. Joseph Bonaparte, the brother of former French emporer Napoleon Bonaparte, lived in this community for a couple of summers soon after it was laid out in 1818. Joseph, who came to America in 1815, after Napoleon's defeat, had formerly ruled Spain as king, appointed by Napoleon. [D&P:528; French:363; Hough-J:304; WPANY:516, 523]

Natural Dam. St. Lawrence. This site of a large rock in the Oswegatchie River, which made a seventeen-foot waterfall, was the country home of Gouverneur Morris and had been called Morris's Mills. [Curtis:558; Harder:162; Landon:147; WPANYA]

Naumburg. Lewis. The place was locally known as Prussian Settlement, but the post office was called Naumberg. [French:376; Hough-L:80]

Nauraushaun. Rockland. Named for the Naranshaw Creek. [Cole:142–3]

Navarino. Onondaga. Ephraim Hall came here early and the place became known as Hall's Corners. When the post office was opened, sometime before 1849, it was named for the 1827 battle during the Greek War of Independence from the Ottoman Empire. [APN:320; Bruce:863; Clark-O:138]

Nedrow. Onondaga. The first settler here was named Worden. When the post office was established in 1817, it could not have this name because there already was one in the state, so the suggestion was made and accepted to spell "Worden" backwards. [WPANYA]

Nelliston. Montgomery. The village was first called Fort Clyde for the fort that was built in 1777 on land owned by Henry Nellis. The name of the village was changed when it was incorporated in 1878. [Montgomery:149; WPANYS]

Nelson. Madison. The town was formed in 1807 and named for Lord Nelson, the British admiral. The settlement was early on called Skunk Hollow because a skunk was caught there and put on display. It had been thought that there were no skunks west of the Hudson River. This one was sent on to Cazenovia in a box as a curiousity. The village was later known as Nelson Flats. [Smith-C&M:641, 650]

Nelson Corners, Nelsonville. Putnam. Elisha Nelson built the first house in 1800, in what became Nelsonville. [Blake:160; Gannett:189; Pelletreau:574]

Neponsit. Queens. The Neponset Realty Company laid out a development here in 1910. [Jackson:805]

Nesconset. Suffolk. The place was named for the Algonquian term for "the second crossing." [APN:323]

Neversink. Sullivan. This town, when it was formed in 1798, took its name from the river, an Algonquian word variously spelled as Newasink, Narrasing, Nevisinck, and Naewersink, meaning "wild or mad river" or "a continual running stream" or "high land between waters." [APN:320; Child:62; French:646; Gannett:188; Quinlan:456]

Nevis. Columbia. Named for the mountain in Scotland. [APN:324]

New Albion. Cattaraugus. The settlement had been called Horth's Corners for the Horth family. Erastus Horth opened the first store in 1833. Sometime before 1833, the post office was opened with A. Horth as postmaster. Later the name was changed for Albion in Orleans County, the former home of some settlers. [Ellis:381, 385]

Newark. Wayne. This village was named for the town in England when it consolidated two villages, Miller's Basin, named for Joseph Miller who settled here in 1820, and Lockville, which was also known as East Newark. [APN:325; Gannett:190; Mc-W:66]

Newark Valley. Tioga. This town was formed in 1823 as Westville. The name was changed to Newark in 1824 for the town in England. The village was called the Society of Western from 1800 to 1808, then it became Westville, and in 1862, its name was changed to Newark Valley. [APN:325; Gannett:190; Gay:201, 256]

New Baltimore. Greene. The town was organized in 1811 and named for Lord Baltimore. The hamlet was settled as a shipbuilding port. [French:334; Greene:368; WPANY:590; WPANYS]

New Berlin, South New Berlin. Chenango. The town was formed in 1807 and named for Silas Burlingame, who had come from Providence, Rhode Island. The name was changed to Lancaster in 1821, then back to New Berlin in 1822. South New Berlin is a village in the south part of the town. [Smith-C&M:382, 384; WPANYS]

New Bremen. Lewis. The New Bremen post office, named for the city in Germany, was opened in the settlement of Dayansville, laid out in 1826 by Charles Dayan. The settlement took the name of the post office in 1848. [Bowen:428; French:378; Hough-L:194–6]

New Brighton, West New Brighton. Richmond. The village of New Brighton was incorporated in 1866 and named for the city in England. West New Brighton is sometimes called West Brighton. The place was called Factoryville for all the manufacturing facilities here in the mid-1800s. The post office opened in 1871 with the name West New Brighton, named for New Brighton. [APN:60; Jackson:806, 1256]

Newburgh. Orange. Named for the city in Scotland. [Gannett:190; WPANYS]

New City. Rockland. In 1774, a new location for the county courthouse was selected, and, in anticipation of great growth because of the presence of the county government, the place was called New City. [Cole:118; Green:416]

Newcomb. Essex. When the town was formed in 1828, it was named for the first town supervisor, Daniel T. Newcomb. [French:303; Smith-Ex:650]

New Dorp, New Dorp Beach. Richmond. This place was settled by the Dutch in 1671 as Niew Dorp, "new town," ten years after Oude Dorp, "old town." In 1860, the New Dorp post office was in the village of Egbertsville, named for James Egbert, a former resident. [French:566–7; Jackson:806]

Newfane. Niagara. The town was named by Mrs. James Van Horn, the wife of a prominent citizen. There is no record as to why she chose this name although it might have been for Newfane, Vermont. The community used to be called Charlotte or Charlottesville for the daughter of the owner of the village site, George R. Davis of Troy, New York. [APN:325; Gannett:190; Pool:322, 328; Williams:389]

Newfield. Tompkins. When the town was first organized in 1811, it was called Cayuta for the creek that flows through it. It was changed to Newfield when the town became part of Tompkins County instead of Tioga County. The new name seems to have referred to all the unowned land in the area. The hamlet of Newfield was originally named Florence. When the first post office in the town came in, it was first called Cayuta, then was changed to Newfield two years after the post office moved into the village. [French:658; Norris:43; P&H-T:250; Selkreg:303]

New Hackensack. Dutchess. The Van Benschoten family were early settlers here who had come from Hackensack, New Jersey, in about 1714. [Smith-D:504; WPANYD:114]

New Hamburg. Dutchess. Probably named for the German city, this place was first known as the Wappingers Creek post office, established in about 1813. [Smith-D:367, 369; WPANYA]

New Hampstead. Rockland. This village was first known as Kakiat, from the Dutch *kijkuit,* meaning "lookout." It then became West Hampstead to distinguish it from Hampstead, the name taken by the town before it became Ramapo in 1828. Because of confusion with Hempstead on Long Island, eventually the village became New Hampstead and the town, Ramapo. Many settlers here were from Long Island. [APN:239; Cole:254–5; Green:400]

New Hampton. Orange. This was previously called Phillipse. The present name was for the railroad station on the New York, Erie, and Western Railway. [R&C:684; WPANYS]

New Hartford. Oneida. Many early settlers came from near Hartford, Connecticut, so when the town was formed in 1827, it was named for their former home. The Native American name for the place was Chegaquatka, "kidneys," reason unrecorded. [French:465; Morgan:473; Oneida:169]

New Haven. Oswego. The town of New Haven was formed in 1813, containing the village of Gay Head. However, the post office established earlier in 1813 was called West Mexico. The confusion this engendered prompted residents to change the names of both the village and the post office to New Haven in 1819. [Churchill:606, 623; French:523; Johnson-O:343]

New Hope. Cayuga. Probably named by the first settlers in the hopes of having a successful life. Today it is the home of New Hope Mills, a maker of pancake and waffle mixes. [WPANYA]

New Hyde Park, North New Hyde Park. Nassau. George Clark bought the estate here from Governor Donegan's family in 1724. He named it Hyde Park for his wife, Anne Hyde. Eventually, the name referred to more than just the estate. In 1815, the settle ment was called Plainville, but by 1817, it was back to being Hyde Park. In 1871, when applying for a post office, it was found that there already was a Hyde Park, so this post office was designated New Hyde Park. North New Hyde Park was first called Plattsville for Henry W. Platt, a prominent resident in the 1850s. That name went out of use by 1896, when it was called New Hyde Park. A branch office of the post office was established here in 1958 as North New Hyde Park, as it is north of the New Hyde Park office and village. [Winsche:72, 75; WPANYS]

Newieden. Sullivan. This might have been a Dutch settlement. [Child:196-Q]

New Kingston. Delaware. In 1777, the city of Kingston was burned by the

British. William Livingston offered fifty-acre lots to 100 families who were left homeless by the fire. They named the new village for their former home. [Delaware:265; French:263; Murray:507]

New Lisbon. Otsego. The town was first called Lisbon for the city in Portugal when it was organized in 1806. The name was changed in 1808. [French:535; WPANYS]

New London. Oneida. Ambrose Jones named this place for his hometown in Connecticut when the post office was established in 1825. He had built the first frame house here. [Oneida:204]

New Milford. Orange. This place was formerly called Jockey Hollow. The post office was established in 1815, probably under the new name, which would have been chosen as something more dignified. [R&C:579]

New Paltz. Ulster. The town was granted by patent in 1677 and named for Pfaltz, the German name of the Palatinate, a region now in Germany from which many settlers came to the United States. [APN:326; French:665; Syl-U:12; WPANY:402]

Newport. Herkimer. The first permanent settler here was Christopher Hawkins, who came here from Newport, Rhode Island, in 1791. [APN:326; French:347; Gannett:191; Herkimer:223]

New Rochelle. Westchester. In 1688, a group of Huguenot refugees settled here and named the place for their former home in France. The town was recognized in 1788. The village was incorporated in 1857, then as a city in 1899. [APN:408; Bolton(1):601; Lederer:101; WPANY:245, 381]

New Russia. Essex. The Crimean War influenced many placenames, including this one. [WPANYA]

New Salem. Albany. Before the post office was established here under this name in the 1830s, the settlement was called Punkinton. [Albany:550; Howell:901]

New Scotland. Albany. The town was formed in 1832 and was named for the community and post office, both of which were named for the many settlers from Scotland who came here in the 1760s. [Albany:545, 551; French:165; Howell:77, 889, 902; WPANYA]

New Springville. Richmond. This place was settled in 1680 and called Carle's Neck for the piece of land between two creeks. By 1840, it was known as Springville and New Springville. [Jackson:821]

New Suffolk. Suffolk. Named for Suffolk, England. [WPANYS]

Newton Falls. St. Lawrence. James L. Newton built a sawmill here in 1894. The post office was established in 1896 as Newtonfalls and changed in 1930. [Harder:164]

Newtonville. Albany. John Newton settled here in 1840, so the place was called

Newton's Corners until the post office was opened in 1850. [Parker:406; French:166; Howell:935; WPANYA]

New Utrecht. Kings. When the Dutch settled here in 1647, they named it for Utrecht in the Netherlands. [Jackson:821–2; WPANYC:470]

New Windsor. Orange. Named for Windsor, England, as early as 1728. [R&C:210]

New Woodstock. Madison. Walter Childs had come here from Woodstock, Connecticut, and suggested the name. [French:390; WPANYS]

New York Mills. Oneida. The first cotton cloth manufacturing mills in New York State were established here in 1808 by the New York Cotton Manufacturing Company. The post office was established in 1831, and the village was incorporated in 1922. [French:471; Oneida:219, 220; WPANYS]

New York. New York. The Dutch called the city New Amsterdam. When the British took over in 1664, they named it for the Duke of York, who became King James II. [APN:327; French:418; Gannett:191; WPANY:59]

Niagara Falls. Niagara. The word *niagara* is a Native American word meaning "across the neck or strait" or "point of land cut in two." In 1805, the first settler, Augustus Porter, envisioned a manufacturing center that would rival the English city of Manchester by using the power of the falls, so he called the place Manchester. The town was first organized in 1812 as Schlosser for the fort that had been erected by Captain Joseph Schlosser, a German officer in the British Army. After the village was burned by the British in 1813, the place became known by the same name as the famous waterfalls, Niagara. The name of the town was changed officially in 1816. [APN:327; French:454; Gannett:191; Parker:307; Pool:174; Williams:377; WPANY:272; WPANYS]

Nichols. Tioga. The town, when it was formed in 1824, was named for Colonel Nichols, a landowner in the area. In exchange for this compliment, Colonel Nichols gave two hundred dollars to the town to be used for the construction of some public building. It was used towards the erection of a church. The village was called Rushville for Dr. Benjamin Rush, a signer of the Declaration of Independence, but when it came time for a post office, it was discovered that there already was one in the state, so it was named for the town instead. [French:651; Gay:301; P&H-Ti:133, 135]

Nicholville. St. Lawrence. In 1817, Samuel Wilson built a sawmill here. The little collection of houses that grew up around it was called Sodom until it was decided to give the place a less suggestive name. It was then named for E. S. Nichols, an agent of William Lawrence, the proprietor of the land. [Curtis:674–5; French:578; Harder:164; Hough-SLF:327]

Nile. Allegany. The settlement was first called South Branch for the creek. When the post office was established, it took the name of the Egyptian river according to the wishes of many of the settlers here who were Seventh-Day Baptists. [Allegany:277; APN:328; Minard:720; WPANYA]

Niles. Cayuga. Elder Robert Niles was a pastor of the First Baptist Church in the community of Sempronius from which this town was formed in 1833. The village of Niles was locally known as Dutch Hollow but then took the name of the town. [French:204; Storke:443, 450]

Nineveh. Broome. Named for the ancient city in Assyria for its biblical connotations. [Gannett:192; WPANYA; WPANYS]

Niobe. Chautauqua. This was formerly called Grant Station, but the name was changed to that of the queen in Greek mythology who is associated with weeping. There is no record of why this name was chosen. [APN:329; McMahon:209]

Niskayuna. Schenectady. The town, formed in 1809, sits on the banks of the Mohawk River with some rich agricultural land. The settlement took its name from the town and was first settled about 1640. The canal crossed the river here on a stone aqueduct. The name is thought to be a corruption of *nistigioone* or *conistigione,* a Native American word for "extensive corn flats." [Clark:57; French:597; Gannett:192; Munsell:192]

Nissequogue. Suffolk. Named with a Native American word meaning "muddy place." [APN:329; Bayles:193; WPANYS]

Niverville. Columbia. This place at the outlet of Kinderhook Lake was a railroad station and was named for the Niver family, early and prominent citizens. [Ellis-C:228; French:247]

Norfolk. St. Lawrence. The town was formed in 1823 and named for Norfolk, England. [French:580; Harder:165]

Normansville. Albany. This place on the Normanskill stream had been called Upper Hollow until the post office was opened in the 1890s. The stream was named for Albert Andriessen Bradt de Noorman, one of the early settlers in the area. [Albany:493; French:163; Howell:781]

North Bay. Oneida. This community sits on the north side of Oneida Lake. [French:470; Oneida:206]

North Blenheim. Schoharie. The town of Blenheim was formed in 1797 and named for the Blenheim patent, a part of which was in the north part of the town. The North Blenheim post office was in the village of Patchin Hollow, which had been named for Freegift Patchin, who had built the second mill here. [French:603; Noyes:155; Roscoe:250; Sias:122]

North Branch. Sullivan. This place lies on the North Branch of Callicoon Creek. [Child:121; French:644]

North Creek. Warren. The settlement is named for the creek on which it sits. Samuel Coplon, the Santa Claus of the North Country, had his toy distribution center here from 1904 to 1936, when he moved it to Bakers Mills. [Smith-W:675; WPANY:493; WPAW:204]

Northeast Center. Dutchess. The town was formed in 1788 and named for its geographical location in the county. [French:273; Smith-D:238]

North Fenton. Broome. The settlement was first called Ketchum's Corners. It lies in the northeast part of the town of Fenton, which was named for Governor Reuben E. Fenton (1819–85). He served in New York State's Assembly and House of Representatives as a Democrat. Then he became a Republican because of the slave issue and served in Congress, as governor, and as U.S. senator. [Smith-B:459, 465; WPANY:393]

North Highland. Putnam. The name comes from the Dutch *hogeland* or *hoogland* meaning "highland." [Gannett:136]

North Hudson. Essex. The town, formed in 1848, was named for its location on the upper Hudson River. [French:304]

Northport, East Northport. Suffolk. This community had been called Great Cow Harbor, but later it took the name of its geographic description. [Bayles:160; French:636; Suffolk/Huntington:48]

North River. Warren. This place is named for the northern section of the Hudson River on the boundary of Warren and Hamilton Counties. [WPANYS; WPAW:205]

North Sea. Suffolk. Named for its location in opposition to the Atlantic Ocean to the south. [Bayles:332; Suffolk/Southampton:34]

Northumberland. Saratoga. There is no record of why this place was named for the county in England. [APN:333; Gannett:193; Syl-S:404]

Northville. Fulton. The village is located in the northeastern part of the town of Northampton. [French:318; Fulton:233]

Northville. Suffolk. A post office named Success was established here in about 1847 but was discontinued in 1880. The community was named for its location in the northeast part of the town of Riverhead. The name was changed to Sound Avenue but then changed back in 1927. [Bayles:285; French:637; Suffolk/Riverhead:6; WPANYS]

Norton Hill. Greene. The Norton family settled on this hill in 1802. [WPANYA]

Norway. Herkimer. The town was named for the country when it was formed in 1792. [French:347; Gannett:193; Herkimer:213]

Norwich, North Norwich. Chenango. The town was formed in 1793; the name was suggested by James Glover, an early settler, for the former home of many settlers from Norwich, Connecticut, which had been named for the city in England. The Native American name for the village was Ganasowadi, the meaning of which has been lost. [APN:333; Gannett:193; Morgan:473; Smith-C&M:306]

Norwood. St. Lawrence. The village had been known as North Potsdam, Potsdam Junction, Potsdam Station, and Raquetteville, the last for its location on the Raquette River. Its name was changed in 1875 for the title of a book by Harriet Beecher Stowe. Reverend Chase, the pastor of the local Methodist Church, had suggested the name because it was simple and "had no i's to dot or t's to cross." [Curtis:498; Harder:168]

Noyack. Suffolk. The name comes from the Algonquian word for "land at a point." [APN:334, 335; Suffolk/Southampton:34]

Nunda. Livingston. The town name comes from *nundao* or *onundao*, meaning "hilly." [APN:335; Gannett:194; Parker:304]

Nyack, Central Nyack, South Nyack, Upper Nyack, West Nyack. Rockland. The name of these villages comes from a Native American word meaning "land at a point" that referred to what the Dutch called Verdrietige Hook, now called Hook Mountain, a 668-foot-high point of rock on the west bank of the Hudson River. [APN:335; Bedell:297; Gannett:194; Green:335]

O

Oswego Harbor © *2004 by Jon Crispin*

Oakfield. Genesee. The town was formed in 1842 and named for the local vegetation. The Oakfield post office was opened in the village of Caryville—in
1833, Colonel Alfred Cary had opened a store here. In 1837, the name of the
village was changed to Plain Brook and soon after to Oakfield for the post office. [Beers:564, 568; French:327; North:488, 490]

Oak Hill. Greene. Lucas Dewitt first settled here in about 1770 and the place was
called Dewittville or Dewittburg. The name was later changed for the many
oak trees in the area. [Greene:360; WPANYS]

Oakland. Livingston. In 1847, Frederick Newbold Lawrence built a mansion
here called the Oaks. It later became a greenhouse and nursery, then in 1896
the Oakland Golf Club. Part of the land became a housing development in
1911 and took the name of the club. [Jackson:859]

Oakland Valley. Sullivan. This place was called Oakland until the post office was
established as Oakland Valley. Both names are descriptive of the surrounding
geography. [Child:145; French:645]

Oak Orchard. Orleans. Named for the creek, which was named for the oak forest
that originally lined its banks. [French:515; Signor:16]

Oaks Corners. Ontario. Named after an early innkeeper, Jonathan Oaks. [Mil-
liken:108]

Oakwood, Oakwood Beach. Richmond. These places are located on flat land between the Atlantic Ocean and the interior hills, an area that was forested when it was first settled. [Jackson:859]

Obernburg. Sullivan. This place was settled by Germans in the 1850s. [Child:149; French:645]

Ocean Beach. Suffolk. The village was named for its location. A post office was established here in 1911, and the village was incorporated in 1921. [WPANYS]

Oceanside. Nassau. This place was first called Christian Hook since the land had belonged to St. George's Episcopal Church in the early 1800s. In 1880, the place was more popularly called Oceanville. By 1890, the settlement was almost an extension of Rockville Centre, so a name change was suggested, such as Rockville Centre South or Rockville South. But in 1892 a post office was established as Ocean Side. The application had been for Oceanville, but there already was one in the state, so the post office department changed it. By 1896, the name was one word. [Winsche:76; WPANY:707]

Odessa. Schuyler. John Foster surveyed the village in 1827 and suggested that it be named for the Russian city on the Black Sea. [APN:338; P&H-S:87]

Ogden. Monroe. The town was named, when it was formed in 1817, for William Ogden, the son-in-law of John Murray, the original proprietor. The community was first known as Town Pump for the well at its center. [French:400; Mc-M:180; Peck:316; WPARM:286; WPANYA]

Ogdensburg. St. Lawrence. Samuel Ogden, who had married a sister of Gouverneur Morris's, bought land here in 1792 and promoted its growth. [French:580; Gannett:195; Harder:170; WPANY:534]

Ohio. Herkimer. The town was named West Brunswick when it was formed in 1823. Its name was changed in 1836 for the state, the name of which comes from the Native American name of the river and means "beautiful river." [APN:339; French:347; Gannett:195; Herkimer:235]

Ohioville. Ulster. The settlement was named for Moses Frere, who meant to go to the state of Ohio but never got there and settled here instead. [Syl-U:13]

Olcott. Niagara. Burgoyne Kemp was the third settler here before 1810. He built the first log barn and the growing settlement became known as Kempville. Sometime later the name was changed. [Pool:327; Williams:390]

Old Field. Suffolk. At one time called Old Field Point, it seems to have been named for its location on an open plain. The Native American word for this place was Cometico. The village was incorporated in 1927. [Bayles:241; French:633; WPANYS]

Old Forge. Herkimer. Named for an old forge that was used in the smelting of iron ore. [WPANYS]

Olean. Cattaraugus. The settlement of the village, later city, was started in about 1804 by Robert Hoops, whose brother, Adam Hoops, was an agent for the

Holland Land Company. It was first called Hamilton for Alexander Hamilton, but locally the place was called Olean Point, a name suggested by Adam Hoops for the oil springs in the region. The Native American name for this place was Hesoh, the same as for Ischuna Creek, "floating nettles." One source claims that the place was named for Olean Shephard, the first white child born in the town. [APN:342; Ellis:154, 169; Gannett:196; Morgan:466; WPANYS]

Olivebridge. Ulster. The town of Olive was formed in 1823. The Olive Bridge post office was in the settlement of Olive City in 1860. The name came from the New Testament Mount of Olives. [APN:342; French:665; Syl-U:296–7]

Olmstedville. Essex. Sanford and Levi Olmstead established a large tannery here in 1840 to take advantage of the hemlock forest. Earlier, the place was spelled Olmsteadville. [French:302; Smith-Ex:635]

Omar. Jefferson. The community was first called Mullet Creek for its stream. It later became Mudge's Mills for the mill owner. When the post office was established, the name was changed for a character in one of Samuel Johnson's allegories. [D&P:457; French:360; Gannett:196; Hough-J:214]

Onchiota. Franklin. The place was first named Pine Park for the trees, but the name was later changed by the railroad to this Iroquoian word that means "rainbow." [APN:344; WPANYS]

Oneida. Madison. The city was situated on Oneida Creek, from which it took its name. The creek was named for one of the tribes of the Six Nations, the word meaning "granite people" or "people of the beacon stone." [APN:344; French:392; Gannett:196; Smith-C&M:718; WPANY:488]

Oneonta, West Oneonta. Otsego. When the town was first formed in 1796, it was called Otego. In 1830 the name was changed to Onteonta from the Iroquoian word meaning "stony place." [APN:344; French:535; WPANY:450; WPANYS]

Onondaga, Onondaga Hill, South Onondaga. Onondaga. The town of Onondaga was formed in 1798. It was not part of the Military Tract but part of the Onondaga Reservation. It became part of New York State in 1798. The name means "people of the hills." Onondaga Hill was the first county seat until the Erie Canal came through Syracuse in 1825, and the seat was moved in 1829. This village was previously called Onondaga West Hill. South Onondaga was called South Onondaga Hollow. [APN:344; Bruce:838, 860; Clark-O:108; Clayton:276–7; French:473, 485; Gannett:197; WPANY:527]

Ontario, Ontario Center. Wayne. When the town was formed in 1807, it was named Freetown. Its name was changed in 1808 for that of Lake Ontario, which forms its northern boundary. The lake was named with a Native American word meaning "beautiful lake." [APN:344; Cowles:319; French:692; Gannett:197]

Oppenheim. Fulton. This place was first settled by Germans who named it for a place from their former home. [Fulton:237]

Oran. Onondaga. Named for the city in Algiers. [APN:346; WPANYA]

Orangeburg. Rockland. This community in the town of Orangetown, which had been part of Orange County, was a post office and a station on the Erie Railroad. All of these were named for William of Orange. [Cole:246; Gannett:197; Green:364; WPANYS]

Orange Lake. Orange. This place was named for the lake, which had been called Moose Pond. Later it was called Machin Pond for Captain Thomas Machin, who set up a copper coin factory on its outlet in 1787. Native Americans called the lake Qussuk, meaning "stony pond." Machin called his settlement New Grange. He had built a gristmill and a sawmill here in 1784. The present name of the place was given by Reverend Dr. James Wilson who lived in the area. [French:509; R&C:281]

Orchard Park. Erie. This used to be the village of East Hamburg, but the residents were tired of their mail going to Hamburg by mistake, so when the Buffalo branch of the Rochester and Pittsburgh Railroad came through in 1883, they changed the name to Orchard Park. This was a descriptive name of the place that contained apple and pear orchards. [Smith-E:531–2]

Orient, Orient Point. Suffolk. In 1836, the residents of Oyster Ponds voted to change the name to Orient for its location as the most easterly peninsula in the state. Orient Point is the easternmost point of the peninsula. The Native American name for the place was Poquatuck. [Bayles:386, 388; French:640; Suffolk/Southold:32; WPANY:702]

Oriskany, Oriskany Falls. Oneida. The village of Oriskany sits on the site of a Native American village called Oriska, "place of nettles," on Oriskany Creek near its confluence with the Mohawk River. The American Oriskany was founded by Gerrit Lansing who bought 400 acres along the creek. The woolen mill built here in 1811 was the first of its kind in the state. The post office was opened in 1820, and the village was incorporated in 1914. The village of Oriskany Falls also sits on Oriskany Creek, but in the southern part of the county, and it was named for the falls on the creek. It was first called Cassety Hollows for Thomas Cassety and his family, early settlers. The post office was established as Oriskany Falls in 1829. [APN:348; French:462, 471; Gannett:198; Oneida:119–21, 219–20; WPANY:485]

Orleans. Ontario. This hamlet was first known as Hardscrabble. [Milliken:108]

Orleans Four Corners. Jefferson. The town of Orleans was formed in 1821 and named for the city of New Orleans, which had become famous for its role in the War of 1812. The settlement was named for the location of the post office. [D&P:455; French:360; Hough-J:208]

Orwell. Oswego. John Reynolds came here from Orwell, Vermont. When the town was formed in 1817, he became the first town supervisor. He was instrumental in the name choice and the growth of the settlement, which was called Orwell Corners and had the Orwell post office. [French:523; Johnson-O:298; Churchill:626, 634; WPANYA]

Oscawana Corners. Putnam. This place was named for the lake, the name of which was either the name of a local Native American or the word meaning "grass" or "green herb." The lake had been called Horton's Pond for John Horton, who used to own the land on the west side of it. [APN:349; Blake:248; Pelletreau:722–3; WPANYS]

Osceola. Lewis. This town was named for the Seminole chief at the suggestion of Miss Jay, who became Mrs. Henry B. Pierrepont of Brooklyn. The Pierreponts owned land here. [APN:349; Bowen:443; French:378; Gannett:198; Hough-L:197, 202]

Ossian. Livingston. When the town was formed in 1808, it was named for the Gaelic bard Ossian. A cycle of poems, purported to be his in translation, was published in the 1760s by James Macpherson and was quite popular. [Doty-L:650; WPANYS]

Ossining. Westchester. The town was formed in 1845 as Ossinsing, derived from an Algonquian term variously spelled as Scint Sinks, Sing Sing, Sin Sinck, and others. It meant "stone upon stone," referring to the granite outcropping over the Hudson River. The town name dropped the third s in 1846. A prison was built here in 1824 named Sing Sing Prison. The village was first called Hunters Landing, then Mount Pleasant. It was incorporated as Sing Sing in 1813, but the residents were not pleased to be associated with the prison, so they changed the name to that of the town in 1901. [APN:349; Bolton(2):1; French:704; Lederer:106; WPANY:581]

Oswegatchie. St. Lawrence. The town was formed in 1802 and named for its principal river, which was named with a version of a Native American word that meant "black river." [APN:349; French:580; Harder:174]

Oswego. Oswego. The name of the county, the river, and the city came from the Native American *ontiahantaque,* meaning "flowing out" or "where the valley widens," referring to the river mouth at Lake Ontario. The French explorers called this place Chonaquen. The town was formed in 1818; the city was organized in 1848. [APN:349; French:517, 523; Gannett:199; WPANY:646]

Otego. Otsego. The town was first called Huntsville when it was formed in 1822. In 1830, however, it was renamed Otego from the Iroquoian word meaning "to have fire there." [APN:350; French:536; WPANYS]

Otisco. Onondaga. The town was formed in 1806 and named for the lake, which was called Otskah or Kaioongk by the Native Americans here, meaning "water is low." [APN:350; Clark-O:344, 346; Clayton:348–9; French:486]

Otisville. Orange. Isaac Otis came here from Massachusetts in 1816 and opened a store around which other buildings clustered. He was the first postmaster when the post office was established in 1819. [R&C:510; WPANYS]

Otselic, South Otselic. Chenango. Otselic Creek gave its name to the town and the settlements. It was an Iroquoian word meaning "plum creek." [APN:350; French:228; Gannett:199; WPANYS]

Otto, East Otto. Cattaraugus. The town of Otto was named for Jacob S. Otto, an agent of the Holland Land Company when it was formed in 1823. The town of East Otto separated from the town of Otto in 1854 and is east of Otto. [Ellis:289, 299; French:189, 193; Gannett:199]

Ouaquaga. Broome. The post office was established here in 1820 as Susquehanna, and then the name was changed in about 1860. There is no record of what the word means, but it seems to be the same as Oquaga. [APN:346, 350; French:181, 183; Smith-B:340]

Ovid. Seneca. The town was formed in 1794 and named by the state land commissioners for the Roman poet. [APN:351; Gannett:199; Seneca:97]

Owasco, Southeast Owasco. Cayuga. The town was formed in 1802 and named for the lake, which was named with the Native American word meaning "lake of the floating bridge." The hamlet, which was near the southeast corner of the town, took its name from the town and the lake. Cornelius Delamater ran the first tavern in the village in 1800. [APN; Morgan:470; Storke:383]

Owego. Tioga. The town was organized in 1791 and named for the creek that flows on its western boundary. The word is Iroquoian, *ahwahga*, meaning "where the valley widens." [APN:351; French:651; Gay:319; WPANY:387]

Owls Head. Franklin. Charles Ring and John Mink first came here in 1852 and the place was known as Ringville. Later the name was changed for the name of a nearby mountain. [French:309; WPANYS]

Oxbow. Jefferson. Named for the bend in the Oswegatchie River on which the village is located. The post office was opened in 1819. [APN:351; D&P:281; French:356; Gannett:200; Hough-J:91; WPANYA]

Oxford. Chenango. General Benjamin Hovey came here from Oxford, Massachusetts, in 1790 and built a log house. The Native American name for the place was Sodeahlowanake, meaning "thick-necked giant." [Morgan:473; Smith-C&M:254]

Oxford. Orange. This was Oxford Depot on the Erie Railroad. The post office was established in 1842. There is no record of name origin. [French:505; R&C:636]

Oyster Bay. Nassau. The body of water was called Oyster Bay in 1639 for the fine oysters found in it. The village took the name of the bay. The post office established an office here named Syosset in 1846, but the villagers objected and the name was changed back to Oyster Bay in 1848. [French:550; Winsche:78–9]

Ozone Park, South Ozone Park. Queens. When ozone was thought to be a healthy gas, the name was often used as a placename. This place was a housing development that was started in the 1880s after the railroad extended service here. The post office was established in 1889. [APN:352; Jackson:871]

P

Pine City © *2004 by Jon Crispin*

Painted Post. Steuben. This place was named for a red-painted post erected by Native Americans as a marker. The Native American name of the place was Tecarnaseteoah, "a board sign." [APN:354; Gannett:200; Morgan:469; Parker:314; Roberts:306; Steuben:19; WPANY:390]

Palatine Bridge. Montgomery. The first bridge across the Mohawk River west of Schenectady was built here. The town of Palatine was named for the Germans who came here from there in about 1723. [APN:355; Frothingham:320; Gannett:201; Montgomery:149; WPANY:460]

Palenville. Greene. Jonathan Palen had a large tannery here before 1817. His family had the first piano in the area, and the place is the legendary home of Rip Van Winkle. [French:332; Greene:147; Vedder:57, 58; WPANY:408]

Palermo. Oswego. The town was formed in 1832 and named for the place in Sicily. The settlement was called Jennings Corners; the post office was opened there as Palermo. At some point, the settlement was known as Palermo Center. [APN:355; Churchill:649, 655; French:526; Johnson-O:318]

Palisades. Rockland. This place was known by a variety of names until it finally settled on the term for a line of cliffs that came from their resemblance to stakes set in the ground. It was first called Dobb's Ferry, the name used for landings on both sides of the Hudson for a ferry run by a fellow named Dobb. The name finally was applied to only the eastern shore landing. The place on the western shore was then known as Sneden's Landing for the fellow who took over here. Then it was named Rockland, for the county, and finally Palisades, for its geographical location. [APN:355; Cole:224–5; French:570, 571; Green:363; WPANY:621]

Palmyra, East Palmyra. Wayne. The town was named for an ancient Syrian town when it was formed in 1789. It was here that Joseph Smith found the gold plates that he translated into the Book of Mormon in 1827. The Native American name of the place was Ganagweh, meaning "a village suddenly sprung up." [APN:355; Cowles:167; Gannett:210; Mc-W:139; Morgan:469; WPANY:660]

Pamelia Four Corners. Jefferson. The town of Pamelia was formed in 1819 and named for the wife of General Jacob Brown, neè Pamelia Williams. She was the daughter of Captain Jude Williams of Williamstown, and her husband was noted in the War of 1812. The name of the town was changed to Leander in 1824, for the son of a legislator, but this did not go over very well and was never used, so the name was changed back quickly. The post office at Pamelia Four Corners was established in 1830. [APN:356; D&P:465–6; French:360; Gannett:201; Hough-J:215]

Panama. Chautauqua. Moses Cunningham Marsh named this place after coming here in 1824 after having been a "wealthy Cuban trader." He built the first frame house in the area, opened the first store, and was the first postmaster in 1826. [D&H:199]

Paradox. Essex. The settlement was named for the lake, the outlet of which is the Schroon River. However, in times of flood, the high level of the river causes the water to flow into the lake instead of out of it, hence its name. [French:304; Smith-Ex:529]

Paris. Oneida. The town was formed in 1792 and named for Isaac Paris, a merchant in Fort Plain. During the famine of 1789 in the village that became Paris Hill, he sent boatloads of food up the Mohawk River to Oriskany Creek where the food was transferred to canoes and taken to Clinton, from which it was taken by cart to the village. He took his payment in ginseng, an herb that grew in the area. The Native American name for the place was Ganundoglee, "hills shrunk together." [French:465–6; Gannett:201; Morgan:472; Oneida:175; WPANY:643]

Parish. Oswego. David Parish owned the land that became the town in 1828. The village was called Parishville, but the post office and railroad station were always called Parish. [Churchill:659, 666; French:526; Johnson-O:431]

Parishville. St. Lawrence. This place had been called Chaumont for J. D. LeRay de Chaumont, who had bought the land in 1804. In 1808, he sold it to David and George Parish. The town was formed in 1818 and named after its proprietors. [Curtis:595; French:581; Harder:177; Hough-SLF:422; Landon:236]

Parkchester. Bronx. In the 1930s, this area between the neighborhoods of Park Versailles and Westchester was developed as a residential site. [Jackson:881]

Park Slope. Kings. This place was developed next to Prospect Park West. [Jackson:883]

Parksville. Sullivan. William Parks was a prominent settler here. [WPANYS]

Parma, Parma Center. Monroe. The town was formed in 1808 and named for the city in Italy. [APN:359; WPARM:288]

Patchin. Erie. Talcott Patchin established a tannery here in about 1820 and carried on with his business for twelve or fifteen years before it failed and he went to Texas. In 1850, the residents petitioned for a post office under the name of Boston Center. This was rejected as being too common a name, so they chose the name of their former neighbor instead. [French:283; Smith-E:600]

Patchogue, East Patchogue. Suffolk. The name comes from that of the Pochough Indians and their word for "turning back," which might have referred to a boundary between peoples. [APN:353, 361; Bayles:268; French:634; Gannett:203]

Patterson. Putnam. The town was originally named Franklin for Benjamin Franklin when it was formed in 1795, but the name was changed in 1808 to reduce the number of Franklins in the state. Matthew Patterson and his family came here from Scotland. The village was sometimes called Patterson City before the Revolutionary War. [Blake:341–2; French:541; Gannett:203; Pelletreau:637; WPANY:546]

Pattersonville. Schenectady. W. H. Patterson was a hotel keeper here. [Clark:57; Munsell:208]

Paul Smiths. Franklin. The place was named for Appollos Smith, better known as Paul, who came here from Vermont in 1859 and opened a hotel for wealthy sportsmen. [Hurd-C&F:504; Landon:478; WPANY:520]

Pavilion. Genesee. The town was formed in 1841 and named for the settlement that was named in 1825 by Harmon J. Betts for a hotel in his hometown of Saratoga. [Beers:589; French:327; North:491–2]

Pawling, West Pawling. Dutchess. The town was formed in 1788 and named for the Paulding family, early settlers whose original family name was Pawling. The village was settled in about 1740 by English Quakers and was known as Gorsetown. When the railroad came through, the depot was called Pawling

Station. As the village grew around the station, it took its name. [French:273; Gannett:203; Smith-D:550, 553; WPANYD:117]

Peakville. Delaware. This place was formerly known as Trout Brook, but the name was changed for its location at the top of a hill. [WPANYS]

Pearl River. Rockland. Early on, this village was called Middletown; that name was replaced with Muddy Creek. When the Erie Railroad came through in the 1870s, the name was changed for the river in which pearl mussels had been found. [Bedell:338; Cole:246; French:571; Green:364]

Peasleeville. Clinton. The settlement was named for Samuel Peasle, and was spelled Peasleville for a time. Peasle had established a forge and a store here, then went to Michigan and became a county judge. [French:238; Hurd-C&F:346]

Pecksville. Dutchess. This was a hamlet in the 1860s, but there is no name origin recorded. [French:271]

Peconic. Suffolk. The community was named from an Algonquian word, *pequon-nock*, meaning "small farm or field." It had been called Hermitage, but the name was changed when the post office was established. [APN:364, 367; Bayles:372; French:637; Suffolk/Southold:30]

Peekamoose. Ulster. Possibly named with an Algonquian word, meaning "broken off smooth," but why is unknown. [APN:364, 379]

Peekskill. Westchester; **Lake Peekskill.** Putnam. Jan Peek settled near a stream in about 1665. The stream took his name, from which the village and later the city were named. [APN:364; Bolton(1):113; French:699; Gannett:204; Lederer:108; WPANY:395]

Pekin. Niagara. In 1822, a post office was established here and called Mountain Ridge for its physical location. The name was changed to Pekin in 1831, by which time the settlement had grown into a bustling hamlet. The name was probably from that of the city in China, part of a trend in the nineteenth century of using exotic names. [APN:364; French:453; Pool:246]

Pelham, Pelham Manor. Westchester. Thomas Pell bought land here in 1664. In the 1680s, his nephew, John Pell, sold 6,000 acres to the Huguenots who established New Rochelle on it. [APN:364; Bolton(1):56; French:704; Gannett:204; Lederer:108; WPANY:381]

Pembroke, East Pembroke. Genesee. The town was formed in 1812 and named for the town in Wales. The Pembroke post office was opened in the community of Richville, which was named for Charles B. Rich, a prominent citizen. It later changed its name to match the post office. [APN:365; Beers:623; French:327; Gannett:204; North:496]

Pendleton, Pendleton Center. Niagara. The town and the settlement were named after Syl-S Pendleton Clark, who had settled on Grand Island in the

Niagara River and called himself the governor of the place before the border was settled between the United States and Canada. He had opened a log tavern in 1821 and became the first postmaster in 1823. [French:455; Pool:332–3; Williams:391; WPANYS]

Penfield, East Penfield. Monroe. Daniel Penfield was an extensive landholder here in 1810 when the town was formed. He had built a sawmill and a gristmill in about 1806 in a place that became known as Mill Site, but then took the name of the town. [French:401; Mc-M:216; Peck:352; WPARM:288]

Pennellville. Oswego. Richard Pennell, a doctor in New York, had a wife who inherited land here in the town of Schroeppel (named for her father, George C. Schroeppel). Pennell built a sawmill here in 1833. [Churchill:753; Johnson-O:331; WPANYA]

Penn Yan. Yates. Early settlers here were from Pennsylvania and from New England (Yankees). Each group wanted to name the place but would not give in to the other. Finally a compromise was reached by taking the first syllable of their "respective designations." [APN:366; Cleveland:220; French:720; Gannett:205; WPANY:656]

Perch River. Jefferson. In 1860, Perch River was the name of the post office in the community of Moffatville. Eventually, the settlement took the name as well, which had come from the name of the river on which the place was located. [D&P:306; French:356; Hough-J:106]

Perinton. Monroe. When the town was formed in 1812, it was named for Glover Perrin, the first settler who came here in 1789. Before that, it had been known as Northfield. [French:401; Gannett:206; Mc-M:221; WPARM:289; WPANYS]

Perkinsville. Steuben. Benjamin Perkins was an early settler here. He built the first sawmill in the town. [French:628; Roberts:542; Steuben:337]

Perry, Perry Center. Wyoming. When the town was formed in 1814, it was named for Commodore Oliver Hazard Perry, victor at the Battle of Lake Erie in 1813. The villages of Perry and Perry Center are both located within the town. The village of Perry was first called Shacksburg, then Columbia, then Nineveh, and finally took the name of the town. [APN:368; French:715; Gannett:206; Wyoming:238, 242]

Perry City. Schuyler. This settlement also was probably named for Commodore Oliver Hazard Perry. [APN:368]

Perry Mills. Clinton. The settlement was first known as Scheifelin's Mills. When George Perry became sole owner of the mills and a resident of the place, it was named for him. The post office was opened in 1841. [French:237; Hurd-C&F:263]

Perrysburg. Cattaraugus. The town was first called Perry for Commodore Oliver

Hazard Perry, the victor at the Battle of Lake Erie in 1813, when it was organized in 1814. The name was changed to Perrysburg in 1818. The Native American name for the place was Ganyestaageh, "place of chestnuts." [APN:368; Ellis:239; French:194; Gannett:206; Parker:290; WPANYS]

Perryville. Madison. The community was first called Blakeslee for Eli Blakeslee, an early settler. Its name was later changed either for a local family name or for Commander Oliver Hazard Perry, who was popular for his victory in the Battle of Lake Erie in 1813. [APN:368; WPANYS]

Perth, West Perth. Fulton. Early settlers came here from Perthshire, Scotland, and named the town, when it was organized in 1831, for their former home. [French:319; Fulton:239; WPANYS]

Peru. Clinton. The town and village were named for the South American country because of the Adirondack Mountains in which they are located. [French:238; Gannett:206; Hurd-C&F:339; WPANY:536]

Peruville. Tompkins. In 1818, this place was known as Peru, possibly for a nearby town. However, it might have been part of a trend at that time to give exotic names to places, especially because of interest in South America's struggle to become free of Spain. [APN:369; Norris:35]

Peterboro. Madison. Peter Smith founded the town of Smithfield, which was organized in 1807, in which this hamlet is located. Both settlements were named for him. He owned slaves while living here. His son, Gerrit Smith, was a reformer and abolitionist who converted part of the land he had inherited into fifty-acre homes for emancipated slaves. [French:393; Gannett:206; Smith-C&M:685–7; WPANY:422]

Petersburg, North Petersburg. Rensselaer. The town was named for Peter Simmons, one of the early settlers, when it was formed in 1791. The settlement was formerly called Rensselaer Mills, then South Petersburg, but the post office here was established as Petersburg for the name of the town. North Petersburg was known as Petersburg Corners in the 1830s. [French:557, 558; Weise:100]

Petrolia. Allegany. There was petroleum here, extracted through O. P. Taylor's oil well Triangle #3. [APN:369; Minard:487]

Pharsalia, East Pharsalia, North Pharsalia. Chenango. The town was first called Stonington, in 1806, then changed its name in 1808 for the battle in which Caesar defeated Pompey in 48 B.C. The communities take their names from their geographical locations within the town. [APN:370; French:229; Smith-C&M:422]

Phelps. Ontario. The town was first called Sullivan for the general, but the name was changed in 1796 to honor Oliver Phelps, one of the original proprietors. The village was first called Vienna but changed its name to match that of the town in 1855. [French:498; Gannett:207; Milliken:108]

Philadelphia. Jefferson. The town was formed in 1821 and was to be called Elizabethtown. But there already was a town with that name in the state, so the new name came from William Penn's "City of Brotherly Love." The area had been settled by Quakers in about 1804. The village had been called Quaker Settlement. The post office was established as Philadelphia in 1822. [APN:370; D&P:475, 477; French:360; Gannett:207; Hough-J:217]

Phillips Creek. Allegany. This place, which was first settled in about 1830, was named for the creek, which was probably named for an early settler. [Allegany:341; French:175; Minard:534–5]

Phillipsport. Sullivan. James Phillips was a prominent businessman here when the Delaware and Hudson Canal opened. The canal company first called the place Lockport, but the local residents preferred the other name. [Child:176; Quinlan:444]

Philmont. Columbia. Previously known as Factory Hill, the name was changed when the Harlem Railroad came through and named the station for George P. Philip, who built a dam for water power. The post office was established in 1858. [Ellis-C:240–1; French:244]

Phoenicia. Ulster. Named for the ancient Mediterranean country. [APN:370; WPANYA]

Phoenix. Oswego. Alexander Phoenix bought land here from Ezra L'Hommedieu in the 1820s. The village was first called Three River Rifts for its location on the Oswego River, but its name was changed in 1828, and the post office was established in 1830 as Phoenix. [Churchill:746, 752; French:527–8; Gannett:206; Johnson-O:327]

Picketts Corners. Clinton. E. J. and Richard Pickett were early settlers here. [Hurd-C&F:358]

Piercefield. St. Lawrence. The origin of this name is unknown. [Harder:182; WPANYS]

Piermont. Rockland. This place on the Hudson River was always some sort of port or terminal. It sits at the mouth of the Sparkill, which was large enough for ships to enter, and because it looked like a ditch, it was called the Slote. It became known as Tappan Slote or Tappan Landing. When the Erie Railroad was built, it required that its eastern terminus be in New York State, so it built the tracks to here, just north of the border with New Jersey. To get to New York City, passengers were to take a boat, so the railroad built a long pier out into the Hudson, past the shallows, and the name of the station was changed to describe the pier with the hills behind the village. [Bedell:200, 214–5; Cole:220; French:570; Green:358; WPANY:606]

Pierrepont, West Pierrepont. St. Lawrence. The town was formed in 1818 and named for its proprietor, Hezekiah B. Pierrepont of Brooklyn. [Curtis:608; French:581; Harder:182; Hough-SLF:425–6]

Pierrepont Manor. Jefferson. William C. Pierrepont, a landowner, had a home here around which the settlement grew. [D&P:369; French:357; Gannett:208; Hough-J:160]

Piffard. Livingston. David Piffard settled here in 1824. The place was called Piffardinia in the nineteenth century. [Doty-L:681; French:387; Gannett:208; WPANYS]

Pike. Wyoming. The town, formed in 1818, was named for General Zebulon Montgomery Pike, a soldier in the War of 1812. [APN:372; French:715; Gannett:208; Wyoming:254]

Pillar Point. Jefferson. The settlement had been called Brooklyn, but the post office was established as Pillar Point and named for the rock formations created by Lake Ontario's erosion of the shore cliffs. [D&P:306; Hough-J:106; WPANYA]

Pilot Knob. Warren. At 2,078 feet, this is a local high point seen from Lake George and possibly used for navigation on the lake. The community started as a summer resort. [WPANYS; WPAW:233]

Pine Bush. Orange. This place had been called Crawford, which was the name of the town, and two other places in the town contained this name. So the name of this settlement was changed to avoid further confusion. It was named for the old pines growing in the area. [French:506; R&C:420]

Pine Bush. Ulster. This is an old, descriptive name for the place. [Syl-U:218]

Pine City. Chemung. Charles Atkins settled here in 1830 and named the place for the large number of pine trees in the area. The post office was established in 1874. [P&H-C:250]

Pine Hill. Ulster. This community was named for the hill on which it sits. It had a post office in 1860. [French:667; Syl-U:308]

Pine Island. Orange. The post office was established in 1870, but there is no record of name origin. [R&C:579]

Pine Plains. Dutchess. The town was formed in 1823 and named for Pine Plains village, which had been named for the forests of pine trees that were here when the place was first settled by Europeans. [French:273; Smith-D:221]

Pine Valley. Chemung. Named for the pine forests. [P&H-C:251]

Piseco. Hamilton. The settlement was laid out in about 1837 by Andrew K. Morehouse, who expected it to become the county seat. It was named for the lake, which was named by John Brown for a Native American of the area. An earlier spelling was Pezceko. [A&K:297; APN:374; Donaldson(1):41; French:337]

Pitcairn. St. Lawrence. Joseph Pitcairn was a proprietor of the land here. The town was formed in 1836. [French:581; Harder:185]

Pitcher, North Pitcher. Chenango. Named in 1827 for Nathaniel Pitcher, lieutenant governor of the state who was at that time acting governor. [French:229; Gannett:209; Smith-C&M:430; WPANYS]

Pittsfield. Otsego. The town was named by Dr. Joseph O. Cone, Samuel Tyler, and Captain Aaron Noble, all of whom settled here in 1793 from Pittsfield, Massachusetts, which was named for Sir William Pitt, Earl of Chatham, and a celebrated English statesman. The community was originally called Pecktown for early settler Alvin Peck. [APN:375; Hurd-O:287; WPANYA; WPANYS]

Pittsford. Monroe. The town was named by Caleb Hopkins in 1814, when it was formed, for his and other settlers' former home in Vermont. [Mc-M:233; WPARM:290; WPANYS]

Pittstown. Rensselaer. The land patent was named by King George III in honor of William Pitt, Earl of Chatham, an English statesman. It was formed as a town in 1788 and kept the name. [APN:375; French:558; Gannett:209; Weise:90]

Plainview. Nassau. In 1695, this was called Manetto Hill, a corruption of Manitou Hill, Hill of the Great Spirit. In 1885, application for a post office was rejected because the name was too similar to other post offices in the state. The name Plainview was chosen instead, for the view of the Hempstead Plains that can be had here. The place changed its name in 1886. [Winsche:80–1]

Plainville. Onondaga. William Wilson settled here in 1806, giving the place the name Wilson's Corners. When the post office was established in 1821, the residents suggested that the name be Farmersville. Because there already was one in the state, the post office department named the post office Plainville. [Bruce:750–1; Clayton:323; WPANYA]

Plandome, Plandome Heights, Plandome Manor. Nassau. Dr. Samuel Latham Mitchill inherited land here from his uncle in the early 1800s. He named the place Planus Domus, Latin for "plain home." It was corrupted to Plandome. Plandome Heights was land south of Plandome and part of the village of Manhasset that was owned by the Duke family. In 1910, they formed a corporation to develop the land and called it Plandome Heights. Plandome Manor was the end result of two separate developments, Plandome Park and Plandome Estates, that were not very successful in the 1920s. In 1936, the village of Plandome Manor was incorporated. [Winsche:81–4; WPANYS]

Plato. Cattaraugus. The post office was established in 1832. In about 1836, the place was mapped and laid out into village lots with the expectations that it would grow and prosper. It was named for the ancient Greek philosopher. [APN:376; Ellis:302]

Plattekill. Ulster. The town was formed in 1800 and named with the Dutch word meaning "flat brook." The settlement was often called Pleasant Valley or the

Valley. The post office was established as Plattekill in 1850. [French:665; Gannett:210; Syl-U:175]

Plattsburgh, West Plattsburgh, South Plattsburgh. Clinton. The town, city, and villages were named for Judge Zephaniah Platt, who moved to this part of the state in the 1700s and settled. He was instrumental in the U.S. adoption of the Bill of Rights. [Gannett:210; WPANY:401]

Pleasant Brook. Otsego. Named for the creek on which it is located. [French:537]

Pleasant Plains. Richmond. In the 1860s, the Staten Island Railroad built a station here that was called Pleasant Plains. The post office was called Lemon Creek, but it eventually took the name of the community. [French:567; Jackson:908]

Pleasant Valley. Dutchess. The town was formed in 1821 and named for the principal settlement, which was first incorporated in 1814 and named for its surroundings. [French:274; Smith-D:314]

Pleasant Valley. Steuben. Named for its surroundings. [WPANYA]

Pleasantville. Westchester. The village had been called Clark's Corners, but the first postmaster, Henry Romer, chose this name for the post office in 1828. The village was incorporated in 1897. [Bolton(1):563; French:702; Lederer:113]

Plessis. Jefferson. This place was formerly called Flat Rock for its rocky surface. The name was later changed to that of a town in France. [APN:377; D&P:270; French:355; Gannett:210; Hough-J:82]

Plumbrook. St. Lawrence. Named for the fruit. [Harder:187]

Plymouth, South Plymouth. Chenango. The town was named for Plymouth, Massachusetts, because many of the settlers had come from New England. The settlement around the South Plymouth post office used to be called either Frankville, for early settlers, or Frinkville, for Coddington Frink, who owned mills here. [French:229; Smith-C&M:418, 421; WPANYS]

Poestenkill, East Poestenkill. Rensselaer. The town and villages were named for the creek, which took its name from the Dutch word meaning "foaming creek." East Poestenkill used to be called Columbia. [French:558; Gannett:211; Weise:109]

Point Breeze. Orleans. Named for its location at the mouth of Oak Orchard Creek on Lake Ontario. [Orleans:99; Signor:655]

Point Peninsula. Jefferson. When the post office was opened in the town of Wilcoxville, it was called Point Peninsula for its geographic location on the point of land extending into Chaumont Bay. [D&P:453; French:359]

Poland. Herkimer. The village was called Russia Flats for its location in the town of Russia. Its name was changed in sympathy to the revolutions in Poland. [APN:380; Herkimer:227]

Poland Center. Chautauqua. This was the post office in the town of Poland, named for the European country. [APN:380; French:214]

Pomona. Rockland. Named for the Roman goddess of fruit trees. [APN:381]

Pompey, Pompey Center. Onondaga. The town was formed in 1789 and named for the Roman general. The place was called Otegegajake, "place of much grass," by the Native Americans. Pompey Center was known as Greens Corners. The Pompey post office was opened in Pompey Hill, which had been called Butler's Hill for Ebenezer Butler, at whose house the first town meeting was held. [APN:381; Bruce:594; Clark-O:243–4; Clayton:395; French:486; Gannett:212]

Pond Eddy. Sullivan. This place is located on the Delaware River and took its name from it. [Child:169; Quinlan:376]

Poolville. Madison. Abijah Pool came here from Massachusetts in about 1810. There were a dozen Pool families living here by 1830 when a post office was established with this name. [Smith-C&M:567]

Pope Mills. St. Lawrence. The Pope family were early settlers here. [French:579; Harder:188]

Poplar Ridge. Cayuga. This place was named for the ridge on which it is located. [French:206; Storke:441]

Poquott. Suffolk. In 1664, John Dier or Dyer first settled at this place that became known as Dyers Neck. It later took its name from a Native American word meaning either "smoke" or "a clear place." [Bayles:242; French:633; Suffolk/Brookhaven:43; WPANYS]

Portageville. Wyoming. The settlement was originally called Schuyler for General Philip Schuyler. In 1829, the name was changed to Portage, for the carrying place around the falls on the Genesee River. In 1846, it was changed to Portageville. [Wyoming:197, 200]

Port Byron. Cayuga. The name was changed from Bucksville, originally named after the Buck family, in 1832 after it became a stop on the original Erie Canal. [Storke:311]

Port Chester. Westchester. This place, at the mouth of the Byram River, was first known as Saw Log Swamp and later as Saw Pit. It was settled in about 1650 and grew into a manufacturing center containing a gristmill, a foundry, and a shovel factory. Later its factories produced candy, boxes, soft drinks, stoves, nuts and bolts, and ammonia. In 1837, it took this descriptive name of its location as the Port of West Chester on Long Island Sound. [Bolton(1):206; French:705; Lederer:114; WPANY:379]

Port Crane. Broome. The town was formed in 1855 and named for Jason Crane, one of the engineers of the old Chenango Canal. The village took its name from the town. [French:183; Gannett:212; Smith-B:466]

Port Dickinson. Broome. This village on the Chenango Canal was first called Carmansville for Joseph Carman, an early settler. After the canal was built, its name was changed for Daniel S. Dickinson, who served successively as lieutenant governor of New York State, U.S. senator from New York, and attorney general of New York State. [Gannett:213; Smith-B:194]

Porter Corners. Saratoga. Asahel Porter was a merchant who settled here in about 1800 and became a prominent citizen. [French:589; Syl-S:441; WPA-NYA]

Porterville. Erie. Jesse Bartoo had built a sawmill here in 1832 and the place was known as Bartoo's Mills. In about 1837, Archibald Porter bought the mills and the place became Porterville. A few years later, R. G. Willis bought the mills. The place was referred to as Bartoo's Mills, Porterville, or Willis Mills, but Porterville stuck. The post office was opened in 1874. [Smith-E:483]

Port Ewen. Ulster. John Ewen, the president of the Pennsylvania Coal Company, gave his name to the place that his company had built up as a transshipment point, primarily of coal from Pennsylvania, on the Hudson River. The village was laid out in 1851. [French:662; Syl-U:114; WPANYA]

Port Gibson. Ontario. This place on the Erie Canal was named for Henry B. Gibson, an early banker in Canandaigua. [Milliken:109]

Port Jefferson, Port Jefferson Station. Suffolk. The Native American name for this place was Sowassett. Then it was called Drowned Meadows. The name was changed for Thomas Jefferson in 1836. [Bayles:243, 245; French:633; Suffolk/Brookhaven:43; WPANYS]

Port Jervis. Orange. In about 1787, this place on the Delaware River was called Carpenter's Point. Its name was changed to that of John B. Jervis, the engineer who built the Delaware and Hudson Canal through here in 1826. [French:506; Gannett:213; R&C:710; Smith-B:301; WPANY:399]

Port Kent. Essex. Elkanah Watson and others built a wharf here in 1822 and named the place for New York State chancellor James Kent. [Smith-Ex:524–5]

Portland. Chautauqua. Named for the city in England. [APN:384; Gannett:213; McMahon:99]

Portlandville. Otsego. This settlement was first known as Mumfordsville for the family who had come here from Bennington, Vermont. They were not interested in having the place be named for them, so Captain Jesse Mumford suggested that it be called Portlandville. This was happily accepted. The post office was established in 1826 with this name and with Mumford as the first postmaster. [Hurd-O:192]

Port Leyden, West Leyden. Lewis. These settlements are in the town of Leyden, which was named by Gerret Boon of Boonville through the Holland Land

Company, many of whose members were from Leyden, Holland. Port Leyden was first called Kelsey's Mills for Eber L. Kelsey, who came here in 1796 and built a sawmill, then a gristmill, by 1800. The village is on the Black River, so in 1848 it changed its name to Port Leyden in anticipation of major growth at the completion of the Black River Canal. [Bowen:260; French:377; Gannett:213; Hough-L:121, 129]

Port Ontario. Oswego. This "city" started as the Port Ontario Company, set up to survey the area around the mouth of the Salmon River into lots to be sold in the belief that a great city would just have to grow up here because of its location. It never grew because Oswego City's location, just south on the Lake Ontario shore, turned out to be better, with better navigation on the Oswego River south to the Erie Canal. [Churchill:705; French:527; Johnson-O:209]

Port Richmond. Richmond. Because of the Dutch Reformed cemetery located here in the 1700s, this area was called the Burial Place. It was incorporated as Port Richmond in 1866 for all the ferry and shipping businesses centered here. [French:566; Jackson:926]

Port Washington. Nassau. In the 1630s, the Native American name for this place was Sinsinck. By 1761, the bay was called Cow Bay and so was the village. In 1859, when applying for a post office, a new, more dignified name was thought appropriate. Because George Washington had passed through here in 1790, the place was named for him, and the "Port" was attached since it was on the water. [Winsche:84]

Portville. Cattaraugus. Named for being a prominent point for the shipment of lumber and shingles down the Ohio and Allegany Rivers to major markets in Pittsburg and Cincinnati. [Ellis:409; Gannett:213]

Post Creek. Chemung. Named for the creek. [French:220–1; P&H-C:203]

Potsdam, West Potsdam. St. Lawrence. The town was named for the German city when it was formed in 1806. [APN:386; Harder:190]

Potter. Yates. Arnold Potter was an original landowner and first settler here. [Cleveland:586; French:720]

Potter Hollow. Albany. Samuel and Timothy Potter settled here with their families in 1806. [Albany:464; French:165; Gannett:214; Howell:915; WPA-NYA; WPANYS]

Pottersville. Warren. The community was named for Joel E. Potter, who opened the first store in 1839 and was the first postmaster. He came from Glens Falls, but left for Schroon Lake, where he lived until he died. [Smith-W:546–7; WPAW:172]

Poughkeepsie. Dutchess. The town was formed in 1788, the city in 1854. The name comes from a Native American word, *apokeepsink,* and early on was spelled Picipsi and Pokipsi. The word was said either to mean "a pleasant harbor" or to be the name of a waterfall. [APN:386; French:274; Gannett:214; Smith-D:357]

Poughquag. Dutchess. This name comes from *apoquague,* meaning either "cleared land" or the Native American name of Sylvan Lake, meaning "round lake." [APN:387; Smith-D:546; WPANYD:117]

Pound Ridge. Westchester. The name of this town, written as one word from 1812 to 1948, came from an enclosure or trap for deer that had been built by Native Americans south of here on a ridge. [Bolton(2):103; French:705; Lederer:115]

Prattsburg. Steuben. Captain Joel Pratt came here to settle in 1802. [French:627; Roberts:462; Steuben:140]

Pratts Hollow. Madison. The Pratt brothers, John and Matthew or James, came here in 1809, built a gristmill, a sawmill, and a distillery, and soon established a woolen mill in which they employed about twenty people. [French:391; Gannett:215; Smith-C&M:636]

Prattsville. Greene. Zadock Pratt came here from Rensselaer County in 1802. He ran a very lucrative general store in Lexington, and then in 1825, he built his own settlement, Prattsville, on Schoharie Creek, in which he built homes for more that a hundred other settlers. The town was organized in 1833 and named for him. [French:334; Gannett:215; Greene:380; Vedder:114; WPANY:411]

Preble. Cortland. The town was formed in 1808 and named for Commodore Edward Preble, an officer in the Tripolitan War. The settlement was called Preble Corners, but the post office was established as Preble. [French:254; Gannett:215; Goodwin:198]

Prendergast Point. Chautauqua. Named for the Prendergast family, founders of Jamestown. [D&H:162]

Presho. Steuben. This place used to be called Erwin Center because it had been near the middle of the town of Erwin. Then the town of Lindley was formed from Erwin, leaving the village at the edge of the new town. In 1888, the post office name was changed to Presho, for Thomas J. Presho who had come here in 1855 and was appointed postmaster. [Roberts:458, 461; Steuben:341; WPANYA]

Preston. Chenango. The place was first settled in 1787 and named by John Glover for Preston, Connecticut, which is about the same distance from Norwich, Connecticut, Glover's hometown, as Preston, New York, is from Norwich, New York. The town was organized in 1806. [APN:388; French:229; Smith-C&M:229; WPANYS]

Preston Hollow. Albany. Dr. Samuel Preston settled here with others in 1796. In about 1880, the community name was changed to Monclova, but after a few years, the residents asked that it be changed back. [Albany:463; French:165; Gannett:215; Howell:914; WPANYA]

Princes Bay. Richmond. An English prince anchored his ship here during the American Revolution. [Jackson:939]

Prospect. Oneida. Colonel Adam G. Mappa, an early settler who came here in about 1801, named this place for the "majestic beauty" of the waterfalls on West Canada Creek. [French:468; Oneida:192; WPANYS]

Protection. Erie. Charles Fuller opened the first hotel here in 1840 and named the place. It was sometimes called Protection Harbor, but generally the second word was dropped. [French:292; Smith-E:616]

Pulaski. Oswego. The village was named for Casimir Pulaski, a Polish officer in the American Revolutionary War. The post office was established in 1817 as Richland and later changed to Pulaski. The village was incorporated in 1832. [APN:390; Churchill:701; Gannett:216; Johnson-O:213]

Pulteney. Steuben. Named for Sir William Pulteney, former owner of the Pulteney Tract. [French:627; Gannett:216; Roberts:477; Steuben:145; WPANYA]

Pulteneyville. Wayne. This place was named for Sir William Pulteney, a proprietor of the Pulteney Estate. It served as a terminus for the Underground Railroad, helping smuggle runaway slaves across Lake Ontario to Canada. [Cowles:314; French:694; Mc-W:189; WPANY:659]

Pulvers Corners. Dutchess. William W. Pulver was a citizen here who died in 1861. [Smith-D:230]

Pumpkin Hill. Genesee. There was once a tavern here that had a sign painted yellow that resembled a pumpkin. [French:325]

Purchase. Westchester. The place was called Thomasville, then Harrison's Purchase, and finally the Purchase. In 1871, "the" was dropped. [French:700; Lederer:64, 116]

Purdy(s), Purdy(s) Station. Westchester. The Purdy family owned much of the land in the area here. [Lederer:117]

Purling. Greene. Enoch Hyde and Benjamin Hall built a forge here in 1788, from which the place was known as the Forge. In 1895, the place changed its name for the sound of the water running over the stones in the Shinglekill. [French:331; Greene:209; Vedder:31; WPANY:410]

Putnam Lake, Putnam Valley. Putnam. Named for Major General Israel Putnam, who was stationed in the county for a part of the time during the Revolutionary War. [French:540; Gannett:217]

Putnam Station. Washington. General Israel Putnam was active in this area during the Revolutionary War. [French:685; Johnson:448; Stone:472]

Pyrites. St. Lawrence. Named for the iron pyrite (fool's gold) deposits found here. [APN:392; Harder:192; WPANYA]

Q

59th Street Columbus Circle © *2004 by Jon Crispin*

Quaker Hill. Dutchess. This place was first settled between 1720 and 1730 by
Quakers from New Jersey. [French:273; Smith-D:558; WPANYD:122]

Quaker Springs. Saratoga. Near the mineral springs here was a Friends meeting
house early in the settlement of the area. [French:591; Syl-S:271]

Quaker Street. Schenectady. Named for the Quakers who settled here in 1790.
[WPANY:448]

Quarry Heights. Westchester. This place began as the home of Italian immigrants who worked on quarrying stone found here and building the Kensico
Dam in 1913. When the project was done, they stayed and the community
grew. [Lederer:118]

Quarryville. Ulster. There was an extensive limestone and flagstone quarrying industry here. [French:666–7; Syl-U:42]

Queens, Queens Village. Queens. The city and the county were named for the queen of King Charles II, Catherine of Braganza. Queens Village was called Brushville in the 1830s. The residents voted to change the name to Queens in 1854. In the 1920s, the Long Island Railroad added "village" to the station name to avoid confusion with the county name. The village changed its name soon after. [French:544; Gannett:217; Jackson:966, 971; WPANYC:557]

Quogue, East Quogue. Suffolk. The Native American word for clams, which were abundant here, was *quahog, quohog,* or *quogue.* However, early records seem to indicate that the name of these villages comes from the shortening of another Algonquian word, *quaquanuntuck,* meaning "trembling river" for the boggy land at the water's edge. [APN:393, 396; Bayles:316; Gannett:218; Suffolk/Southampton:28]

R

Near Richfield Springs © *2004 by Jon Crispin*

Rainbow Lake. Franklin. Named for the lake. [WPANYS]

Ramapo. Rockland. The town was first called New Hampstead when it was formed in 1791, then changed to Hampstead in 1797, and finally Ramapo in 1828. The word is Algonquian, spelled variously as Ramapough, Romopock, Romapuck, Ramapuck, or Ramapaugh, meaning "round pond" or "clear or sweet water." The place where the settlement of Ramapo is was early on called Sidman Clove, the clove being the pass through the mountains that later became Ramapo Pass and Ramapo Mountains. It later became known as Ramapo Works for the factories that were established there. In 1879, the name of the post office was changed from Ramapo Works to Ramapo. [APN:399; Bedell:324; Cole:273, 275; French:571; Green:393, 398]

Randall. Montgomery. The community was called Yatesville until the post office was established in 1863 when this name was suggested by the first postmaster,

Louis Lounsberry, but there is no record of why he chose this name. [Froth-ingham:342]

Randallsville. Madison. This was the name of the Smith Valley post office, but the origin of the name is not recorded. [Smith-C&M:582]

Randolph, East Randolph. Cattaraugus. Early settlers named the community for Randolph, Vermont, their former home. [Ellis:185; French:194]

Ransomville. Niagara. This place was first known as Quade's Corners when it was settled in 1817. It began serious growth with the arrival of Jehial C. S. Ran-som and the establishment of the post office in 1826. He and his family did considerable business and were rewarded with the place being named for them. [French:456; Gannett:219; Pool:263; Williams:378–9; WPANYS]

Rapids. Niagara. The swift current on Tonawanda Creek at this location gave this place its name. [Pool:172]

Raquette Lake. Hamilton. The name of the lake comes from the French word for snowshoe. The story is that when the ice and snow of the lake melted, making the use of snowshoes irrelevant, a group of Loyalists left their snowshoes in a pile. Years later, when what was left of the pile of snowshoes was found, the lake became known for them. The community was named for the lake, previously spelled Racket. [A&K:5–6; APN:400; Donaldson(1):42–3; French:337; Gannett:219; WPANY:497]

Rathbone. Steuben. General Ransom Rathbone settled here in 1842. [French:627; Gannett:219; Roberts:481; Steuben:341–2]

Ravena. Albany. The village had been called Coeymans Junction for the junction of two branches of the West Shore Railroad here. In 1893, the post office name was changed to Ravena, a variant of Ravenna, an Italian city, because no one was satisfied with the name Coeymans Junction. [Albany:480–1; APN:400]

Rawson. Allegany. The Rawson family were early settlers here. [Allegany:328; French:175; Minard:789]

Raymondville. St. Lawrence. Benjamin Raymond moved here with his family in 1816. The settlement was first called Racketon for the Raquette River. [Cur-tis:629; French:580; Harder:196; Hough-SLF:365]

Reading Center. Schuyler. The town was formed in 1806 and named for the for-mer home of the Roberts family, settlers who came here from Reading, Penn-sylvania. [P&H-S:207; WPANYA]

Red Creek. Wayne. The village was first called Jacksonville, for General Andrew Jackson, but when the post office was established in 1836, it and the village were named Red Creek for the stream. [Cowles:298]

Redfield. Oswego. Dr. Frederick Redfield owned a large tract of land here, but he died before he was able to move here. When the town was formed in 1800, it was named for him. The post office called Redfield was opened in 1807 in the village of Central Square, which soon changed its name to Redfield Square to avoid confusion with the other Central Square in the county. [Churchill:670, 676; French:526; Johnson-O:423; WPANYA]

Redford. Clinton. This was a glassmaking center in the 1840s that is said to have taken its name from the reddish rocks in the Saranac River. [Hurd-C&F:358; WPANYS]

Red Hook, Upper Red Hook. Dutchess. The town was formed in 1812. The name comes from one of two sources. The Dutch may have called this area Roode Hoeck for the ripe cranberries in the marsh when they first came here. There was also an old tavern built of red brick that stood at the crossroads and became a landmark. [French:276; Gannett:220; Smith-D:181; WPA-NYD:95]

Red Hook. Kings. The Dutch named this place for the color of the soil and the shape of the point of land jutting out into what was later called Upper New York Bay. [Gannett:220; Jackson:991; WPANYC:464]

Red Mills. St. Lawrence. This place was formerly called Gallooville, Gallopville, or Galloupville for the Gallop Rapids in the St. Lawrence River. But in 1804 D. W. Church built a sawmill and painted it red. [Curtis:326; Harder:196; Hough-SLF:331]

Red Oaks Mill. Dutchess. This was a picnic and swimming spot on Wappingers Creek that became a suburb of Poughkeepsie. It probably took its name from the local trees and a mill on the creek. [WPANYD:113]

Red Rock. Columbia. The community was called Pilfershire until 1825 when a large rock along the roadside was painted red and topped with a wooden column with the date. [Ellis-C:325; French:243; Gannett:221]

Redwood. Jefferson. Thomas Clark had surveyed this village and called it Jamesville. But John S. Foster came and built a glass factory in 1833. He named the place for his hometown, Redford, Vermont. [D&P:269; French:355; Hough-J:82; WPANY:513]

Rego Park. Queens. The Real Good Construction Company developed this neighborhood in the 1920s, and the name came from the first two letters of the first two words of the company name. [APN:403; Jackson:994]

Remsen. Oneida. The town, formed in 1798, was named for Henry Remsen who held the Remsenburgh patent. [French:466; Gannett:221; Oneida:179]

Rensselaer. Rensselaer. The Van Rensselaer family owned a great deal of land here and left its name in many places. The city was formed in 1897 from the villages of Bath-on-the-Hudson, East Albany, and Greenbush. Bath-on-the-Hudson was named for the bathhouses built to take advantage of the mineral springs there. [Gannett:221; Weise:45, 54; WPANY:563]

Rensselaer Falls. St. Lawrence. Tate, Chafee, and Co. erected a forge here in 1839 and the place was called Tateville. Stephen and Henry Van Rensselaer owned land here, built a sawmill in 1839, and Henry laid out the village in 1846. Stephen went on to become lieutenant governor, state senator, supporter of the Erie Canal, and founder of Rensselaer Polytechnic Institute. [Curtis:460; French:575; Harder:197]

Rensselaerville. Albany. In 1630, land was granted here to Stephen Van Rensselaer. The colony was known as Rensselaerwyck. The town was formed in 1790 and named for him. [Albany:461; French:165; Gannett:221; Howell:778, 911]

Resort. Wayne. This was a summer colony at the head of the east shore of Sodus Bay. [WPANY:649]

Retsof. Livingston. This is Foster spelled backwards, for one of the landowners here. It was settled in 1878 when the first salt mine was developed. [WPANYS]

Rexford. Saratoga. Eleazar Rexford ran a tavern here during the building of the Erie Canal, which here crossed the Mohawk River on a stone aqueduct. [French:587; Syl-S:477]

Rexville. Steuben. Charles and Daniel Rexford were early settlers. [Steuben:342]

Reynoldsville. Schuyler. The first postmaster was James Reynolds when the post office was established in 1827 and named for him and his family. [P&H-S:149]

Rhinebeck. Dutchess. The town was formed in 1788. The name came from that of a nearby creek called Rein Beek or Rynbeek. This name came from a combination of the Rhine (the river in Germany) and William Beekman, the name of the fellow who founded the town, who had come with other settlers from Germany. The Hudson River had been called "the Rhine of America." [APN:404; French:276; Gannett:222; Smith-D:252; WPANYD:92]

Rhinecliff. Dutchess. The Hudson River had been called "the Rhine of America," which influenced the naming of a number of places near its shore. [APN:404]

Richburg. Allegany. Alvan Richardson came here in about 1819 and put up the first sawmill and inn in 1824 and the first gristmill in 1825. [Allegany:380; French:176; Gannett:222; Minard:855]

Richfield, Richfield Springs. Otsego. The town of Richfield was formed in 1792 and named for the quality of the soil here. The village was named for the mineral springs that led to the establishment of spas for the cure of skin disorders. [APN:405; French:537; WPANY:420; WPANYS]

Richford. Tioga. Ezekiel Rich kept a hotel here and ran a tannery that made mittens. He donated the land that made up the northern part of the public square of the settlement that took his name. (Stephen Wells donated the southern part.) When the town was first organized in 1831, it was named Arlington, but in 1832 it took the name of the settlement. [French:652; Gay:406; P&H-Ti:188–9]

Richmond Hill. Queens. In 1867, Albon P. Man hired the landscape architect Edward Richmond to buy land and lay out a community here. The village was incorporated in 1894. [Jackson:1004; WPANYC:583]

Richmond Valley. Richmond. The Staten Island Railroad opened a station here in 1860 and named it Richmond Valley. [Jackson:1004]

Richmondville, West Richmondville. Schoharie. The town was formed in 1849 and named for the post office, which was already established. [French:606; Roscoe:284; Sias:142]

Richville. St. Lawrence. Samuel Rich settled here with Jonathan Haskins in 1804. The place was called Rich's Settlement until the post office opened as Richville in 1824. [Curtis:512; French:576; Harder:199; Hough-SLF:291]

Riders Mills. Columbia. In about 1880, the place was known as Mosher's Mills. Then Jonathan Rider bought the grist—and sawmills, and it became known as Riders Mills Settlement. [Ellis-C:289; French:244]

Ridge. Suffolk. Sometimes called Ridgeville, both names referred to the settlement's geographic location. [Bayles:262; Suffolk/Brookhaven:49]

Ridgebury. Orange. The Presbyterian Church here was first called the Ridgebury Church. The community took its name from the church. [R&C:684]

Ridgeway. Orleans. The town was formed in 1812 and named for the road that ran along the lake ridge, going east and west through the town. The village was locally known as Ridgeway Corners. [French:515; Gannett:222; Orleans:247; Signor:292, 341]

Ridgewood. Queens. Early eighteenth-century English settlers named this place for the high wooded terrain here. From the 1880s to the end of World War I, the area used the name Evergreen because Ridgewood on Long Island claimed priority. This changed after the war. [Jackson:1005; WPANYC:460]

Rifton. Ulster. This place was formerly called Arnoldton, for one of the founders of early manufacturing here. Later the name was changed to Rifton Glen to sound more poetical. [Syl-U:115]

Riga. Monroe. The town was formed in 1808 and named for the city in Latvia. [APN:406; WPARM:291]

Riparius. Warren. This was first settled by the Mead family in 1820. The name means the same thing, "on the banks," as that of its sister community, Riverside, on the other side of the Hudson River. [APN:406; WPANYS; WPAW:192–3]

Ripley, South Ripley. Chautauqua. The town was named for General Eleazar W.

Ripley. The settlement of Ripley was formerly named Quincy, probably for a family name. South Ripley was named for its location in the town. [D&H:225–6; French:215; Gannett:223]

Risingville. Steuben. Noble A. Rising was the first postmaster here in 1853. [Steuben:343]

Riverdale. Bronx. The New York Central Railroad opened a depot here and named it Riverdale-on-Hudson to service the summer mansions of the city's industrialists and others. It eventually became a suburb. [French:708; Jackson:1008]

Riverhead. Suffolk. Named for its location at the head of the Peconic River. [Bayles:287; WPANYS]

Riverside. Broome. Named for its location on the Susquehanna River. The post office was established in about 1875. [Smith-B:491]

Rochdale. Dutchess. This was formerly known as Whippleville for the family who lived there. Then James Taylor, a prominent citizen, named it for his previous home, an industrial center in England. [Smith-D:369]

Rochester, East Rochester. Monroe. Colonel Nathaniel Rochester was one of the first proprietors here. It was called Rochesterville when it was incorporated as a village in 1817. It changed its name in 1822 and was incorporated as a city in 1834. The Native American name for this location was Gaskosago, meaning "at the falls" for the waterfalls on the Genesee River on which the city is situated. [APN:408; French:402; Gannett:224; Mc-M:81; Morgan:468; Parker:306; WPARM:43]

Rock City. Dutchess. Named for the rocky nature of the land and the deep ravines through which streams flow. [French:273; Smith-D:215; WPANYD:95]

Rock City Falls. Saratoga. This place took its name from the rocks and falls in the Kayadrossera River on which it sits. The post office was opened in 1849. [Syl-S:488; WPANYA]

Rockdale. Chenango. This settlement sits on the west bank of the Unadilla River and was probably named for its physical characteristics. [Smith-C&M:248; WPANYS]

Rock Glen. Wyoming. Named for the extensive quarries of grey sandstone here. [Wyoming:193]

Rock Hill. Sullivan. This place took its name from its surroundings. [WPANYS]

Rockland. Sullivan. The town was formed in 1809 and was named for its hilly and forested landscape. [Child:196-B; French:647; Quinlan:490]

Rockland Lake. Rockland. The hamlet, located between the lake and the Hudson River, took its name from the lake, which was used extensively in the production of ice in the mid-1800s. The lake was called Quashpeake Pond by the Native Americans. In 1711, John Slaughter bought a tract of land here and built a landing that was known as Slaughter's Landing until 1835 when the name was changed for that of the lake, which was named for the county. The county name came from its rocky landscape. [Bedell:159–60; Cole:91; French:569; Gannett:225; Green:420]

Rock Stream. Yates. The place was first known as Hurd's Corners, then as Hathaway's Corners, but when the post office was established in 1830, it was named for the creek full of rocks. [Cleveland:1120]

Rock Tavern. Orange. The tavern here, around which the village grew, was named for the rock on which it was built. [R&C:222]

Rockville. Allegany. There was a large grindstone quarry in the area. [Allegany:209; French:171; Gannett:225]

Rockville Centre. Nassau. When the post office was established here in 1849, it was named for Reverend Mordecai Rock Smith. It was first called Rockville, but there already was such a post office in the state, so the Centre was added. [French:547; Winsche:85–6; WPANY:707]

Rockwood. Fulton. This place was called Pleasant Valley until the post office was established in 1850 when the name was changed, maybe as a descriptive of the place. [Fulton:222]

Rocky Point. Suffolk. Named for its location on the Long Island Sound. [Bayles:253; French:634]

Rodman, East Rodman. Jefferson. The town was formed in 1804 as Harrison, named for Richard Harrison of New York City who was a proprietor here. The name was changed in 1808 for Daniel Rodman of Hudson who was a clerk in the assembly and favored by the legislators. The post office in Rodman was established in 1816. East Rodman was the name of the post office in Whitesville, which had been named for Thomas White, who had come here in 1802 from Litchfield, New York, then moved further west in 1810. [D&P:493; French:361; Gannett:225; Hough-J:231]

Rome. Oneida. The Native American name for this site between the Mohawk River and Wood Creek was Deowainsta or Dayahoowaquat, meaning "carrying place" for the portage between the two streams. The village that grew up here around Fort Stanwix, which had been built in 1758, was called Lynchville for Dominick Lynch who bought 2,397 acres in 1786, parceled them out into lots, and started a settlement. In 1819, the village was incorporated as Rome for the city in Italy. It became a city in 1870. [APN:410; French:466; Gannett:225; Morgan:472; Oneida:225–6; WPANY:486]

Romulus. Seneca. The town was formed in 1794 and named by the state land commissioners for the founder of Rome. [APN:410; Gannett:225]

Ronkonkoma, Lake Ronkonkoma. Suffolk. Named for the lake, the name of which comes from an Algonquian word for "white sand." [APN:410; Bayles:266]

Rooseveltown. St. Lawrence. Named for Franklin Delano Roosevelt, thirty-second president of the United States. [Harder:204]

Roscoe. Sullivan. This place had been called Westfield Flats, but there is no record of name origin. [Child:196-B; WPANYS]

Rose, North Rose. Wayne. The town was formed in 1826 and needed a name. A suggestion was made that it be named for Robert Rose of Geneva who owned a good bit of land here. It was thought that, in exchange for such a compliment, he might give some land to the town or something equally valuable. When he was told of this decision, he sent the town a small merino ram, said to be about the size of a woodchuck. The village of Rose was first called Valentine's when a post office was established there in 1827 with Dr. Peter Valentine as postmaster. The name was later changed to Albion, then Rose Valley, and finally Rose, in 1834. North Rose was first known as Lamb's Corners for a family of that name. The name was changed when the post office was opened there in 1860. [Cowles:403–4, 413–4; French:693; Gannett:225; Mc-W:155]

Rosebank. Richmond. Before 1880, this was part of Peterstown, named by German settlers. [Jackson:1022]

Roseboom. Otsego. Abram Roseboom settled here in about 1800, building the first sawmill and carding mill. The town took his name when it was formed in 1854. The settlement had been called Lodi. [French:537; Hurd-O:315–6]

Rosedale. Queens. Thomas and Christopher Foster settled here in 1647. The place became known as Foster's Meadow. A hamlet grew up, and the railroad built a station in 1870. In 1892, developers changed the name to Rosedale, for the flower. [APN:411; Jackson:1022]

Rosendale. Ulster. The town was formed in 1844 and given the name of an old farm in the area from 1711. [French:666; Syl-U:231]

Rosiere. Jefferson. This was the name given to the first station on the railroad out from Cape Vincent. [D&P:327]

Roslyn, Roslyn Estates. Nassau. The place had been called Hempstead Harbor, but the post office would not allow that name because of the confusion with other communities named Hempstead, so William Cairns suggested the name of Roslyn, Scotland, in 1844, and it was adopted by vote of the residents. [Winsche:87–8]

Rossburg. Allegany. This place was called Mixville Landing for Ebenezer Mix, early landowner, then Wiscoy Landing during its days as a canal town on the Genesee Valley Canal. There is no record of its present name origin. [Minard:737, 743; WPANYA]

Ross Corners. Broome. Named for David Ross, a prominent early lumberman, who kept a store here from 1838 to 1850. His son, George Ross, continued the lumber trade. [Smith-B:477]

Rossie. St. Lawrence. The town was formed in 1813 and named for David Parish's sister, Rosa. Her husband owned a castle in Scotland that was also called Rossie for her. [Curtis:585; French:582; Harder:204; Hough-SLF:448]

Rotterdam, Rotterdam Junction. Schenectady. The Dutch named this place for the city in the Netherlands because the area was lowlands. The town was formed in 1820. [APN:411; Clark:58; French:597; Gannett:226]

Round Lake. Saratoga. Named for the lake, which is a nearly perfect one-mile-diameter circle. [French:590; Syl-S:388]

Round Top. Greene. This place took its name from the nearby rocky hill, which was sometimes called Dome Mountain. [French:331; Greene:209; WPA-NYS]

Rouses Point. Clinton. The village was named for Jacque Rouse, a Canadian refugee soldier who settled here in 1783. [Gannett:226; Hurd-C&F:263]

Roxbury. Delaware. The town was organized in 1799 and named for Roxbury, Connecticut, the former home of many of the settlers. [French:264; WPA-NYS]

Roxbury. Queens. This was a 1960s development at the western end of Rockaway peninsula. [Jackson:1026]

Royalton Center. Niagara. The town was named for Royalton, Vermont, by settlers from Vermont and New England. The village is in the central part of the town. [French:456; Pool:268; Williams:382]

Ruby. Ulster. Named for the color of the soil. [WPANYA]

Rural Grove. Montgomery. This place in the town of Root was first called Unionville. Then it was called Leatherville for the leather industry. When that waned, the name was no longer appropriate, so in about 1850 the name Rural Grove started to be used, for the grove of elms at the edge of the community. The post office had been called Root, but in 1872 it changed its name to match that of the settlement. [Frothingham:330; Montgomery:164]

Rush, North Rush, West Rush. Monroe. The town was formed in 1818 and named either for Dr. Benjamin Rush, a signer of the Declaration of Independence, or for the large patches of rushes growing along Honeoye Creek. The settlement of Rush was called Webster's Mills for the industry built on the creek by John Webster in 1810. North Rush used to be called Hart's Corners. [APN:414; Mc-M:257; WPARM:292; WPANYA]

Rushford. Allegany. The town was formed in 1816. During the initial discussions about the name of the town, there were some who wanted it to be named for Windsor, Vermont, but because there already was a town by that name in the state, this one took the name Rushford, either because of the rushes growing in the area or for Dr. Benjamin Rush of Philadelphia, a popular signer of the

Declaration of Independence. The village was first called Kellogville for Hiram Kellog, an early settler. But when the post office was established, in 1816, the village changed its name for that of the town. [Allegany:330; French:175; Minard:790; WPANYA]

Rushville. Yates. Named for Dr. Benjamin Rush, a signer of the Declaration of Independence. [WPANYS]

Russell, North Russell. St. Lawrence. The town was named, when it was formed in 1807, for Russell Atwater, who bought the land in 1798 from Daniel McCormick who had wanted it to be named Ballybean for his hometown in Ireland. [Curtis:526; French:582; Harder:206; Hough-SLF:469]

Russia. Herkimer. The town was formed as Union in 1806. Its name was changed in 1808 for the country. [French:347; Herkimer:227]

Rutland Center. Jefferson. The town of Rutland was formed in 1802 and named for Rutland, Vermont, the home of an early settler. On some maps, Rutland Center was labeled as Brookville for Curtis G. Brooks. [APN:414; D&P:495; French:361; Gannett:227; Hough-J:233]

Rye, Rye Brook. Westchester. Settled in 1660, the town was formed in 1788 and was named for Rye in the county of Sussex in England. The Native American name for the place was Peningoe. [APN:414; Bolton(2):127; French:705; Lederer:124; WPANY:380]

S

Syracuse © *2004 by Jon Crispin*

Sabael. Hamilton. The place was named for Sabael Benedict, a member of the Abenaki tribe, who settled here in about 1775. [A&K:427]

Sabattis. Hamilton. Mitchell Sabattis was an old Native American guide in the area. The place was early known as Long Lake West, but when the post office was established in 1898, it was named for Sabattis. Eventually, the settlement took the name as well. [A&K:816; Donaldson(1):43; Donaldson(2):81–7]

Sabbath Day Point. Warren. The traditional story is that this headland on Lake George was named when General Amherst and his troops stopped here on a Sunday in 1759 to rest. However, there is a mention of this place by this name in the journal written by Robert Rogers, who had been sent here to observe the land in 1758. [French:674; Smith-W:560; WPAW:197]

Sacandaga. Fulton. This place took its name from the river, part of which was dammed to become Sacandaga Lake. The word is Iroquoian, meaning "swampy" or "drowned lands" for the marsh that lies along the river. The settlement started out as a meeting and picnic ground in 1884 and was called Sacandaga Park. [APN:415; French:314; Gannett:227; WPANYA; WPA-NYS]

Sackets Harbor. Jefferson. The village and the harbor were named for Augustus Sacket, an early settler and proprietor. The Native American name was Gahuagojetwadaalote, "fort at the mouth of the Great River." The village was incorporated in 1814. [D&P:399–400; French:358; Gannett:227; Hough-J:174; WPANY:517]

Sagaponack. Suffolk. This place was named with a Native American word meaning "place where the ground nuts grow" or "the place at which a stream flows out of a lake or pond." [APN:416; Gannett:228; Suffolk/Southampton:35; WPANYS]

Sag Harbor. Suffolk. This village had been called Sagaponack Harbor and the Harbor of Sagg. The name comes from a Native American word meaning "place where the ground nuts grow" or "the place at which a stream flows out of a lake or pond." [APN:416; Gannett:228; Suffolk/Southampton:35; WPANYS]

Saint Albans. Queens. This development took the name of a London suburb in 1892. The railroad station opened in 1898 and the post office in 1899. [Jackson:1033; WPANYC:586]

Saint Andrew. Orange. This place took its name from St. Andrews Episcopal Church that was located here. It was early called Saint Andrews. [French:508; R&C:387]

Saint George. Richmond. This was part of New Brighton until the 1880s, when Erastus Witman organized the local ferry lines and rail routes and named the place for George Law, a railroad and ferry investor who had land that Witman needed for a ferry terminal. [Jackson:1034]

Saint Huberts. Essex. Named for the patron saint of the hunt because of the abundant deer hunting here. [WPANY:512]

Saint James. Suffolk. The Episcopalians built a church here, St. James, and named it for their benefactor, James Clinch of New York. The post office took its name from the church. [Bayles:194; French:637; Suffolk/Smithtown:19, 20]

Saint Johnsburg. Niagara. The St. John's German Lutheran church gave the community its name in 1846. At first, it was called simply Johnsburg. [French:457; Pool:344; Williams:392]

Saint Johnsville. Montgomery. The town was formed in 1838 and named for the village. There are two stories for the origin of this name. One is that it was named for St. Johns Reformed Church that was built in 1770 and then moved to the site of the village in 1804. The village grew up around it and took its name. Other references state that it was not named for the church but for Alexander St. John, a surveyor of a turnpike road that had been commissioned to run from Johnstown to near the town of Zimmermans—as this place was called previously for an early settler. When a post office was established, it was called St. Johnsville in honor of the surveyor. The choice of name could have been influenced by both, as there was a St. Johns Church here for many years. [French:416; Frothingham:312, 313]

Saint Josephs. Sullivan. This community took its name from a Catholic church here. [WPANYS]

Saint Regis, Saint Regis Falls. Franklin. Jean Francois Regis was a saint canonized by Pope Clement XII in 1737. The village of St. Regis and the river were named by Father Anthony Gordon, a Jesuit. The village of St. Regis Falls took its name from the waterfall in the river. [French:309; Gannett:229; Hough-SLF:113; Hurd-C&F:446; WPANYS]

Salamanca. Cattaraugus. When the town was organized in 1854, it was called Bucktooth. The present city of Salamanca was named for Señor Don Jose de Salamanca, a Spanish marquis who helped finance the Atlantic and Great Western Railroad when it was built through here in 1860. [APN:419; Ellis:346, 349, 350; French:188; Gannett:229; WPANY:392]

Salem. Washington. The town was formed in 1786 and was named as a compromise. The Scottish settlers wanted it to be named New Perth. The New Englanders were partial to White Creek. In 1777, there had been a fort erected in the area that was named Fort Salem. This name was applied to the village in 1782, and when people grew tired of arguing about the name of the town, they decided to name it for this fort. [French:685; Johnson:137]

Salem Center, North Salem, South Salem. Westchester. These villages and the town of North Salem probably took their names from the place in Massachusetts. [APN:419; Gannett:229; WPANYS]

Salisbury, Salisbury Center. Herkimer. The town was named for Salisbury, Connecticut, when it was formed in 1797. Many of its residents had come from there. [French:348; Herkimer:207, 211; WPANYS]

Salisbury Mills. Orange. Named for the mills and for the town in England that was the former home of some of the settlers here. [APN:420; R&C:635]

Saltaire. Suffolk. This was a summer resort that became permanent. The post office was established in 1913, and the village was incorporated in 1917. Its name comes from a description of the air here on the ocean. [WPANYS]

Salt Point. Dutchess. Named either for the creek or for the local tradition of putting out salt licks to attract deer. [French:270, 274; WPANYD:151]

Salt Springville. Montgomery. Named for the brine springs in the area. [French:532]

Sammonsville. Fulton. The Sammons family were early settlers here. [Fulton:210]

Samsonville. Ulster. General Henry A. Samson established a large tannery here early in the nineteenth century. [French:665; Gannett:230; Syl-U:298; WPANYA]

Sanborn. Niagara. The Sanborn family arrived in 1846. The Reverend E. C. Sanborn was first, then his son, Lee R., bought land, laid out a village, built a sawmill, and became the postmaster from 1862 to 1877. [Pool:299; Williams:384]

Sandfordville. St. Lawrence. Jonah Sandford was the first settler here. [Harder:211]

Sand Lake, West Sand Lake. Rensselaer. The town was named for the lake, which carries a descriptive name, when it was formed in 1812. The community of Sand Lake was called Sliter's Corners until the Sand Lake post office was established here in 1815. West Sand Lake used to be called Ulinesville for Bernard Uline who built the first house here. [French:558; Weise:135, 141, 142]

Sands Point. Nassau. John Sands bought land here in 1691. [Winsche:91–2]

Sandusky. Cattaraugus. Named for Sandusky, Ohio, from the Native American *otsandooske*, meaning "flowing rock" or "there where there is pure water." [Parker:289; WPANYS]

Sandy Creek. Oswego. The town was formed in 1825 and named for the stream, Sandy Creek, that flows through it. The village was first called Washingtonville, but the name was changed to that of the town. [Churchill:711, 724; French:527; Johnson-O:374, 376–7]

Sandy Pond. Oswego. The pond had been called Wigwam Cove, but then that name was changed for the more descriptive one. The settlement was named for the pond. [Churchill:712]

Sanford, North Sanford. Broome. The community of Sanford had been called Creek Settlement for its location on Oquaga Creek, then became named for the town of Sanford. North Sanford, in the northeastern part of the town, used to be called Potter Settlement for a Mr. Potter who had settled here in about 1801. He later moved to Pennsylvania where Potter County was named for him. [Smith-B:305, 322]

Sangerfield. Oneida. The town was established in 1795 on land originally owned by Jedediah Sanger who, wanting to have a new settlement named after him, promised a cask of rum for the first town meeting and fifty acres to the first church. The rum was drunk at the first town meeting in 1795. The Native American name for the site was Skanawis, "a long swamp." [French:467; Gannett:231; Morgan:472; Oneida:183]

Sanitaria Springs. Broome. This place was first called Osborne Hollow for Eli Osborne, an early settler. The current name was derived from a sanitarium that was established here by Dr. Kilmer of Binghamton. [WPANYA; WPA-NYS]

Santa Clara. Franklin. The town took its name from the hamlet when it was organized in 1888. The hamlet was named by John Hurd for his wife. [WPA-NYS]

Saranac. Clinton. The town took its name from the river, the name of which is a Native American word that means "river that flows under a rock" or "entrance of a river into a lake." The settlement had been called Saranac Hollow. [French:240; Gannett:232; WPANYS]

Saranac Inn, Saranac Lake. Franklin. Named for the lake (see Saranac). [Gannett:232; WPANY:507]

Saratoga Springs. Saratoga. The city was named for its many mineral springs and for the Native American word *saraghtoga*, meaning "place of the miraculous water in a rock" or "hillside country of the great river" or "swift water." [French:591; Gannett:232; Syl-S:259, 266; WPANY:306]

Sardinia. Erie. When the town was formed in 1821, it was named by General Ezra Nott, the first settler here, for the Mediterranean island. [APN:426; Gannett:232; Smith-E:617]

Saugerties. Ulster. The town was formed in 1811 and named with a derivation from the Dutch word *zagger*, meaning "one who saws," for a sawmill that was built here by Robert Livingston. The village was incorporated as Ulster in 1831 but changed its name in 1855. [French:666; Gannett:232; Syl-U:34, 36; WPANY:594]

Sauquoit. Oneida. This had been two settlements, West Saugquoit and East Saquoit, across from each other on Sauquoit Creek, and they shared the Sauquoit post office that was located in West Sauquoit. The post office was named in 1820 from a Native American word, *saghdaqueda*, the meaning of which might be "smooth pebbles in a stream." The naturalist Asa Gray was born here in 1810. [APN:427; French:466; Oneida:175, 177; WPANYS]

Savannah. Wayne. The town was formed in 1824 and named for the grassy plain that covered most of its surface. In 1867, paper was manufactured here from the savannah grass. [APN:428; Cowles:346; French:693; Gannett:232; Mc-W:160]

Savona. Steuben. This used to be the Mud Creek post office, but its name was changed for the city in Italy. [APN:428; French:622; Steuben:344–5]

Sayville, West Sayville. Suffolk. This name was to be Seville, for the city in Spain, but the word was misspelled in the application for a post office. [Suffolk/Islip:7; WPANYS]

Scarborough. Westchester. In 1850, the local parish of St. Mary's Episcopal

Church took on the name from the town of Scarborough in England that had impressed the Reverend Edward Mead. Eventually, the surrounding area took the name. The post office was spelled Scarboro from 1864 until 1928. In 1909, the New York Central Railroad changed the name of the station from Scarboro to West Briarcliff. This was soon changed back when local residents protested by throwing the sign into the Hudson River. [APN:429; Lederer:128, 154]

Scarsdale. Westchester. Caleb Heathcote settled here with his family in 1701, naming the place the Manor of Scarsdale for his former home in England. The village was incorporated in 1916. [APN:429; Bolton(2):211; French:705; Gannett:233; Lederer:128; WPANY:549]

Schaghticoke, Schaghticoke Hill. Rensselaer. The town was formed in 1788 and took a form of the Algonquin name for the place, Pachgatgoch, "the place where the river branches or divides." The villages were also named for this term that describes the confluence of the Hoosick and Hudson Rivers. [APN:429; French:558; Gannett:233]

Schenectady. Schenectady. The name of the city and county was derived from two different spellings, *schaghnactaadagh* and *schenectada,* of a Native American word that has been variously translated as "beyond the pine plains," "beyond the plains," "over beyond the plains," and "beyond pines." [APN:429; Clark:58; French:598; Gannett:233; WPANY:317]

Schenevus. Otsego. The village was first called Jacksonboro. When the post office was established in 1829, it took the name of the creek, which might have been named for a Native American who lived here or for a word meaning "the first hoeing of corn." [APN:429; WPANYS]

Schodack Center, East Schodack, North Schodack. Rensselaer. The town was formed in 1795 and named for the Native American word *schoodic,* meaning "meadow or fire plain" or "a place that was burned over." East Schodack was called Scott's Corners for a hotel kept by a man named Scott. [APN:429; Gannett:233; Weise:75]

Schoharie. Schoharie. The village was first called Brunnen Dorp, "Fountain Town," by the German settlers. The town was formed in 1788 and named, as was the county, for the Native American word *towasschohor,* meaning "driftwood." [French:600, 606; Noyes:158; Roscoe:254; Sias:13, 145]

Schroon Lake, South Schroon. Essex. The town was formed in 1804 and named for the lake, which was named by French scouts in the early 1700s for the widow of Paul Scarron, French dramatist. She was usually known as Madame de Maintenon, and she became a consort of Louis XIV. The outstanding scenery of the long, slim lake was compared with her youth and beauty. [French:304; Gannett:233; Smith-Ex:528; WPANY:556]

Schuyler Falls. Clinton. Peter Schuyler bought the land and waterpower at the site of this settlement from Zephaniah Platt. The town and the settlement were named for him. [French:240; Hurd-C&F:368]

Schuyler Lake. Otsego. This place took its name from the lake, which had been named for General Philip Schuyler's family, who owned land here. [APN:430; French:533; Gannett:234; WPANYS]

Schuylerville. Saratoga. Named for the family of General Philip Schuyler, who were early settlers here. [APN:430; French:591; Gannett:234; Syl-S:271; WPANY:625]

Scio. Allegany. The town was formed in 1823 and possibly name for the island in the Mediterranean, but there is a local story that it was named for State Claim #10. The village was known as Blood's for Francis L. Blood who kept the hotel here. [Allegany:335; APN:430; French:175; Minard:479, 486]

Sciota. Clinton. The name was a variant of *scioto,* part of a longer Iroquoian word meaning "deer." [APN:430; Hurd-C&F:288]

Scipio Center, Scipioville. Cayuga. The town of Scipio, formed in 1794, and the villages were named after a Roman general during the classical naming of the Military Tract in 1790. Scipioville was first known as Watkins Settlement and Watkins Corner. Then its name changed to Fitch's Corners for Paine Fitch, who built a tavern there in 1806. Eventually, that name was changed to Mechanicsville, which the village held until the post office was established and was named for the town. [APN; Storke:428]

Scotia. Schenectady. Alexander Lindsey Glen came here from Scotland and named the place with the Latin name for his homeland. [APN:430; Clark:58; Munsell:187–8; WPANY:455]

Scott. Cortland. The town was formed in 1815 and named for General Winfield Scott. The Scott post office was opened in the community of Scott Center. [French:254; Goodwin:214]

Scottsburg. Livingston. Matthew and William Scott were early settlers here in 1806. [Doty-L:656; French:386; Gannett:234; WPANYS]

Scottsville. Monroe. Isaac Scott bought 150 acres from the Wadsworths when he came here from New Hampshire in 1790. He built a log house, opened a tavern, and farmed. The post office opened in 1822. The Native American name of the place was Oatka, "the opening." [French:405; Mc-M:193, 194; Morgan:468; Peck:437; Parker:306]

Scriba. Oswego. George Scriba held the patent on land here. When the town was formed in 1811, the residents wanted it to be called Boston, but the legislature named it for George Scriba instead. The hamlet of Scriba was locally known as Scriba Corners or Scriba Center. The post office was established here in 1813 as Scriba. [Churchill:758, 769; French:528; Gannett:234; Johnson-O:412, 414]

Sea Breeze. Monroe. Named for the breezes from Lake Ontario, this is a community that grew up around a popular summer amusement resort. [WPARM:409]

Sea Cliff. Nassau. First called Littleworth for the place in England, in the 1830s it became known as Carpenterville for the Joseph Carpenter family. In 1871, the Metropolitan Camp Ground Association of New York and Brooklyn bought the land to provide a "healthful summer resort for Christian families." They named the place Sea Cliff Grove as a descriptive term. By 1883, the village was Sea Cliff. [Gannett:235; Winsche:92–3]

Seaford. Nassau. This was first called Jerusalem South, but when the South Side Long Island Railroad completed its line through here, the name caused confusion with the other Jerusalem on the line. So the western portion of Jerusalem South became Ridgewood, then later Wantaugh. The eastern section wanted to be Atlanticville, but this did not catch on. So the name of the settlement, the station, and the post office were officially changed to Seaford in 1867 for Seaford, Delaware. Jacob Seaman Jackson Jones had suggested the name after having to travel there to recover a stolen horse. [Winsche:93–4]

Seagate. Kings. The Sea Gate Association built an upper-class neighborhood on this peninsula on the western end of Coney Island in the 1890s. [Jackson:1057]

Seager. Ulster. Hiram Seager was an early settler here in about 1800. [WPANYA]

Searsville. Orange. Benjamin Sears lived here, owned the mills, and was once a sheriff of the county. It was sometimes called Searsburgh. [R&C:419]

Seeley Creek. Chemung. This place was named for the creek, which was named for the Seeley or Seely family that was numerous in the area early on. The post office was opened in 1833. [French:221; P&H-C:247, 254]

Selden. Suffolk. The settlement was called Westfield, but its name was changed for Judge Selden, who had promised to do something special for the place but then never did. [Bayled:264; Suffolk/Brookhaven:48]

Selkirk. Albany. The Selkirk family settled here in 1870. The post office was opened in 1883. [Albany:495; Howell:781; WPANYA]

Selkirk. Oswego. Named for the town and county in Scotland. [APN:434]

Sempronius. Cayuga. The town was formed in 1799 and named for a Roman tribune during the Military Tract naming of 1790. The settlement was known locally as Nonesuch, a name given the place by Dwight Kellogg, a relative of Judge Charles Kellogg after whom Kellogsville is named. The post office was opened in the hamlet of Vansville, which later changed its name to match that of the town and post office. [APN; French:204; Storke:48]

Seneca Castle. Ontario. This community was first called Castleton, but the post office was named Seneca Castle. Both names were from the Native American village nearby, the town of Seneca, named for one of the Iroquois tribes. The Dutch called these Native Americans *Sinnekaas,* which was derived from *otsinaki,* the Algonquian equivalent of the Iroquoian *onenieuteaka,* meaning "place of stone." This was the tribal name of the Oneida, but the Dutch thought that all Native Americans west of the Mohawk were called this. As each group was identified as white settlers moved west, the most western, unknown Native Americans were called Sinnekaas. The Senecas, who called themselves Sonnontouan or Nundawaagah, were the most western tribe in New York State and thus became to the Dutch the Sinnekars, which was further corrupted to Seneca, made to correspond to the Roman philosopher's name and thereby conforming to the classical naming pattern of upstate New York. [APN:434; French:498; Milliken:109; Parker:296]

Seneca Falls. Seneca. The village was named for the waterfalls in the river (see the entry for Seneca Castle for the derivation of *Seneca*). The Native American name of the place was Shaseounse, "rolling water." [APN:434; French:617; Gannett:236]

Seneca Hill. Oswego. This place is on the Oswego River opposite Minetto (see Seneca Castle for the derivation of "Seneca"). [Churchill:818]

Sennett. Cayuga. Judge Daniel Sennett was one of the first settlers of the town. He was a justice of the peace and a judge of the circuit court. [French:204; Storke:36]

Setauket, East Setauket. Suffolk. An early settlement here was called Ashford, and Seatuket Harbor was called Cromwell Bay. The present name came from an Algonquian word that means "river mouth." [APN:435; Bayles:237]

Seward. Schoharie. The town was formed in 1840 and named for Governor Seward. The Seward post office was in the settlement of Seward Valley, which was locally known as Neeley's Hollow. [APN:436; French:607; Gannett:236; Noyes:156; Roscoe:268; Sias:148]

Shadigee. Orleans. This was the location of Yates Pier on Lake Ontario, built in about 1850. There is no record of name origin. [Orleans:315; Signor:617]

Shandaken. Ulster. The town was formed in 1804 and named for a Native American word meaning either "rapid water" or "at the hemlocks." [APN:437; French:667; Gannett:236; Syl-U:306]

Shandelee. Sullivan. This place took its name from Shandelee Lake, which used to be called Shandley Pond, probably named for an early settler. [Child:119]

Sharon, Sharon Springs. Schoharie. The town of Sharon was formed in 1797 as Dorlach. Later in 1797, its name was changed for Sharon, Connecticut. The village of Sharon Springs had a number of springs used for medicinal purposes. [APN:438; French:607; Gannett:236; Roscoe:226, 239; Sias:150–1]

Shawnee. Niagara. Timothy Shaw opened a store and an ashery here in 1828, giving his name to the place. [Pool:344; Williams:392]

Sheds. Madison. Jonathan Sheds was an early settler here. The place was known as Shed's Corners. [Smith-C&M:606]

Shekomeko. Dutchess. Moravian missionaries settled here at a place the Native Americans called Shacameco, meaning "eel stream." [Smith-D:221; WPA-NYD:110]

Shelby, Shelby Center, West Shelby. Orleans. The town was formed in 1818 and named for Isaac Shelby, who was the first governor of Kentucky and a commander in the War of 1812, instrumental in the victory of the battle on the Thames River in Ontario, Canada. Shelby Center was earlier known as Barnegat, meaning "foaming passage" or "breaker's inlet." [APN:35, 439; French:516; Gannett:35, 237; Orleans:293; Signor:508]

Shelter Island, Shelter Island Heights. Suffolk. This name was a translation of the Native American name for the place, Manhansackahaquashuwornuck (and other spellings), meaning "an island sheltered by islands." It was a haven for Quakers in 1652. [Bayles:394; French:637; Gannett:237; Suffolk/Shelter Island:1; WPANY:713]

Sherburne. Chenango. The town was formed in 1795 and is said to have been named by a member of the legislature for the song "Sherburne" that was popular at the time. The Native American name of the place was Ganadadele, "steep hill." [Morgan:473; Smith-C&M:449; WPANYS]

Sheridan. Chautauqua. In 1824 when it was formed, the town was named for R. B. Sheridan, an English poet and dramatist, a name suggested by Nathaniel Grey, one of the original lobbyists to make this a separate town. He was an admirer of the poet. [APN:439; D&H:230]

Sherman. Chautauqua. The village was first called Millerville, then Kipville, and finally Sherman for a signer of the Declaration of Independence and a member of the Constitutional Convention. [D&H:235; French:215; Gannett:239; McMahon:312]

Sherrill. Oneida. This eventual home of the Oneida Community was first called Turkey Street from the Native American Turikesreet, "the place of the thief," for the white men who stole corn and poultry from the Native Americans at Oneida Castle. When the time came for a post office with a more dignified name, Congressman James S. Sherman of Utica (vice president of the United States from 1901 to 1912) was instrumental in getting permission for the name change in 1888. For his efforts, he was given the privilege of naming the town. He named it after his son, Sherrill. [French:469; Oneida:235, 238; WPANY:467]

Sherwood. Cayuga. Judge Seth Sherwood, from Vermont, settled here on 200 acres in the mid-1790s. [Storke:420]

Shinhopple. Delaware. The place took its name from the hobble bush that grew in abundance in the area. This plant was a flowering vine that was difficult to wade through as it tangled about the shins, hence the name. [Murray:317; WPANY:638]

Shinnecock Hills. Suffolk. This place was what was left of the Shinnecock Indians. The word meant "level land." [APN:440; French:638; Gannett:238]

Shokan, West Shokan. Ulster. This place is just down the road from Ashokan and was named from the same Native American word, meaning "little mouth," referring to the outlet of a small stream. [APN:24; Syl-U:297]

Shongo. Allegany. The settlement was known as Beanville, but the post office, established before 1860, was named for a Seneca chief who stayed in this area in the summers and whose wife may have been buried here. [Allegany:156; APN:441; French:176; Minard:541, 657; WPANY:681]

Shortsville. Ontario. Theophilus Short built the first sawmill here in 1804. It was first known as Shorts Mills. [French:497; Milliken:109]

Short Tract. Allegany. William Short was a prominent land agent who owned part of the Church Tract here. [Allegany:297; Minard:516; WPANYA]

Shrub Oak. Westchester. Named for the trees; before 1829 it was called Scrub Oak. [Lederer:131]

Shushan. Washington. When petitioning for a post office, the community asked to be called South Salem for its location in the town. The post office department refused to have any more Salems and named the post office for a place mentioned in the Bible. [APN:442; Gannett:239; Johnson:147]

Sidney, Sidney Center, East Sidney. Delaware. When the town was organized in 1801, the name was suggested by an English schoolmaster, John Mandeville, for Sir Sidney Smith, the British admiral who had successfully dealt with Napoleon in Syria at about that time. The place had been called Susquehanna Flats for its location on the river banks. [French:264; Gannett:239; Murray:528]

Siloam. Madison. The place was previously called Ellinwood Hollow. Elder Beman set up the sulphur springs here as a place of healing and named the settlement for the fountain and pool in Jerusalem responsible for the miracle of the blind man. The Hebrew word means "sending forth." [APN:444; Smith-C&M:692]

Silver Bay. Warren. This was a summer colony that grew into a village, named for the color of the water of Lake George at this point. [WPAW:169]

Silver Creek. Chautauqua. The village was named for a creek, the Native American name of which was Gaanundata, meaning "a leveled hill." [DA&H:195; McMahon:314; Morgan:463; Parker:293; WPANY:438]

Silver Lake. Wyoming. Named for the lake, the Native American name of which was Ganayat. The meaning of this name is lost. [Morgan:467]

Silver Springs. Wyoming. The village was named for the clear spring located here. [WPANYS]

Sinclairville. Chautauqua. Major Samuel Sinclear was a soldier in the Revolution who settled here in 1810. The place was first called Sinclearville. [D&H:125, 130; French:211; Gannett:239; McMahon:316]

Skaneateles, Skaneateles Falls. Onondaga. The town was formed in 1830 and named for the lake, whose Native American name means "very long lake," which it is. The village was started in about 1800, the post office was opened in 1804, and the village was incorporated in 1833. [APN:446; Bruce:985, 999; Clark-O:305; Clayton:288, 290; French:487; Gannett:240]

Slate Hill. Orange. This was first called Brookfield, for its location near a brook, but the name of the post office and the railroad station was Slate Hill for its geographic location. [R&C:684; WPANYS]

Slaterville Springs. Tompkins. Named for Levi Slater who was the first teacher here in 1801. Because many of the early settlers were Dutch, the place was first known as Dutch Settlement to distinguish it from Yankee Settlement (Caroline) just down the turnpike. When the post office opened in 1823, it was called Slaterville, but then came the discovery of the Magnetic Mineral Springs. This water cure brought people and prosperity to the area, and the post office name was changed to Slaterville Springs in 1890. [Norris:15; P&H-T:136; Selkreg:273]

Sleepy Hollow. Westchester. This had been called Beekmantown until 1874 when it was incorporated using the name with which the post office was established in 1871, North Tarrytown, for its location north of Tarrytown. North Tarrytown changed its name to Sleepy Hollow in the 1990s for the location of the Washington Irving story in which the headless horseman threw his head at Ichabod Crane. Residents wanted to detach themselves from Tarrytown and to have an identity of their own. [French:702; Lederer:16, 103, 132; WPANY:583]

Slingerlands. Albany. Locally, the place was known as Red Hook, but when the post office was established in 1852, it was named Normanskill for a nearby stream. William H. Slingerland was the postmaster at the time, a member of a family that settled here early. In 1870, the name was changed to honor the Slingerland family. [Albany:492; Howell:781; WPANYS]

Sloansville. Schoharie. John R. Sloan was an early settler who bought land here in 1800. [French:605; Gannett:241; Roscoe:329; WPANYA]

Sloatsburg. Rockland. Jacob Sloat built a cotton mill here in about 1815. The Native American name for the place had been Pothat or Pothod, but the town took the name of the Sloat family. The post office was opened in 1848. [Be-dell:241; Cole:272; Green:324, 397; WPANY:384]

Smartville. Oswego. William Smart ran a store and a sawmill here. The post office was opened in 1893. [Churchill:487]

Smithboro. Tioga. Ezra Smith settled here in 1791 on land that he owned. [Gay:488]

Smithtown. Suffolk. The town was organized in 1677 and recognized in 1788. Richard Smith of Rhode Island was an early proprietor of the place. The settlement used to be called Head of the River, for its location on the Nesse-quague River. So many early settlers here were named Smith that it became habit to call people by their occupation or father's name or other attribute, so John Smith became Honest John, and John Smith the blacksmith became John Blacksmith. Edmund Smith, son of Thomas, became Ed Tom, and so on. [French:637; Gannett:241; Suffolk/Smithtown:1]

Smithville. Jefferson. Jesse Smith was a founder and prominent citizen of the community in the early 1800s. [D&P:248; Hough-J:75; WPANYA]

Smithville Flats. Chenango. The settlement is in the town of Smithville, named for Elisha Smith, the agent of the Hornby tract. The settlement was first called Big Flats for the wide valley of the Genegantslet River in which it sits. It took its name from the town, which was formed in 1808. [French:230; Smith-C&M:293, 299; WPANYS]

Smyrna. Chenango. The town was formed in March of 1808 and named Stafford. A month later, its name was changed to Smyrna, the name of the principal village in the town, which had been named for the ancient city in Syria. [APN:450; French:230; Gannett:241; Smith-C&M:468; WPANYS]

Snyder. Erie. Michael Snyder was a merchant here starting in the 1830s. The community was first called Snyderville. [Smith-E:406]

Sodom. Warren. The place was named for the biblical city by early Puritan settlers as a warning to their younger generations in an attempt to keep them from committing sins. [APN:452; WPAW:193]

Sodus, Sodus Center, Sodus Point, South Sodus. Wayne. The name of the town, formed in 1789, and the villages and the bay on Lake Ontario came from a Native American word, *assorodus,* meaning "silvery water" or from *asaredos* or *seodos,* meaning "knife." [APN:452; Cowles:197; French:693; Gannett:242; Morgan:469; Parker:315]

Solon. Cortland. The town was formed in 1798 and named for the Athenian statesman. [French:254; Gannett:242; Goodwin:177]

Solsville. Madison. Solomon Alcott was an early settler here. [Smith-C&M:622]

Solvay. Onondaga. The Solvay Processing Company established here used a chemical process developed by Ernest Solvay, a Belgian chemist, to make ammonia, soda ash, and other products, including Arm and Hammer soda. A village grew around this industry. [APN:453; Bruce:864–65; Gannett:242; WPANY:329, 470]

Somers. Westchester. In 1788, the town was formed as Stephentown for Stephen Van Cortlandt. Its name was changed in 1808 for Captain Richard Somers, a naval hero of the Tripolitan War. It was the birthplace of the American circus. [French:705; Gannett:242; Lederer:134; WPANY:546–7]

Somerset. Niagara. The town was named for the county in England. The settlement was first called Somerset Corners, but the post office was Somerset so the settlement lost the Corners to match the post office. [APN:453; Pool:317; Williams:386]

Somerville. St. Lawrence. Named for John Somerville and family. The post office was established in 1828. [Curtis:593; Harder:222; Hough-SLF:455]

Sonora. Steuben. Probably named for the Mexican state. [APN:453]

Sonyea. Livingston. This name came from a Native American word, either the name of Captain Snow, Sonyeawa, or a word meaning "burning spring" or "hot valley." [APN:453; Parker:304; WPANYA]

South Bay. Madison. Named for its location on the south shore of Oneida Lake. [Smith-C&M:731]

South Beach. Richmond. This is where the Dutch village Oude Dorp, meaning "old town," had been. It became a popular beach resort from the 1880s to the 1920s. [Jackson:1098]

Southfields. Orange. The Southfields Iron Works were established in the south part of the town of Tuxedo in about 1805. [French:508; R&C:795]

South Hill. Tompkins. This is a hill south of the city of Ithaca. It, or parts of it, has had a variety of names in the past: Prospect Hill, Brewery Hill, Bowery Hill, Michigan Hill, and Goat Hill. [Norris:8]

Southold. Suffolk. The town was named for Southold, England, when it was first incorporated by patent in 1676. The settlement location was called Yennecock by the Native Americans. [Bayles:361–2; WPANYS]

Southport. Chemung. The town was organized in 1822 and named for its location on the Chemung River. [French:221; P&H-C:247; WPANYS]

South Valley. Otsego. Named for its geographic location. [French:537; WPANYS]

Spafford. Onondaga. The town was formed in 1811 and named for Horatio Gates Spafford, who wrote the first *New York State Gazetteer*. The hamlet had been called Spafford Corners. [Bruce:909–10; Clark-O:348; Clayton:344, 346; French:487; Gannett:242]

Sparkill. Rockland. Named for the stream, a Dutch name meaning "spruce stream." [APN:459]

Sparrow Bush. Orange. This place had been called Honesville and had a post office established under that name in 1827. It closed in 1844. Then in 1850 it was reestablished as Sparrowbush, although why is not recorded. [French:506; R&C:714]

Speculator. Hamilton. In 1844, the place was called Lake Pleasant. In 1863, Joel Newton came in with the idea of developing the area. He built a sawmill and got a post office opened, named Newton's Corners. This name lasted until 1896 when the residents decided that it was too rural a name and changed it for the view from the mountain overlooking Lake Pleasant. [A&K:650–7]

Speedsville. Tompkins. The village was first called Jenksville for Laban Jenks, an early settler. It was renamed for John J. Speed, who had settled here with his brother William on the new Catskill Turnpike. They opened a store and in 1806 were granted a post office that was called Speedsville. [Norris:15; P&H-T:139; Selkreg:290]

Speigletown. Rensselaer. The Van der Speigel family were early residents here. The community was first called Dort. [Weise:39]

Spencer. Tioga. The town was formed in 1806 and named for Judge Ambrose Spencer, who later became chief justice of the New York Supreme Court. [French:652; Gay:439; P&H-Ti:197; WPANYS]

Spencerport. Monroe. Daniel Spencer bought 100 acres here in 1804. When the Erie Canal came through in the 1820s, it was known as Spencer's Basin, then as Spencerport. [French:400; Gannett:243; Mc-M:182; Peck:325]

Spencertown. Columbia. Named for the Spencer family, early settlers. [Ellis-C:381; French:243; WPANYA]

Speonk. Suffolk. This name seems to be a remnant of an unknown Algonquian word. [APN:455]

Split Rock. Onondaga. Named for the nearly perpendicular cliff of about 150 feet high. There was a quarry here that supplied the Solvay Processing Company with raw materials. During World War I, the site of the quarry was used to produce munitions. In July 1918, a fire produced an explosion still remembered today. [Bruce:864; Clark-O:137; French:485]

Spragueville. St. Lawrence. Samuel B. Sprague was an early settler here. It was first called Sprague's Corners, then Shingle Creek, then Keenesville, for Hiram Keene. That name was too close to Keeseville, another town, so it was changed to Spragueville. [Harder:225]

Sprakers. Montgomery. The Spraker family owned land and a tavern here, and, at the completion of the Erie Canal, they owned a store and a warehouse, too. The place was then known as Spraker's Basin. [Frothingham:340; Montgomery:164]

Spring Brook. Erie. This place is on Cazenove Creek; the post office was opened in 1850. [French:290; Smith-E:493]

Springfield Center, East Springfield. Otsego. Named either for the city in Massachusetts or for a large spring in the town of Springfield, which was formed in 1797. [French:537; WPANYS]

Spring Lake. Cayuga. The community was originally known as Pineville for the pine forests that covered the area. The name was changed in 1874 for the nearby lake when the post office was established. [Storke:284–5]

Springtown. Ulster. The post office here was established in the 1870s. [Syl-U:13–14]

Spring Valley. Rockland. This village had been known as Pot Cheese Hollow and as Pascack. When the railroad built a station here, it was named by Samuel Coe Springsteel either for himself or for the springs in the area. The post office was established in 1848. [Bedell:308; Cole:281; Green:405]

Springville. Erie. This place was known as Fiddler's Green. A fiddler, David Leroy, and others would meet here and play popular tunes. The village is on a stream that runs into Cattaraugus Creek. [French:289; Smith-E:630; WPANY:688]

Springwater. Livingston. When the town was formed in 1816, it was named for the numerous springs in the area. The settlement was first called Knowlesville for Seth Knowles, who came here in 1806. [Doty-L:667; French:386; WPA-NYA]

Sprout Brook. Montgomery. Named for the stream. [Frothingham:250; Montgomery:98]

Spuyten Duyvil. Bronx. This settlement was named for the creek, which was named from the Dutch phrase meaning "in spite of the Devil," in about 1647, evoked for the strong currents through which sailors passed. Washington Irving wrote an elaborate story of a revolutionary who met Satan crossing the flooded creek, which he was going to cross in spite of the Devil, on his way to warn the citizens with blasts of his trumpet of the British arrival. He drowned but his trumpet can be heard to this day. [French:708; Gannett:243; Jackson:1108; WPANY:622–3]

Staatsburg. Dutchess. The Staats family is said to have settled here in about 1715; the place was then called Staatsboro. But it could also be the transformation of the Dutch and German words for "city" into a proper name. [Smith-D:308; WPANYD:103]

Stacy Basin. Oneida. This was a stop on the Erie Canal that was enlarged and straightened in the 1860s. It was probably named for a local resident. [Oneida:201]

Stafford. Genesee. The town was formed in 1820. The village was known as Transit until 1841. [Beers:638; French:327; North:497]

Stamford. Delaware. Because most of the settlers here had come from near Stamford, Connecticut, the town was first named New Stamford when it was organized in 1792. [French:264; Murray:547–8]

Standish. Clinton. Named for the family of early settlers. [Hurd-C&F:172–3]

Stanley. Ontario. Seth Stanley was an early settler here. The village was first known as Stanleys Corners. [French:498–9; Milliken:109]

Stannards. Allegany. John Stannard kept the first hotel here, and the name of the place at that time was Stannard's Corners. [Allegany:343; Minard:542; WPA-NYA]

Stark. St. Lawrence. The Stark family were early settlers here. [Harder:227]

Starkey. Yates. When the town was formed, in 1824, it was named for John Starkey, a prominent citizen. [Cleveland:892; French:721]

Starkville. Herkimer. The town of Stark was named for General John Stark of the Revolutionary War when it was formed in 1828. The village took its name from the town. [French:348; Gannett:244; Herkimer:117]

Star Lake. St. Lawrence. Named for the lake, which was named in 1880 for its shape. [Harder:227]

State Bridge. Oneida. This was the site of a state-built bridge over the Erie Canal. [Oneida:201]

State Line. Chautauqua. This place is on the boundary between New York and Pennsylvania. [APN:459; French:215]

Staten Island. Richmond. Henry Hudson named this island, which became Richmond County, for his sponsor, the states-general of the Netherlands. Or it may have been named for the home of Charles II's brother, James, in York-shire. The Native American name was Matanucke or Monocknong. [APN:459; French:563; Jackson:1113; WPANYC:598]

Steamburg. Cattaraugus. Named for the number of steam works and mills that were operating here at one time. The post office was established in 1861. [Ellis:421; WPANYS]

Stella Niagara. Niagara. The "star of the Niagara" is on the Niagara River. [WPA-NYS]

Stephentown, Stephentown Center, West Stephentown. Rensselaer. The town was named for Stephen Van Rensselaer, patroon of the manor, when it was formed in 1784. Stephentown Center used to be called Mechanicville. The post office was established in 1878. The post office in the village of Stephentown was opened in 1804. [French:559; Gannett:244; Weise:130, 133]

Sterling, Sterling Valley. Cayuga. The town was formed in 1812 and named for William Alexander, Lord Sterling, a general during the American Revolution. The settlement of Sterling was first known as Sterling Center, two miles north of Sterling Junction, which became Sterling Station. Sterling Valley was earlier called Coopers Mills for settler John Cooper, who built saw—and gristmills there. Both mills later burned down. [French:205; Storke:36, 252, 258, 260]

Sterling Forest. Orange. Named for General William Alexander, Lord Sterling, and for its geographic location. [French:510; WPANYS]

Stewart Manor. Nassau. Alexander Turney Stewart bought land here in 1869. His heirs held the land until it was sold in the early 1900s to developer William M. Brown, who named it in 1907. [Winsche:95; WPANYS]

Stillwater. Chautauqua. Named for Stillwater Creek, a descriptive name. [APN:460; French:214]

Stillwater. Saratoga. The water of the Hudson River is very calm here. [French:592; Syl-S:286]

Stissing. Dutchess. This place was previously called Stissingville for the mountain and the lake nearby. [French:277; Smith-D:292; WPANYD:96]

Stittville. Oneida. A sawmill was built here in 1778 when the place was known as Red Mills. In 1828, Robert Stitt came here, built the first store and hotel, and the place became known as Stittsville. Eventually the name lost the middle *S*. The post office opened in 1849. [French:468; Oneida:165]

Stockbridge. Madison. The town was formed in 1836 and named for the Stockbridge Indians, who had lived here until 1824. The hamlet was originally known as Knoxville for Henry Knox, an early settler and first merchant. [French:393; Smith-C&M:705, 707, 712]

Stockholm Center, North Stockholm, West Stockholm. St. Lawrence. The town was named for the city in Sweden by the original surveyors. It was formed in 1806. The settlements took their names from their geographic locations within the town. [French:583; Curtis:518; Harder:230]

Stockport. Columbia. James Wild was a prominent citizen here who had come from Stockport, England. The town was formed in 1833 and the community was a center of fabric manufacturing until 1837. [Ellis-C:347, 350; French:248; Gannett:245; WPANYA]

Stockton, South Stockton. Chautauqua. The community was formerly known as Delanti, but the name was changed in 1833 for Richard Stockton, a signer of the Declaration of Independence. [D&H:235, 239; French:216; McMahon:317]

Stokes. Oneida. First called Nisbets Corners for Robert Nisbets, a dairy farmer in the early 1800s. Then it became Lee Corners. Finally, Charles Stokes became the first postmaster. [French:465; Oneida:160]

Stone Arabia. Montgomery. The town of Palatine was first called Stone Arabia when it was formed in 1772. The name comes from the German *die steine Rübe*, meaning "stone turnips," a joking reference to the rocks in the fields. [APN:461; Anderson; French:416]

Stone Mills. Jefferson. The place was first called Collins Mills, for John B. Collins. He and Peter Pratt built a stone gristmill in about 1820, which gave the place its present name. [D&P:457; French:360; Hough-J:214]

Stone Ridge. Ulster. Named for the mountain. [French:664]

Stony Brook. Suffolk. This place took its name from the descriptive name of the local stream. The Native American name for this location was Wopowag. [Bayles:234; French:633; Suffolk/Brookhaven:42; WPANYS]

Stony Creek. Warren. The community had been called Creek Center and Stony Creek Center and was settled in about 1795. It was named for the town, which was named for the stream that flows through it, when it was formed in 1852. [French:675–6; WPANYS; WPAW:174]

Stony Hollow. Ulster. This was a station name on the Ulster and Delaware Railroad. [Syl-U:286]

Stony Point. Rockland. The town was formed in 1865 and named for the rocky bluff on the Hudson River where Anthony Wayne took a fort back from the British during the Revolutionary War. The settlement was called North Haverstraw until the town was formed. Then it was called Florus Falls, for Florus Crom who owned much of the land here. In 1870, the settlement took the name of the town. [Bedell:106, 199–200; Green:430, 433; WPANY:604–5]

Stormville. Dutchess. The Storm family, Thomas and Isaac with their families, settled here in the 1730s. [French:271; Smith-D:538; WPANYD:116]

Stottville. Columbia. Before Jonathan Stott settled here in 1828 and ran Stotts Woolen Mills, the settlement was called Springville. His extensive mills produced flannel and were the main industry here. At one time, the name was spelled Stottsville. [Ellis-C:349; French:248; WPANYA]

Stow. Chautauqua. Named for the town in England. [APN:462]

Stratford. Fulton. Early settlers came here from Stratford, Connecticut, and had the post office named for their former home. The hamlet had been called Nicholsville, but that changed to match the post office. [French:319; Fulton:241; WPANYA]

Strathmore. Nassau. Named for the place in Scotland. [APN:462]

Strykersville. Wyoming. General Stryker bought the land here, with William Richardson and Philo Stevens, in 1808. [Wyoming:266]

Stuyvesant, Stuyvesant Falls. Columbia. The town was formed in 1823 and named for Governor Peter Stuyvesant. Stuyvesant Falls was on both sides of Kinderhook Creek where there were waterfalls that provided water power. [Ellis-C:355, 357–8; French:248; Gannett:246]

Suffern. Rockland. John Suffern came here when the place was called the Point of the Mountains. He called it New Antrim for Antrim, Ireland, his former home. In 1896, the village was named for him. [Bedell:312–3; Cole:277; Gannett:247; WPANYS]

Sugar Loaf. Orange. This settlement was named Sugar Loaf after the large, bald mountain behind it, which resembled a colonial sugar loaf. Sugar used to come in rounded conical blocks, about five inches in diameter. This "loaf" was placed on the table and bits would be taken from it with spoons. [APN:464; R&C:617; WPANYS]

Sullivan. Madison. The town was formed in 1803 and named for General John Sullivan, the exterminator of the Iroquois in this area. [French:393; Smith-C&M:738; WPANYS]

Summer Hill. Cayuga. The birthplace of Millard Fillmore, the thirteenth president of the United States, was first called Plato when it divided from the town of Locke. It changed its name in 1832, maybe for its location high on the hills in the southeast part of the county. In the winters, this area is treacherous with blowing and drifting snow. [French:205; Storke:513]

Summit. Schoharie. The town was formed in 1819 and named for its 2,100-foot elevation. [French:607; Noyes:154; Roscoe:153; Sias:151]

Summitville. Sullivan. Named for its geographic location. [Child:175; WPANYS]

Sundown. Ulster. This place had been called Sundown Valley for its beautiful view. [Syl-U:331]

Sunnyside. Queens. This place took the name of a tavern here that served patrons of the Fashion Race Course in Corona in the 1850s and 1860s. [Jackson:1143]

Sunnyside. Richmond. Named for the boarding house here in 1889 that was called Sunnyside. [Jackson:1143]

Swain. Allegany. Samuel Swain settled in the county in about 1818, then moved to this place in 1849. It was known as Swainsville and as Swain's Station. [Allegany:302; French:174; Minard:537; WPANYA]

Swan Lake. Sullivan. This place used to be called Stevensville, and the lake was then called Stevensville Pond. [Child:160]

Swartwood. Chemung. Named for the Swartwood family. [P&H-C:282–3]

Swastika. Clinton. The word is the name for an old good luck symbol. [APN:468; WPANYS]

Sylvan Beach. Oneida. This resort village on the shores of Oneida Lake took its name from the peace of the nearby forested area. [APN:469; Oneida:209; WPANYS]

Syosset. Nassau. In 1821, the town was called Little East Woods. By 1831, this name was abandoned. In 1846, it became known as Syosset, either a Native American word, "settlement on the bay protected by islands," or from the Dutch word *schouts,* sheriff, with the spelling going from Schout to Siocits to Syocits. [APN:469; French:550; Winsche:96; WPANYA]

Syracuse, East Syracuse, North Syracuse. Onondaga. The city of Syracuse has gone through a number of names, starting with Bogardus Corners, 1806–1809; Milan, 1809–12; South Salina, 1812–14; Cossitts Corners for

Sterling Cossitt, 1814–17; Corinth, 1817–20; and finally Syracuse, suggested by John Wilkinson, the first postmaster, who had read of the Sicilian city and thought that the site here, near a marsh and salt springs, resembled that city's location. He was also influenced by the fashion for classical names. The village of East Syracuse grew up around the railroad yards that the New York Central and Hudson River Railroad put up east of the city in 1872. North Syracuse was named for its location. [APN:469; Bruce:86, 89, 401–4; Clark-O:87; Clayton:391; French:488; Gannett:249; WPANY:331]

T

Trumansburg © *2004 by Jon Crispin*

Taberg. Oneida. The Oneida Glass and Iron Manufacturing Company started here in 1809. A blast furnace was built in 1811, and the place was named for the iron mining town in Sweden. The post office was established in 1815. [French:461–2; Oneida:115; WPANYA]

Taborton. Rensselaer. Gershorn Tabor was an early resident here. [Weise:123]

Taghkanic, East Taghkanic, West Taghkanic. Columbia. The town was formed in 1803 as Granger. The name was changed in 1814 for the Native American word meaning "there is enough water." West Taghkanic was first called Millers Corners for Jacob Miller, the first merchant in about 1800. Then it became Lapham's for Jonathan Lapham who opened another store in about 1808. [Ellis-C:397, 399; French:249; Gannett:249]

Tahawus. Essex. Named for the Native American name of Mt. Marcy, "he splits the sky." [WPANY:495]

Talcottville. Lewis. The Leyden post office was here. There is no record of its name origin, but it is likely to have been named for an early settler. [French:377; Hough-L:131]

Talcville. St. Lawrence. Alfred Freeman had built a blast furnace and a forge here, so the place was called Freemansburgh. Then in the 1870s, talc deposits were found here and a talc mill settlement was established. [Harder:234]

Tannersville. Greene. Colonel William W. Edwards and his son came from Northampton, Massachusetts, to establish the first extensive tannery in the state here. Other tanneries were built and the post office took its name from the industry, which produced a good deal of leather for many years until the supply of hemlock bark, an important source of vegetable tannin, was exhausted. [French:333; Vedder:95]

Tappan. Rockland. The name of this place came from the Native American word *thuphane,* meaning "cold stream." [APN:474; Cole:227; French:570; Gannett:250; Green:331]

Tarrytown. Westchester. When the Dutch lived here, the place was called Tarwe Dorp, meaning "wheat town," for the quantities of the grain that were grown here. The Native Americans had called the place Alipcock, meaning "the place of elms." [Bolton(1):294; French:700; Gannett:250; Lederer:141; WPANY:584]

Taylor. Cortland. The town was formed in 1849 and named for General Zachary Taylor, who then became the twelfth president of the United States. The settlement had been called Taylorville or Bangall with the Taylor post office. [French:254; Gannett:250; Goodwin:260]

Texas. Oswego. George Scriba started a village here in the town of Mexico at the mouth of Little Sandy Creek on the Lake Ontario shore that he called Vera Cruz, for the city in the country of Mexico. The settlement was destroyed by fire in 1820. Soon after, S. P. Robinson built a boatyard, then a paper mill and a store. When the post office was established, it was named Texas. [APN:510; Churchill:576, 598; French:520, 523; Johnson-O:263, 265]

Thayer Corners. Franklin. L. K. Thayer was the postmaster here in the late 1800s. [Hurd-C&F:453]

Thendara. Herkimer. There is no record of name origin, although one theory is that it is a mishearing of *kendaia,* an Iroquoian word for "open country" or "clearing." [APN:236, 480; WPANYS]

Theresa. Jefferson. The town was formed in 1841 and named for a daughter of James LeRay de Chaumont. She married the Marquis de Gouvello and moved to France with him. [D&P:512; French:361; Gannett:252; Hough-J:243]

Thiells. Rockland. Jacob Thiells operated a forge here during the Revolutionary War on 3,000 acres that he had bought. The place was first called Thiells Corners. [Bedell:264, 266; Freen:385]

Thompson Ridge. Orange. Many members of the Thompson family lived here. [R&C:419]

Thompsonville. Sullivan. When the town of Thompson was formed in 1803, it was named for William Thompson, the first judge in the county. The settlement was also named for him. He had settled here early, built the first mill and factory, and was instrumental in establishing the first permanent settlement in the town. [French:647; Child:196-D, 196-I; Quinlan:515]

Thomson. Washington. There is no record of this place's name origin, although it was probably named for a family living in the area. [WPANYS]

Thornwood. Westchester. This place between Hawthorne and Pleasantville has been called Thornwood since 1914. The origin is uncertain, but might be related to Hawthorne. [Lederer:142]

Three Mile Bay. Jefferson. The bay was named for its distance from the village of Chaumont. The settlement took the name of the bay. [D&P:453; French:359; Hough-J:204; WPANYA]

Three Rivers. Onondaga. Named for the location where the Oneida River meets the Seneca River to form the Oswego River. The place was earlier called Three River Point. [Bruce:825; French:481; WPANY:647]

Throgs Neck. Bronx. The Dutch called this peninsula Vriedelandt, but it eventually got its name from John Throckmorton, who settled here in 1642. [French:706; Gannett:252; Jackson:1180; WPANYC:546]

Throopsville. Cayuga. Enos T. Throop, a former governor of New York State, moved to the Auburn area where he served as a judge of the seventh circuit. He had a large farm named Willow Brook near Owasco Lake to which he returned when he retired. The hamlet was named in his honor, as was the town of Throop when it was formed in 1859. [French:206; Storke:334, 336–7]

Thurman, Thurman Station. Warren. The settlement was known early as Kenyontown and was settled about 1800. The name was changed to match that of the town, which was named when it was formed in 1792 for John Thurman, who was an early landowner of this territory. It is said that he would travel to New York City with beechnuts or hazelnuts in his pockets that he would show off as samples of the buckwheat or wheat that grew on his lands along the Upper Hudson River. [French:676; Gannett:232; WPANYS; WPAW:106, 176, 193]

Thurston. Steuben. William B. Thurston was a principal landowner here. Before the settlement was named for him, it had been called Merchantville. [French:627; Roberts:490, 493; Steuben:153]

Ticonderoga. Essex. The town was formed in 1804 and named for the Native American word *cheonderoga*, meaning "between two waters" or "sounding waters," referring to the noise of the rapids at the outlet of Lake George. The village had been called Lower Falls for the same rapids. [APN:482; French:304; Gannett:253; WPANY:538]

Tioga Center. Tioga. The town, the village, and the county took the Native American name of the place, which meant "at the forks" or "the meeting of the waters" or "the point of land at the confluence of two streams." [APN:484; Gannett:253; P&H-Ti:33]

Tivoli. Dutchess. A Frenchman, Delabegarre, settled here after the Revolutionary War and built a house that he called Le Chateau de Tivoli, which may have been named for the Italian city. [APN:485; Gannett:254; Smith-D:188; WPANYD:108]

Tomhannock. Rensselaer. This place was on Otter Creek, a tributary of Tomhannock Creek, named for an Algonquian term meaning "overflowed." It was early known as Reed's Corners, but when the post office was established, it took the name of the creek. [APN:488; French:558; Weise:95]

Tompkins Corners. Putnam. Cornelius Tompkins and his brothers settled here in about 1777. [French:543; Pelletreau:718; WPANYS]

Tomkins Cove. Rockland. Daniel and Calvin Tompkins bought land here and developed limestone quarries, run by C. Tompkins and Co., in the 1840s. [Bedell:321; French:570]

Tonawanda. Erie; **North Tonawanda.** Niagara. The town of Tonawanda was formed in 1836 and named for the creek, the name of which is an Iroquois word meaning "swift water." The city is on the Erie Canal at the confluence of the Niagara River and the creek from which it took its name. North Tonawanda is on the opposite, north, bank of the Erie Canal. [APN:488; French:293; Gannett:254; Smith-E:416; WPANY:683]

Tottenville. Richmond. This place had been called Totten's Landing, Bentley Dock, Unionville, Mount Hermon, Arensville, and the Neck. Eventually, it was named for the Totten family. [Gannett:255; French:567; Jackson:1192; WPANYC:614]

Towners. Putnam. This settlement was first called Four Corners for the intersection of two roads here. James Towner lived here and kept a tavern. When the Harlem Railroad came through, it called its depot Towner's Station. [Blake:342; Pelletreau:646]

Town Line. Erie. This community is on the line between the towns of Alden and Lancaster. [Smith-E:447, 464]

Townsend. Schuyler. Claudius Townsend bought the land on which this place was located. He was the first postmaster in 1826. [P&H-S:107; WPANYA]

Tracy Creek. Broome. Named for the creek, which was probably named for an early family that lived near it. [Smith-B:474]

Travis. Richmond. This was first called Jersey Wharf, then New Blazing Star during the American Revolution. In the early 1800s, it was called Travisville for Captain Jacob Travis, who owned land here. During the Civil War, it was called Long Neck for its shape, then Deckertown for a local family. In the 1880s, it was known as Linoleumville for a successful linoleum factory here. In 1931, after the linoleum factory was sold, the name was changed to Travis by a vote of the residents. [French:566; Jackson:1198; WPANYC:622]

Treadwell. Delaware. Minor Treadwell was an early tavernkeeper in the area. It had previously been called Jug City and Croton. [WPANYS]

Triangle. Broome. The town is shaped like a triangle, lying between the Chenango and Tioughnioga Rivers and south of the Military Tract. The hamlet took its name from the town. [French:183; Smith-B:341]

Tribes Hill. Montgomery. This was an assembly point for Native Americans when white settlers first came in about 1725. [French:412; Frothingham:277; Montgomery:87]

Troupsburg. Steuben. The place was named for Robert Troup, a general agent of the Pulteney Estate. During the anti-rent conflict, he was very unpopular for his methods of dealing with the citizens, and had the place been named in the 1830s instead of 1808, it would not have been named for him. [French:628; Roberts:493; Steuben:156]

Trout Creek. Delaware. John Teed and his brother settled here in 1810, giving the place the name Teedville. However, when the post office was established, it was named Trout Creek for the stream in which the fish were plentiful. [Delaware:312; WPANYS]

Trout River. Franklin. Named for the river. [Hurd-C&F:472]

Troy. Rensselaer. The land here was owned by Jacob D. Venderheyden who was persuaded to lay out building lots in 1787. He insisted that the village be named for him, but it was locally known as Ferry Hook for the ferry across the Hudson or Ashley's Ferry for Captain Stephen Ashley. The name Troy, for the ancient city, was adopted in 1789, the beginning of classical naming in New York State. The post office was established in 1796. [APN:495; French:561; Gannett:256; Weise:15–17; WPANY:344]

Trumansburg. Tompkins. The village was named for Abner Treman or Tremaine, a member of the first family of settlers. It has been called Tremansburg, Tremansville, Tremans' Mill, and Tremain Village. [French:658; Gannett:256; Norris:49; Selkreg:217]

Trumbull Corners. Tompkins. Named for Jacob and James Trumbull, who moved here in 1813. The first post office was called North Newfield in 1846 but was changed to Trumbull's Corners in 1847. The village was also sometimes known as Rumsey Corners. [Norris:46; P&H-T:253; Selkreg:305, 308]

Truxton. Cortland. The town was formed in 1808 and named for a Naval hero, Commodore Thomas Truxtun, also spelled Truxton. [French:255; Gannett:256; Goodwin:207]

Tuckahoe. Suffolk; **Tuckahoe.** Westchester. This name came from the Native American word for "place of the *tuckah*," an aquatic plant that used to be roasted and ground into flour. [APN:496; Lederer:146]

Tully. Onondaga. The town was formed in 1803 and named as part of the classical naming of 1790 for Marcus Tullius Cicero, the Roman orator. The post office was opened in 1815. [APN:497; Bruce:892, 896; Clark-O:335, 338; Clayton:355; French:489; Gannett:256]

Tupper Lake. Franklin. Tupper was one of the surveyors of the Macomb Purchase here in 1800. [Hurd-C&F:498]

Turin. Lewis. The village had been called Turin Four Corners and was named for the city in Italy. [APN:498; Gannett:257; Hough-L:207, 214]

Turnwood. Ulster. The post office was established here in 1859. [Syl-U:328]

Tuscarora. Livingston. The village was named for the Dusgaoweh Indians, a tribe of the Six Nations, whose name meant "shirt-wearing people." [Gannett:257; Parker:305; WPANYS]

Tusten. Sullivan. The town was named for Colonel Benjamin Tusten when it was formed in 1853. He was killed in the Battle of Minisink in 1779. [Child:196-P; French:647–8; Gannett:257; Quinlan:638]

Tuxedo Park. Orange. The Native American name for this place was P'taukseet-tough, "place of bears" or "place of wolves." The land was owned in the 1880s by Pierre Lorillard IV, who decided that his 13,000 acres should house the important millionaires of the early twentieth century. The land was sold in large tracts on which large mansions were built. The name of the formal jacket comes from this select group of landowners. [APN:500; Gannett:257; WPANY:385]

Tyre. Seneca. The town was formed in 1829 and was named by the state land commissioners for the ancient Mediterranean city. [APN:501; French:617; Seneca:124]

Tyrone. Schuyler. The town was named by its first supervisor, General William Kernan, when it was formed in 1822, for the county in Ireland. [APN:501; French:612; P&H-S:219]

U

Utica © *2004 by Jon Crispin*

Ulster Heights, Ulster Park, Ulsterville. Ulster. The county and the settlement were named for the Irish title of the Duke of York. Ulster Park was first known as Amesville, then as Norris' Corners. [French:660; Syl-U:116]

Unadilla, Unadilla Center, Unadilla Forks. Otsego; **South Unadilla.** Delaware. The town was formed in 1792, and it and the villages were named for the river, the name of which was a Native American word meaning "place of greeting." [APN:503; French:538; Gannett:258; WPANY:451; WPANYS]

Union Center. Broome. This place is located in the town of Union, which was named either as an expression of popular American sentiment in the 1770s or because it was here that Generals Sullivan and Clinton met in 1779, Sullivan coming up from Pennsylvania and Clinton coming down from the Mohawk Valley. [Smith-B:441; WPANY:387]

Uniondale. Nassau. In the 1650s, this place was called East Meadow for its location. In the 1770s, it became Turtle Hook, but by 1853 this was no longer acceptable, so the name was changed to Union Dale. Why that name was chosen is not recorded. The post office was opened in 1895. [Winsche:97]

Unionport. Bronx. This was an area of development on Westchester Creek with a neutral name. [French:706; Jackson:1210]

Union Springs. Cayuga. This village, on the eastern shore of Cayuga Lake, was named for the many natural springs in the area, two of which produce small ponds that freeze only in the coldest, most windy winters. The town was named Springport when it was formed in 1823. These springs provided water power for much industry, including sawmills, a planing mill, a tannery, and flour mills. [French:205; Storke:427]

Unionville. Albany. In 1860, the post office here was called Union Church, for the church in the area. Later, the name was changed. [Albany:552; French:164; Howell:902]

Unionville. Orange. This village, on the border of New York and New Jersey, took its name from the time, in 1740, when the boundary was being settled as a symbol of friendship between the two states. [R&C:665; WPANYS]

Unionville. St. Lawrence. The Union was formed when several farmers pooled their money and land in 1804. By 1807, it was called the Union Settlement and was an experiment in communal living headed by William Bullard. The experiment ended in 1810, but the village continued under its present name. [Harder:245; Hough-SLF:435]

University Gardens. Nassau. A development corporation proposed to create an expensive housing development here in 1926. It took its name from a proposed golf course, University Golf Club, that did not get off the ground before it was sold to the development corporation. [Winsche:98]

University Heights. Bronx. As part of Fordham Manor, this was called Fordham Heights. But in 1894, New York University moved here and the name was changed to reflect the new neighbor. [Jackson:1217; WPANYC:520]

Urbana. Steuben. When the town was organized in 1822, it needed a name. Elder Sanford was adamant that the place be named Jordan for the place in the Bible. However, the rest of the community decided that it should be named Urbana, from the Latin *urbanus,* meaning urbane in the old sense and therefore giving the place some sophistication. [APN:505; Roberts:525]

Utica. Oneida. The Native Americans called the locality Yanundadasis or Unundagages or Nundadasis, meaning "around the hill." Then, after an old stockade was razed, it was called Tevadahahtodague, "ruin of fort." The white settlement that grew up here was called Old Fort Schuyler, but in 1798 it was decided that the village needed a better name. After much unproductive discussion, names were drawn out of a hat and Utica was the first drawn. The name of the ancient port of Carthage had been suggested by Erastus Clark. [APN:505; French:468; Gannett:259; Morgan:472; Oneida:241–2; WPANY:354]

Utopia. Queens. In 1905, the Utopia Land Company proposed to build a development here. They never got enough funds to continue, but the name was used for the Utopia Parkway. Eventually, this place did become established. [Jackson:1219]

V

Virgil © *2004 by Jon Crispin*

Vail Mills. Fulton. William Vail came here in 1804 from Connecticut. A gristmill, a sawmill, and a planing mill were built. [Fulton:227]

Vails Gate. Orange. For many years, there had been efforts to changed the name of this place to Mortonville, but the name for a Mr. Vail, an old resident who was the keeper of the gate on the Blooming Grove turnpike, persisted. [R&C:221; WPANYS]

Valatie. Columbia. The name of this village comes from the Dutch for "little falls," for the fifteen-foot falls here on Kinderhook Creek. [Ellis-C:226; French:247; Gannett:259]

Valcour. Clinton. This place used to be called Port Jackson. It is on Lake Champlain, opposite Valcour Island, and took its name from the island, which was named by the French. [Hurd-C&F:346; WPANYS]

Valhalla. Westchester. The wife of the first postmaster was a Wagner fan and suggested that the place be named for the Germanic home of the gods. The Ken-

sico post office took this name in 1861, the railroad station in 1904.
[APN:518; Lederer:149]

Valley Cottage. Rockland. This community is said to be named for the nearest
house to the railroad station, when the railroad came through, "a cottage in
the valley." [WPANYA; WPANYS]

Valley Falls. Rensselaer. Named for its location on the Hoosick River. [Weise:95]

Valley Stream, North Valley Stream. Nassau. Robert Pagan came here from
Scotland in the early 1800s and named the place for the small streams that ran
through the area. [Winsche:100]

Valois. Schuyler. Named for a place in France. [WPANYA]

Van Etten. Chemung. Named for James B. Van Etten, who represented
Chemung County in the state legislature in 1852. [French:221; Gan-
nett:260; P&H-C:283]

Van Hornesville. Herkimer. Thomas VanHorn came here, in 1793, after the
Revolutionary War in which he had served as an orderly sergeant.
[Herkimer:119; WPANYS]

Van Nest. Bronx. Pieter Pietersen Van Neste settled here with his family in 1647.
In the 1870s, the area was developed by the Van Nest Improvement Company. [Jackson:1225]

Varna. Tompkins. No one really knows why this settlement was so named, but it
fits in with the classical naming of the Military Tract. In the nineteenth century, Varna was a Bulgarian city known for its port and its importance in the
Crimean and Russo-Turkish Wars. Its Greek name was Odysseus, and in the
1950s, its name was changed to Stalin. With the decline of Communist rule,
it returned to its former name. [APN:508; Norris:22]

Varysburg. Wyoming. William Vary bought 400 acres of land on which the hamlet was located. [French:715; Gannett:260; Wyoming:265]

Vega. Delaware. The village was formerly called Shackville. A nicer name was
needed and so it was named either for the Spanish word for meadow or for
the star. [APN:509; WPANYS]

Venice Center. Cayuga. The town of Venice was formed in 1823, named for the
city in Italy. The hamlet was named for its location in the town. [French:206;
Storke:432]

Verbank. Dutchess. This place may have been named for its green surroundings.
[WPANYD:144]

Vermontville. Franklin. Named by settlers from Vermont when they came here in
about 1848. [WPANYS]

Vernon. Oneida. The town was formed in 1802 and named for Washington's
home, Mount Vernon. The Virginia estate had been named for Admiral Edward Vernon by George's brother, Lawrence, who had served under Vernon.

The Native American name for the New York town was Skanusunk, "place of the fox," and for the village, Skunaudowa, "great hemlock." [APN:511; Gannett:260; Morgan:472; Oneida:197]

Verona. Oneida. The town was formed in 1802 and named for the city in Italy. The community was first called Hand's Village. The Native American name was Teonatale, "pine forest." [APN:511; Gannett:261; Morgan:473; Oneida:203]

Verplanck. Westchester. Philip Verplanck was an early landowner here. [Gannett:261; Lederer:150]

Versailles. Cattaraugus. Named for the palace in Paris when France was still popular for its aid in the American Revolution. The post office was established in about 1840. The Native American name for this place was Gustango, "among the rocks or cliffs." [APN:511; Ellis:243; Gannett:261; Parker:290]

Vesper. Onondaga. The post office was opened in 1827 and named for the Latin name of the evening star. [APN:511; Bruce:898; Clark-O:338]

Vestal, Vestal Center. Broome. The town and the villages were named for the Roman goddess of the hearth, whose name is associated with the vestal virgins, young women consecrated to the goddess, and therefore with pristine, virginal landscapes. The village of Vestal was previously called Crane's Ferry and Vestal Mills. [APN:511; WPANYS]

Victor. Ontario. In 1687, a Native American village, Gannagaro or Gaosagao, meaning "in the basswood country," was destroyed by the French. The town was formed in 1812; the village was incorporated in 1879. Both may have been named because in the battle between the French and the Native Americans, the French thought that they had won, although it turned out that there were many more Senecas in the region than the French had realized. However, a more plausible reason for the name, given the time difference between the battles and the formation of the town and village, is that they were named for Claudius Victor Boughton, the son of a prominent citizen, Hezekiah Boughton, whose last name a hill and at least two roads carry. [French:499; Gannett:261; Milliken:110; Morgan:469]

Victory, North Victory. Cayuga. As did the town of Conquest, Victory took its name from the successful division from the town of Cato in 1821. [French:206; Storke:36, 267]

Victory Mills. Saratoga. The Victory Manufacturing Company, extensive cotton mills in the nineteenth century, was instrumental in building up the village. The mills were closed in 1929 and the machinery was shipped to Alabama. [French:591; Syl-S:271; WPANY:625]

Vienna. Oneida. The town was formed in 1807 as Orange. The name was changed to Bengal in 1808, then Vienna in 1816, for the Austrian city. The settlement was first called Parker's Corners, then South Corners. Finally, it took the name of the town. [APN:512; French:470; Gannett:261; Oneida:205–6]

Village of the Branch. Suffolk. The village was named for its location on the northeast branch of the Nissiquogue River. It was incorporated in 1927. [WPANYS]

Vine Valley. Yates. Named for its geographic description. [Cleveland:587]

Virgil. Cortland. The town was formed in 1804 and named for the Roman poet Publius Vergilius Maro. [APN:513; French:255; Gannett:261; Goodwin:180; WPANYA]

Vischer Ferry. Saratoga. John E. Vischer ran a ferry on the Mohawk River here. [French:587; Syl-S:477; WPANYA]

Vista. Westchester. The post office was established here sometime before 1827 and was named for the view. [Lederer:151]

Volney. Oswego. The town was formed in 1806 as Fredericksburgh. The name was changed in 1811 for Count Volney, the French author, who visited the town in 1808 while on a tour of the United States. The village was sometimes called Volney Center. [Churchill:773, 817; French:528; Gannett:261; Johnson-O:225]

Voorheesville. Albany. Alonzo B. Voorhees built the first house in the village in 1862. The village was incorporated in 1899. [Albany:553; Howell:902; WPANYS]

W

Watkins Glen © *2004 by Jon Crispin*

Waddington. St. Lawrence. Joshua Waddington of New York was the proprietor here. The settlement was formerly called Hamilton, for Alexander Hamilton, but the name was changed in 1810, probably because there were other Hamiltons in the state. [French:579; Harder:248; Hough-SLF:342]

Wadhams. Essex. This was called Wadhams Mills, for the early settler who had started a milling industry here. [French:305; Smith-Ex:630]

Wading River. Suffolk. Named for the river, which the Native Americans called Pauquacunsuk. [Bayles:283; French:637; Suffolk/Riverhead:4]

Wadsworth. Livingston. Named for the Wadsworth family, who owned a good bit of land in the county. [Doty-L:522; WPANYS]

Wainscott. Suffolk. Named for Wainscott Pond, the name origin of which is not recorded. [Suffolk/Easthampton:22]

Walden. Orange. Jacob T. Walden was a former resident who was president of the company that bought the water power and a large tract of land. [R&C:385]

231

Wales Center, South Wales. Erie. The town of Wales was formed in 1818 and named for the country. The Wales Center post office was established in 1843 and named for its location in the town. This village had previously been called Hall's Hollow for Isaac and Levi Hall, who built a sawmill and a gristmill here in about 1812. [APN:518; Smith-E:565, 567]

Walker. Monroe. The place was first called North Clarkson, then East Hamlin for its location in the town. It was finally named for the pastor of the Freewill Baptist Church, Reverend William Walker. [WPANYA; WPANYS]

Walker Valley. Ulster. The post office here was earlier called Jamesburg. [Syl-U:165]

Wallington. Wayne. The first railroad station here was called Calciana, derived from a word for lime. The name Wellington came from an old stone tavern in the area. [Cowles:213]

Wallkill. Ulster. Named for the stream, which took its name from the Dutch. [APN:519]

Walloomsac. Rensselaer. This place was named for the river, which has been variously spelled as Wallomsock, Wallamsock, Wallomschock, Walmscock, and others. It came from the Algonquian word that means "the place of paint." [APN:519; French:555; Weise:88]

Walton. Delaware. William Walton was granted a patent of 20,000 acres here in 1770. The town was formed in 1797 and took his name as did the village. [Delaware:324; French:265; Murray:569]

Walworth, West Walworth. Wayne. The town was named for Chancellor Reuben H. Walworth when it was formed in 1829. The hamlet of Walworth was known as Douglas's Corners until 1825 for brothers Stephen and Andrew who were early settlers here. [Cowles:394, 399; French:694; Gannett:264; Mc-W:185]

Wampsville. Madison. Myndert Wemple, "Old Wemp," settled here in abou 1800. The place was called Wempsville, which was eventually corrupted into the present form. [Smith-C&M:732]

Wanakah. Erie. This name is a corruption of an Algonquian word, "good land." [APN:520]

Wanakena. St. Lawrence. This place may have taken its name from an Iroquoian word meaning "pleasant place." [APN:520; Harder:245]

Wantagh. Nassau. This community was a part of Jerusalem South that became called Ridgewood after the South Side Railroad of Long Island established a station here. Then another village became Ridgewood and confusion ensued. So in 1891, the post office, the village, and the train station became Wantagh, a variant of Wyandance, the name of an early Native American leader. [APN:520; Winsche:101]

Wappingers Falls. Dutchess. The town of Wappinger was formed in 1875 and named for the stream, which was named for the Wappinger Indians who had lived here on the east bank of the river. The name probably was a derivation from the Dutch *wapendragers,* meaning "weapon-bearers," applied to the Indians. But it could also have come from *wapani,* an Algonquin term for "east." The village was named for its location at the falls on Wappingers Creek. [APN:521; French:272; Gannett:264; Smith-D:491, 493; WPA-NYD:6]

Warners. Onondaga. Seth, Amos, and Herman Warner settled here in about 1810. [Bruce:720; French:490; WPANYA]

Warnerville. Schoharie. Captain George Warner settled here in 1764, but the place was called Mann's Valley for Captain George Mann, who came here in 1786. The post office was established in 1831 as Mann's Valley. The place changed its name to Cobleskill Center and then to Warnerville. [French:606; Gannett:205; Roscoe:290; Sias:143; WPANYA]

Warren. Herkimer. The town, when it was organized in 1796, was named for General Joseph Warren who fell in the Battle of Bunker Hill. The post office in the village was established in 1840. [APN:521; French:349; Gannett:265; Herkimer:107, 113]

Warrensburg. Warren. James Warren settled here in 1804. In 1811, he drowned on the West River; his ten-year-old son, Nelson, witnessed the event and it is said that his hair turned white afterwards. Two years after Warren's drowning, the town was organized and named for him. The settlement and post office were named for the town. [Smith-W:575, 583; WPANY:557; WPAW:180]

Warrens Corners. Niagara. Ezra Warren came here from Vermont as a soldier in 1812. He spent four weeks at a tavern kept by the widow of a Mr. Forsyth, the first settler here who opened the tavern in 1806. Warren went back to Vermont after his discharge, but then returned, married the widow, and ran the tavern. [Pool:243–4; Williams:374]

Warsaw, South Warsaw. Wyoming. The town was formed in 1808 and was named for the city in Poland. The Native American name was Chinosehehgeh, meaning "on the side of the valley." [APN:522; Morgan:467; Wyoming:273]

Warwick. Orange. Benjamin Aske named his land for the town and county in England. [APN:522; R&C:565; WPANY:398]

Washington Heights. New York. Fort Washinton was located here during the Revolutionary War. It was sometimes called Harlem Heights. [Jackson:1242]

Washington Hollow. Dutchess. The town of Washington was formed in 1788 and named for George Washington. The hamlet lies on the line between the towns of Washington and Pleasant Valley. [French:274, 278; Smith-D:320]

Washington Mills. Oneida. When the first woolen mill was established here, in the 1810s, the community was called Checkerville. The Washington Steam Mills and the Oneida Woolen Mills were the major industry here and the community took its name from them. [French:465; Oneida:169]

Washingtonville. Orange. Named for George Washington. [R&C:634]

Wassaic. Dutchess. The name came from an Algonquian term meaning "hard work" or "rock place." [APN:523; Gannett:266]

Waterford. Saratoga. The town was formed in 1816 and named for the fact that there was a ford across the Mohawk River to Havre Island at this point. [French:593; Syl-S:327]

Waterloo. Seneca. The village to the south of the outlet of Seneca Lake was called Scauyes, for the Native American village that had been on this site, and New Hudson to the north of the outlet, for Hudson in Columbia County, the former home of early settlers. In 1816, a meeting was held to name the entire place. An old soldier suggested that the name be that of the place of Napoleon's defeat in 1815. The name was accepted and then used to name the town when it was formed in 1829. [APN:524; Gannett:266; Seneca:83–5]

Water Mill. Suffolk. In 1644, an agreement was made between Edward Howell and the town in which he would build a mill while the hamlet would build the dam. The hamlet was called Mill Neck before taking the more descriptive name. [Bayles:333; Suffolk/Southampton:30]

Waterport. Orleans. Named for its location at the junction of Otter and Oak Orchard Creeks. [Orleans:98; Signor:653]

Watertown. Jefferson. The city was named for the town, which was formed in 1800 and named for the water power of the Black River, used for a number of manufacturing enterprises. However, there is also a possibility that the name was inspired by that of Watertown, Massachusetts. [APN:524; D&P:131, 226; French:362; Gannett:267; Hough-J:248]

Waterville. Oneida. The Native Americans called this place Skanawis, "large swamp." When it was just a collection of houses, mills, and stores on the banks of Big Creek, it was called the Huddle, but it was eventually named for the former home of early settlers, Waterville, Maine. [French:467; Oneida:183; WPANY:643]

Watervliet. Albany. This name came from the Dutch for "flowing stream" or "overflowed flats." It was given to the village of West Troy when it was incorporated as a city in 1896. West Troy was on the west bank of the Hudson River, opposite the city of Troy. In 1836, West Troy was incorporated as a village that was made up of the three villages: West Troy; Port Schuyler, named for the original owners of the land, John and Peter Schuyler, and previously known as Washington (first settled in about 1814); and Gibbonsville, named for James Gibbon, a merchant in Albany on whose land the village was laid out. [Albany:394, 411, 423; APN:524; Gannett:267; Howell:929, 974]

Watkins Glen. Schuyler. John W. Watkins bought land here, but it was his brother, Dr. Samuel Watkins, who settled here and first named the village Salubria in the 1820s. He then changed the name to Jefferson, because an old resident of the place, Isaac Q. Leake, had laid out a rival village and called it Savoy. Jefferson was incorporated in 1841 and changed its name to Watkins, for the doctor, in 1852. The glen is a narrow and winding gorge overlooking which Watkins had built a house. [French:611; Gannett:267; P&H-S:55, 68]

Watson. Lewis. The town was named, when it was formed in 1821, for James Watson of New York who owned about 62,000 acres here. [Bowen:496; French:379; Gannett:267; Hough-L:219]

Waverly. Tioga. Isaac Shepherd had first called the place Villemont, but then in 1854, it was officially renamed for the place in Sir Walter Scott's writings. [Gay:93]

Wawarsing. Ulster. The town was formed in 1806, and the name was spelled Wawarsink, said to mean either "black bird's nest" or "holy place of sacred feasts and war dances" or neither. [APN:526; French:667; Gannett:268; Syl-U:256]

Wayland. Steuben. In 1848 the villages of Patchinville and Begola were consolidated and called Wayland Depot. The "Depot" was dropped in 1884. It was named for a hymn called "Wayland" that Mr. Patchin, an early settler, had suggested. However, there are some who think that the place was named for Reverend Dr. Francis Wayland of Rhode Island, a church leader. [French:628; Roberts:542; Steuben:169, 348]

Wayne. Steuben. The town was organized in 1796 as Frederickstown for Frederick Bartles, who had built a mill here in 1793. The name was changed in 1808 to honor General Anthony Wayne. The hamlet of Wayne was early known as Wayne Hotel. [French:629; Roberts:551; Steuben:171–2]

Wayne Center. Wayne. Like the county, and being in the middle of the county, it was named for General Anthony Wayne. [Cowles:414; French:688]

Webatuck. Dutchess. This name may come from the Algonquian for "goose." [APN:527]

Webster, West Webster. Monroe. The town was organized in 1840 and is said to have been named for Daniel Webster; however, there were local Websters here as settlers. [French:405; Peck:424; WPARM:293]

Websters Crossing. Livingston. Elisha Webster built a sawmill here sometime around 1871. [WPANYS]

Weedsport. Cayuga. Elisha (Elihu, in some references) and Edward Weed settled here in 1821. When the Erie Canal was built, they dug out a basin on the south side of the canal and erected a storehouse. The place became known as Weed's Basin. Elisha Weed was the first postmaster of the post office that was established under the name Weed's Port. [French:201; Storke:326]

Wegatchie. St. Lawrence. This name is a contraction of the name of a nearby river, Oswegatchie, which in turn means "black river." [Harder:252]

Wells. Hamilton. The town was formed in 1805 and named for Joshua Wells, a land agent and first settler here, before 1792. [A&K:905; French:339]

Wellsburg. Chemung. The town was named for the family that once owned most of the town site. [Gannett:269]

Wellsville. Allegany. The town was formed in 1855 and named for the village, which was named for Gardiner Wells, who settled here in the late 1820s. When the railroad came through in 1852, they named the station Genesee. The name of the village was changed to this in 1871, but most of the residents wanted it to be Wellsville so as not to be confused with Geneseo and Little Genesee. The village was reincorporated as Wellsville in 1873. The railroad station name was changed in 1874. It is a convenient name because of the oil wells found in the area. [Allegany:345; French:175; Minard:332, 334, 349; WPANY:681]

Wendelville. Niagara. The first merchant here was Martin Wendell. [Pool:335; Williams:391]

Wesley. Cattaraugus. Named for John Wesley, founder of Methodism. [APN:530]

Westbrookville. Orange. John Westbrook kept a tavern here before the Revolutionary War. [R&C:712]

Westbury. Cayuga. This place was named for its location at the western edge of Cayuga County, bordering Wayne County. It was first settled by brothers William and Jacob Burghduff in 1806. [French:206; Storke:272]

Westbury, Old Westbury. Nassau. Old Westbury had been called Westbury, but because there already was a post office with this name, in 1841, the post office became North Hempstead. But the village was still Westbury. To simplify matters, the village and the post office took the name Old Westbury in 1868. Today's Westbury was called Westbury Station as a station on the Long Island Railroad since the 1860s. The post office was opened in 1882. By 1908, the other Westbury post office in the state had been discontinued, so Westbury Station petitioned that it and its post office change names to Westbury. [Winsche:102]

West Camp. Ulster. This was the site of Palatine Germans who lived here in about 1710. It is on the west bank of the Hudson River, opposite East Camp. [French:667; Syl-U:41]

Westchester Heights. Bronx. This was an area between two railroads, south of Westchester County. [WPANYC:538]

West Clarksville. The town of Clarksville was formed in 1835 and named for Stanley Nichols Clarke, one of the agents of the Holland Land Company. When the post office was opened in Clarksville Corners, it did so as West Clarksville, and eventually the town took the name of the post office. [Allegany:242, 244; French:173; Minard:937]

Westerleigh. Richmond. This place was named in 1892, but there is no record of name origin. [Jackson:1254]

Westerlo, South Westerlo. Albany. The village had been called Chesterville for Reverend John Chester, a pastor in Albany. Then Reverend Eilardus Westerlo came here from Holland in 1760. The village name was changed for him, and the town took that name when it was formed in 1815. The post office was established here as Westerlo in 1827. South Westerlo was called Smith's Mills for David Smith, an early settler. The name was changed in 1827 when the post office was opened. [Albany:528, 531–2; APN:530; French:166; Gannett:270; Howell:923]

Westernville, North Western. Oneida. Both of these communities are in the town of Western, which was named for being the western portion of the original town. North Western is in the center of the town, but was the most northern of the villages. A general store was opened here in 1895. [Oneida:211, 213]

West Falls. Erie. This place on the west bank of Cazenove Creek was called Crockershire for the Crocker family that had first lived here. There was a move to name the place Florence, but when the time came to petition for a post office, there already was a Florence in the state, and so the post office, and therefore the village, became West Falls. [French:283; Smith-E:557]

Westfield. Chautauqua. This used to be called the Crossroads, but the name was changed for one of the Westfields in England. The village is in the western part of the county, on ground that slopes to Lake Erie. [D&H:243; French:216; McMahon:319]

Westford. Otsego. This town was first settled in 1790, organized in 1808, and named for the settlers' former home in Vermont. [French:538; WPANYS]

West Kill. Greene. Named for the stream. [Greene:361]

West Monroe. Oswego. George Scriba called this Delft for the place in the Netherlands. When the town was formed, in 1839, it was called West Monroe. [Churchill:826; French:528; Johnson-O:367]

Westmoreland. Oneida. The town was formed in 1792 and named for the county in England. The hamlet was first called Hampton. [APN:520; French:471; Gannett:270; Oneida:216]

Weston. Schuyler. Named for Benjamin Weston Woodward, judge of Schuyler County in 1866 at the age of twenty-nine. [WPANYA]

Westons Mills. Cattaraugus. The Weston brothers were extensively involved in the lumber industry here. The settlement was first called Westonville while the post office was Westons Mills. Eventually, the settlement took the post office name. [Ellis:411; WPANYS]

West Point. Orange. The home of the U.S. Military Academy was named for its geographic location on a sharp point of land projecting into the Hudson from the west shore. [French:505; R&C:814]

Westport. Essex. The town was formed in 1815. It lies on the west shore of Lake Champlain. By 1804, the village was called North West Bay, but then later took the name of the town. [French:305; Smith-Ex:615]

West Schuyler. Herkimer. The town of Schuyler was formed in 1792 and named for General Philip Schuyler of New York, the Revolutionary commander, who owned much of the land in the town. This community was named for its location. [APN:430; Herkimer:145]

West Seneca. Erie. The town was formed as Seneca in 1851, but its name was changed in 1852 to prevent confusion with another Seneca further east. It was named for the Native Americans living in the area. (See Seneca Castle for more details.) [French:293; Gannett:236; Parker:296; Smith-E:508]

West Sparta. Livingston. This town was formed from Sparta in 1846 and lies to its west. Both were named for the city in ancient Greece, famed for courage. [APN:455; Doty-L:673; French:386]

Westtown. Orange. Named for being the only settlement in the west part of the town of Minisink. [R&C:665]

West Valley. Cattaraugus. The hamlet and post office, established in the 1830s, were named for George N. West, who had been the town supervisor and a representative of the county in the state assembly. [Ellis:340]

Westville, Westville Center. Franklin. This town originally formed the western part of the town of Constable before separating from it in 1829. It took its name from its location, as did the hamlet. [French:312; Hough-SLF:515]

Westville. Otsego. This place is in the western part of the town of Westford. [French:538]

Wethersfield Springs. Wyoming. The town of Wethersfield was formed in 1823 and named for Wethersfield in Hartford County, Connecticut, which was named for an English town. [APN:531; Wyoming:299]

Wevertown. Warren. This place was settled in 1833 as a tannery site by David Noble and his family when it was called Nobles Corners. Then the place was called Weavertown for settlers named Weaver. At some time, the name lost its "a." Most of the early development of the village was due to the tanning industry [French:676; Smith-W:549, 550, 552; WPAW:193]

Whallonsburg. Essex. James Whallon had built a forge here in 1840 and then was the postmaster. [Smith-Ex:559]

Wheatville. Genesee. Named for its good agricultural qualities. [Beers:121]

Wheeler. Steuben. Captain Silas Wheeler was an early settler here. He had served in the Revolutionary War. [French:629; Roberts:569; Steuben:178]

White Creek. Washington. The town, organized in 1815, and the settlement were named for the stream, which was named because of the white quartz pebbles that formed its bed. [French:686]

Whitehall. Washington. The town, when formed by patent in 1763, was first called Skenesborough. Major Philip Skene of the British Army obtained patents to some 37,000 acres and settled here. He lost it all when the Americans won the Revolution, and the name was changed in 1786. The area had been called Kahchoquahna by the Native Americans, meaning "the place where we dip fish." [French:686; Johnson:473, 475; WPANY:540]

White Lake. Sullivan. The community was named for the lake, which was named for its white sandy shore and bottom. [Child:106, 109; French:643]

White Plains, North White Plains. Westchester. The town was formed in 1788 and was named either for the limestone in the area, the white balsam, or a translation of the Native American name for the place, Quaropas, meaning "white marshes." [Bolton(2):264; Gannett:272; Lederer:156]

Whitesboro. Oneida. Judge Hugh White, a veteran of the Revolutionary War, came here in 1784 from Middletown, Connecticut. The village was sometimes called Whitehall Landing. [Gannett:272; Oneida:219–20; WPANY:485]

Whitestone. Queens. A large white rock inspired the name for this place. Then, in the 1840s, it was called Clintonville for DeWitt Clinton. In 1854, the name reverted back to Whitestone. [French:546; Jackson:1260; WPANYC:571]

White Sulphur Springs. Sullivan. This settlement was called Robertsonville for Bradley Robertson, an early settler in 1809. Its name was later changed for the medicinal springs found here and used in natural cures. [Child:160; Quinlan:344; WPANYS]

Whitesville. Allegany. Samuel S. White came here from Madison County in 1819. In 1826, he built a hotel, and the place became known as White's. [Allegany:321; French:174–5; Minard:598–9; WPANYA]

Whitney Point. Broome. First the place was called Patterson's Settlement for General John Patterson, an early settler. Later it was called Tinker Town or Tinker Point, which was then generalized to the Point. In 1824, when the post office was established, its name was set as Whitney's Point for Thomas Whitney, who had settled here in 1802 and was the first postmaster. It is located on the point of land between the Otselic and Tioughnioga Rivers. [French:183; Gannett:272; Smith-B:341, 343]

Willard. Seneca. The hamlet used to be called Ovid Landing, but then Dr. Sylvester Willard had a state asylum built here and it took his name when the post office was established as Willard. [Seneca:152]

Willet. Cortland. The town was formed in 1818 and named for Colonel Marinus Willet of the Revolutionary War. [French:255; Goodwin:243; WPANYA]

Williams Bridge. Bronx. John Williams, a local farmer in colonial times, built a bridge over the Bronx River here. [French:707; Jackson:1263; WPA-NYC:538]

Williamsburg. Kings. Jonathan Williams surveyed this area in the late 1700s. [Jackson:1264; WPANYC:455]

Williamson, East Williamson. Wayne. When the town was formed in 1802, it was named for Charles Williamson, the first agent of the Pulteney Estate. [Cowles:304; French:694; Gannett:274; Mc-W:189]

Williamstown. Oswego. The early name of this place was Franklin because that was the name given it by the proprietor of the land. However, Henry Williams was a prominent citizen here, so when the town was formed, in 1804, it was named for him. The post office in the settlement was established in 1813. [Churchill:833, 841; French:528; Johnson-O:353]

Williamsville. Erie. Jonas Williams built mills here in about 1804. The place became known as Williams Mills until after the War of 1812 when it became Williamsville. The Seneca name for this place was Gahdayehdeh, "open sky," or Gaskasadaneo, "many falls." [French:282; Gannett:274; Parker:298; Smith-E:398]

Willowemoc. Sullivan. This place was named for the creek, which was named by the Native Americans with a word meaning "bottomland." [APN:535; Child:191; French:647]

Willsboro, Willsboro Point. Essex. The town was formed in 1788 and named for William Gilliland, a major landowner here. It was formerly spelled Willsborough. [French:305; Smith-Ex:441]

Willseyville. Tioga. Jacob Willsey came here from Fairfield, Connecticut, and served as justice of the peace. [P&H-Ti:102]

Wilmington. Essex. When the town was formed in 1821, it was named Dansville. The name was changed in 1822. [French:305; Smith-Ex:637]

Wilson, East Wilson. Niagara. The village was founded by Reuben Wilson and his son, Luther. They had built mills here in about 1810, then Luther laid out the village in 1827. The town was named for Reuben, who was the first town supervisor. The village of East Wilson was first known as Marsh Settlement for Joseph Marsh, an early settler. Then it was known as Beebe's Corners. [French:457; Pool:302, 309, 313; Williams:385–6]

Wilton. Saratoga. This place was known as Palmerton, for the mountains, but when the town was formed in 1818, it was named for the former home in New Hampshire of some settlers, which had been named for the English town. The community had been known as Doe's Corners. [APN:535; French:593; Gannett:275; Syl-S:462–6]

Windham, East Windham. Greene. The settlement was known as Osbornville in 1830 and Windham Center in 1844. The town took its name from Windham, Connecticut, by settlers from there. [Greene:196, 394; Vedder:120]

Windsor, East Windsor, West Windsor. Broome. The town was named for Windsor, Connecticut, by early settlers who had come from there. The village of Windsor had been called Old Oquaga, then the name was changed for the town. The name of West Windsor was given to the post office in the village of Stillson Hollow, named for Lyman Stillson, who kept a public house here. The post office in East Windsor was opened in 1872. [APN:536; French:184; Gannett:275; Smith-B:273, 287, 297–8]

Wingdale. Dutchess. The Wing family settled here in about 1806, with Jackson Wing running a tavern after 1807. [French:271; Smith-D:481; WPA-NYD:119]

Winthrop. St. Lawrence. Henry Wilkerson Winthrop was a descendant of Isaac Kelsey, the first settler here. [Harder:258]

Wiscoy. Allegany. Named for the creek, the name of which is a compound word from *wis,* Native American for the fifth numeral, alluding to the creek with five waterfalls. [Allegany:305, 307, 312; APN:539; French:174; Gannett:276; Minard:736]

Witherbee. Essex. Named for the owner of an iron ore bed here that he mined. [Smith-Ex:581]

Wittenberg. Ulster. Named for the city in Germany. [APN:539]

Wolcott. Wayne. The town, when it was formed in 1807, was named for Oliver Wolcott, secretary of the treasury during the Washington and Adams administrations. [French:694; Gannett:276]

Wolcottsville. Niagara. The first settler here was Anson Wolcott, who bought land from the Holland Land Company in 1847. [Pool:272; WPANYA]

Woodbourne. Sullivan. Gabriel Ludlum named the settlement for its natural surroundings. [Child:137; French:644; WPANYS]

Woodbury. Nassau. In 1746, this settlement was called East Woods. The post office was established as Woodbury in 1836. [Winsche:104]

Woodgate. Oneida. Named for the forests in which it is located. [Oneida:151]

Woodhaven. Queens. John R. Pitkin moved here in 1835 to build a manufacturing center and, with it, a workers' village that he called Woodville. In 1853, the residents voted to change the name to Woodhaven. [Jackson:1271; WPA-NYC:583]

Woodhull. Steuben. When the town was formed in 1828, it was named for General Nathaniel Woodhull, an officer in the Revolutionary War. [French:629; Steuben:181]

Woodland. Ulster. This was the name given to a district in Woodland Valley and a post office. [French:667; Syl-U:309]

Woodlawn. Bronx. This place was first called Washingtonville, then Wakefield, and finally Woodlawn after the Woodlawn Cemetery was laid out in 1863. George Updyke established the village in 1873. [French:706; Jackson:1272; WPANYC:539–40]

Woodmere. Nassau. Samuel Wood bought land here in 1869 and called the place Woodsburgh. When applying for a post office in 1897, the name was too close to Woodbury for the postal officials, so the name was changed to Woodmere. [Winsche:104–5]

Woodridge. Sullivan. This used to be a depot on the New York and Midland Railroad called Centerville Station. [Child:137]

Woodrow. Richmond. The Woodrow United Methodist Church was built here in 1842 on Woodrow Road and named for the woods. [Jackson:1272]

Woodstock. Ulster. The town was formed in 1787 and named for the town in England. [APN:540; French:668; Gannett:277; Syl-U:318]

Woodville. Jefferson. This was formerly called Wood's Settlement, named for the sons of Nathaniel Wood, Ebenezer, Ephraim, and Jacob, of Middletown, Vermont, who were the first settlers here. [D&P:370; French:357; Hough-J:159]

Woodville. Ontario. This was a landing on Canandaigua Lake from which wood was shipped. [Milliken:110]

Worcester. Otsego. Early settlers came here in the 1780s from Worcester, Massachusetts. [WPANYS]

Worth. Jefferson. The town was formed in 1848 and named for General William J. Worth, an officer in the Mexican War. [APN:541; D&P:532; French:363; Gannett:277; Hough-J:306]

Wright. Washington. This place was named for an early settler and town supervisor. [WPANYS]

Wrights Corners. Niagara. The community was named for Solomon Wright, who ran a store here that was started in 1817 by Alvin Buck and taken over by Wright in 1823. He was the postmaster for forty-one years. [Pool:329]

Wurlitzer Park. Niagara. This community grew up around the Rudolph Wurlitzer Plant that made theater and church organs, radio cabinets, mechanical pianos, and coin-operated record players. Wurlitzer was a German who founded the company in Cincinnati in 1856, then opened a plant in this area in 1908. [WPANY:683]

Wurtsboro. Sullivan. William and Maurice Wurtz were Philadelphia merchants who had acquired coal fields in Pennsylvania and were determined to bring the coal to markets in New York and New England. To do this, they helped with the building of the Delaware and Hudson Canal, with Maurice Wurtz serving as president of the canal company. Before the canal was built, this place was called Rome. [Child:174; French:646; Gannett:278; Quinlan:435; WPANY:386]

Wyandanch. Suffolk. Named for a local Indian who, according to tradition, had always been a friend of the white settlers. [Bayles:423]

Wyantskill. Rensselaer. This place was named for the stream, which was named for Wynant Gerritse Van der Poel, who had bought a sawmill that had been built on the stream's shore. [Weise:12, 54]

Wyckoff. Cayuga. Many members of the Wyckoff family lived in the area. It was first Wyckoff Station, a stop on the railroad, and had no church, store, hotel, or shop, just the post office in the depot. [Storke:382]

Wyoming. Wyoming. The village was known as Newell's Settlement before the establishment of a post office, when it was called Middlebury Post Office, for Middlebury, Vermont, the former home of some settlers. In 1829, the name of the village and post office was changed to Wyoming through the efforts of Judge John B. Skinner, who was an admirer of Native American names. In 1841, the name was applied to the county. The local Native American name of the place was Tecaresetaneont, "place with a sign post." [APN:542; Morgan:467; Parker:316; Wyoming:70, 212, 217]

Y

Yates © 2004 by Jon Crispin

Yagerville. Ulster. This was a "special" name of a neighborhood that had a sawmill. [Syl-U:218, 224]

Yaphank. Suffolk. The settlement was formerly called Millville. It later took the Native American name of a small river nearby. [Bayles:256; Suffolk/Brookhaven:49]

Yates. Orleans. The town was formed in 1822 as Northton. The name was changed in 1823 for Joseph C. Yates, then governor of New York State. [French:516; Gannett:279; Orleans:312; Signor:588]

Yatesville. Yates. Like the county, the village was named for Joseph C. Yates, who was governor in 1823 when the county was formed. [French:717]

Yonkers. Westchester. Adrian Cornelissen Van der Donck was a lawyer and historian of New Netherlands who was politely called *jonker*, the Dutch term for "squire" or "young lord." This place was referred to as the Jonkers, eventually spelled with the y. It was formed as a town in 1788. [APN:546; French:707; Gannett:279; Lederer:160; WPANY:371]

York. Livingston. The town was formed in 1819, named as a compliment for Joseph York, who was a member of the assembly when the residents were petitioning for the formation of this town. [Doty-L:680; WPANYS]

Yorkshire. Cattaraugus. Named for the English county. [APN:546]

Yorktown, Yorktown Heights. Westchester. The town was formed in 1788 and named for the Yorktown in Virginia after the Revolutionary War. [French:708; Lederer:160]

Yorkville. Oneida. Yorkville was named for the city of York in England. The village was incorporated in 1902. [APN:546; Oneida:220]

Youngstown. Niagara. John Young was the first merchant here. [French:456; Gannett:280; Pool:260; Williams:381]

Youngsville. Sullivan. Samuel M. Young was the first settler here in 1834. He came from Liberty, and built the first sawmill and opened the first store. [Child:125; Quinlan:163]

Z

Ausable Chasm © *2004 by Jon Crispin*

Zena. Ulster. Named for a woman. [APN:548]
Zurich. Wayne. Named for the Swiss city. [APN:550]

Appendix

Bibliography

Appendix

Places for Which No Information on Name Origins Was Found

Of the approximately 2,500 places whose names I chose to research, the following were the ones for which I could find no information. The origin of their names remains obscure. The community name is followed by the county name. I would appreciate hearing from anyone with information on these names. Please contact me either by e-mail, at vasiliev@ geneseo.edu, or by mail, at P.O. Box 247, Bloomfield, New York 14469.

Acra, Greene
Adamsville, Washington
Alder Brook, Franklin
Allaben, Ulster
Alligerville, Ulster
Andes, Delaware
Armor, Erie
Ashford, Ashford Hollow, Cattaraugus
Atwell, Herkimer
Balcom, Chautauqua
Beachville, Steuben
Blockville, Chautauqua
Bloomington, Ulster
Bowerstown, Otsego
Brisben, Chenango
Brooksburg, Greene
Buena Vista, Steuben
Bull Run, Ulster
Burnwood, Delaware
Cahoonzie, Orange

Candor, Tioga
Castle Point, Dutchess
Centralia, Chautauqua
Chambers, Chemung
Cherry Grove, Suffolk
Clarks Mills, Washington
Cliff Haven, Clinton
Clinton Park, Rensselaer
Colonial Village, Niagara
Connelly Park, Chautauqua
Corbett, Delaware
Cottekill, Ulster
Cumminsville, Livingston
Dahlia, Sullivan
Davis Park, Suffolk
Dogtail Corners, Dutchess
Dunewood, Suffolk
Durlandville, Orange
Eagleville, Washington
East Seneca, Erie

Edgewood, Greene
Eggertsville, Erie
Elkdale, Cattaraugus
Elsmere, Albany
Elwood, Suffolk
Emmons, Otsego
Empeyville, Oneida
Fair Harbor, Suffolk
Fairview, Dutchess
Fairview, Wyoming
Fairville, Wayne
Farmingville, Suffolk
Ferry Village, Erie
Fishers Landing, Jefferson
Five Points, Ontario
Fly Summit, Washington
Forsyth, Chautauqua
Fort Hunter, Albany
Fowlerville, Erie
Franklin Park, Onondaga
Freedom, Cattaraugus
Freetown, Suffolk
French Woods, Delaware
Frost Valley, Ulster
Galeville, Onondaga
Glenburnie, Washington
Glenford, Ulster
Glenora, Yates
Glen Park, Jefferson
Glenwood, Niagara
Golden Glow Heights, Chemung
Grandyle Village, Erie
Granite, Ulster
Greenfield Park, Ulster
Greenhurst, Chautauqua
Grooville, Sullivan
Grover Hills, Essex
Gurn Spring, Saratoga
Guyanoga, Yates
Halesite, Suffolk
Half Hollow Hills, Suffolk
Harkness, Clinton
Hartmans Corners, Albany

Herrings, Jefferson
Highland-on-the-Lake, Erie
Hillcrest, Rockland
Holcom(b)ville, Warren
Holmes, Dutchess
Hope Farm, Dutchess
Howard, Steuben.
Howes, Broome
Hunts Corner, Sullivan
Hurd(s) Corners, Dutchess
Hyde Park, Otsego
Index, Otsego
Indian Park, Orange
Indian Village, Onondaga
Islandia, Suffolk
Jacksonburg, Herkimer
Jewettville, Erie
Keene, Essex
Keene Valley, Essex
Kenmore, Erie
Kerley(s) Corners, Dutchess
Kings Park, Suffolk
Kirk, Chenango
Kiryas Joel, Orange
Lacona, Oswego
Lake Erie Beach, Erie
Lakeland, Onondaga
Lakeside, Wayne
Lamberton, Chautauqua
Lanesville, Greene
Laona, Chautauqua
Lap(a)la, Ulster
Lava, Sullivan
Linwood, Livingston
Little York, Schoharie
Lock Berlin, Wayne
Locust Manor, Queens
Lomontville, Ulster
Lonelyville, Suffolk
Lowman, Chemung
Lyndon, Onondaga
MacDougall, Seneca
Manorton, Columbia

Maplecrest, Greene
Maplehurst, Cattaraugus
Maples, Cattaraugus
Maple Springs, Chautauqua
Maplewood, Sullivan
Martisco, Onondaga
Mattydale, Onondaga
Maybrook, Orange
Maywood, Albany
McKeever, Herkimer
Medway, Greene
Melody Lake, Sullivan
Merrill, Clinton
Middleville, Suffolk
Millersport, Erie
Mina, Chautauqua
Mohegan Lake, Westchester
Mountain Lodge, Orange
Mount Tremper, Ulster
Mount Vernon, Erie
Munsons Corners, Cortland
Nashville, Chautauqua
New Concord, Columbia
Nimmonsburg, Broome
North, St. Lawrence
Northfield, Delaware
North Pole, Essex
North Wilmurt, Herkimer
Oak Beach, Suffolk
Oakdale, Suffolk
Oakland Gardens, Queens
Obi, Allegany
Oliverea, Ulster
Oniontown, Dutchess
Oramel, Allegany
Orchard Knoll, Chemung
Paines Hollow, Herkimer
Panther Lake, Oswego
Parkston, Sullivan
Park Terrace, Broome
Pataukunk, Ulster
Pearl Creek, Wyoming
Phillips Mills, Chautauqua

Pine Hill, Oneida
Pleasantdale, Rensselaer
Pokeville, Cortland
Port Henry, Essex
Purdys Mill, Clinton
Ray Brook, Essex
Raymertown, Rensselaer
Reber, Essex
Ricard, Oswego
Riceville, Cattaraugus
Riceville, Fulton
Richland, Oswego
Ridgewood, Niagara
Riverside, Steuben
Riverside, Suffolk
Roanoke, Suffolk
Rock Valley, Delaware
Roessleville, Albany
Roosevelt Beach, Niagara
Sailor's Haven, Suffolk
Saint Remy, Ulster
San Remo, Suffolk
Sawkill, Ulster
Scranton, Erie
Severance, Essex
Shady, Ulster
Sheldrake, Seneca
Sherwood Park, Rensselaer
Shirley, Suffolk
Sholam, Ulster
Shoreham, Suffolk
Shore Haven, Chautauqua
Sloan, Erie
Smallwood, Sullivan
Smith Mills, Chautauqua
Snyders Corner(s), Rensselaer
Sound Beach, Suffolk
South Manor, Suffolk
Southwood, Onondaga
Spring Glen, Ulster
Springs, Suffolk
Spruceton, Greene
Stanford Heights, Albany

Stedman, Chautauqua
Stetsonville, Otsego
Stilesville, Delaware
Stillwater, Herkimer
Sugartown, Cattaraugus
Sullivanville, Chemung
Summerdale, Chautauqua
Surprise, Greene
Swormville, Erie
Sycaway, Rensselaer
Taunton, Onondaga
Terryville, Suffolk
Texas Valley, Cortland
Tillson, Ulster
Truthville, Washington
Tunnel, Broome
Twin Orchard(s), Broome
Underwood, Essex
Union Hill,, Wayne
VanBuren Point, Chautauqua
Vandalia, Cattaraugus
Verdoy, Albany

Veteran, Ulster
Wallace, Steuben
Waterboro, Chautauqua
Watsonville, Schoharie
Watts Flats, Chautauqua
Webb Mills, Chemung
Wesley Hills, Rockland
West Corners, Broome
West Hill, Schenectady
Westmere, Albany
West Park, Ulster
Westvale, Onondaga
Wheelertown, Herkimer
Whitelaw, Madison
Willow, Ulster
Willow Grove, Rockland
Willow Point, Broome
Windom, Erie
Woodinville, Dutchess
Woodlawn, Woodlawn Beach, Erie
Woodsville, Livingston
Yulan, Sullivan

Bibliography

Aber, Ted, and Stella King. 1965. *The History of Hamilton County*. Lake Pleasant, N.Y.: Great Wilderness Books.

Amana Colonies Convention and Visitors Bureau, http://www.amanacolonies.com.

Anderson, David G. Williamstown, Ontario, Canada: Glengarry Historical Society, NY-HIST-L@UNIX10.nysed.gov.

Bayles, Richard. [1873] 1962. *Historical and Descriptive Sketches of Suffolk County with a Historical Outline of Long Island*. Reprint, Port Washington, N.Y.: Ira J. Friedman.

Bedell, Cornelia F. 1968. *Now and Then and Long Ago in Rockland County*. New City, N.Y.: Historical Society of Rockland County.

Beers, F. W., ed. 1890. *Gazetteer and Biographical Record of Genesee County, New York, 1788–1890*. Syracuse, N.Y.: J. W. Vose.

Blake, William J. 1849. *The History of Putnam County, New York*. New York: Baker & Schribner.

Bolton, Robert. [1881] 1996. *The History of the Several Towns, Manors, and Patents of the County of Westchester From Its First Settlement to the Present Time*. 2 vols. New York: Chas. F. Roper. Reprint, Bowie, Md.: Heritage Books.

Bowen, G. Byron, ed. 1970. *History of Lewis County, New York, 1880–1965*. Board of Legislators of Lewis County, N.Y.

Bruce, Dwight, ed. 1896. *Onondaga's Centennial*. Boston: Boston History Co.

Chernow, Barbara A., and George A. Vallasi, eds. 1993. *The Columbia Encyclopedia*. 5th ed. New York: Columbia Univ. Press.

Child, Hamilton. [1872] 1975. *Gazetteer and Business Directory of Sullivan County, New York*. Syracuse, N.Y.: Journal Office. Reprint, Rock Hill, N.Y.: Fallsburg Printing Company.

Churchill, John C. 1895. *Landmarks of Oswego County, New York*. Syracuse, N.Y.: D. Mason.

Clark, J. M. 1914. "The Place Names of Schenectady County." *New York State Museum Bulletin*: 56–58.

Clark, Joshua V. H. [1849] 1973. *Onondaga; or Reminiscences of Earlier and Later Times*. Vol. 2. Syracuse, N.Y.: Stoddard and Babcock. Reprint, Millwood, N.Y.: Kraus Reprint Co.

Clayton, W. W. [1878] 1980. *History of Onondaga County, New York*. Syracuse, N.Y.: D. Mason. Reprint, New Berlin, N.Y.: Molly Yes Press.

Cleveland, Stafford C. 1873. *History and Directory of Yates County*. 2 vols. Penn Yan, N.Y.: Yates County Chronicle.

Cole, David. [1884] 1992. *History of Rockland County, New York*. New York: L. B. Beers. Reprint, New City, N.Y.: Historical Society of Rockland County.

Cowles, George W. 1895. *Landmarks of Wayne County, New York*. Syracuse, N.Y.: D. Mason.

Curtis, Gates. 1894. *Our County and Its People: A Memorial Record of St. Lawrence County, New York*. Syracuse, N.Y.: D. Mason.

Donaldson, Alfred L. [1921] 1963. *A History of the Adirondacks*. 2 vols. New York: Century Co. Reprint, Port Washington, N.Y.: Ira J. Friedman.

Doty, Lockwood L. 1876. *A History of Livingston County, New York*. Geneseo, N.Y.: J. W. Clement.

————, ed. 1925. *History of the Genesee Country*. Chicago: S. J. Clarke Publishing.

Downs, John P., and Fenwick Y. Hedley. 1921. *History of Chautauqua County, New York, and Its People*. vol. 1. New York: American Historical Society.

Durant, Samuel W., and Henry B. Pierce. 1878. *History of Jefferson County, New York*. Philadelphia: L. H. Everts.

Ellis, Franklin. 1878. *History of Columbia County, New York*. Philadelphia: Everts & Ensign.

————. [1879] 1976. *History of Cattaraugus County, New York*. Philadelphia: L. H. Everts. Reprint, Olean, N.Y.: Historical and Cultural Association of the Olean Area.

Flick, Alexander C., ed. 1937. *History of the State of New York*. Vol. 10, *The Empire State*. New York: Columbia Univ. Press.

French, J. H. [1860] 1986. *Gazetteer of the State of New York*. Syracuse, N.Y.: R. P. Smith. Reprint, Interlaken, N.Y.: Heart of the Lakes Publishing.

Fried, Marc B. 1975. *The Early History of Kingston and Ulster County, New York*. Marbletown, N.Y.: Ulster County Historical Society.

Frothingham, Washington. 1892. *History of Montgomery County, New York*. Syracuse, N.Y.: D. Mason.

Gannett, Henry. 1902. *The Origin of Certain Place-Names of the United States*. Bulletin of the United States Geological Survey #197, Series F, Geography, 32. Washington, D.C.: Government Printing Office.

Gay, W. B. [1888] 1978. *Historical Gazetteer of Tioga County, New York*. Syracuse, N.Y.: W. B. Gay. Reprint, Owego, N.Y.: Tioga County Historical Society.

Goodwin, H. C. 1859. *Pioneer History; or, Cortland County and the Border Wars of New York*. New York: A. B. Burdick.

Green, Frank Bertangue. [1886] 1989. *The History of Rockland County*. New York: A. S. Barnes. Reprint, New City, N.Y.: Historical Society of Rockland County.

Grumet, Robert Steven. 1981. *Native American Place Names in New York City.* New York: Museum of the City of New York.

Hakes, Harlo. 1896. *Landmarks of Steuben County, New York.* Syracuse, N.Y.: D. Mason.

Harder, Kelsie B., and Mary H. Smallman. 1992. *Claims to Name: Toponyms of St. Lawrence County.* Utica, N.Y.: North Country Books.

History of Allegany County, N.Y. [1879] 1978. New York: F. W. Beers. Reprint, Ovid, N.Y.: W. E. Morrison.

History of Delaware County. [1880] 1976. New York: W. W. Munsell. Reprint, Ovid, N.Y.: W. E. Morrison.

History of Greene County. [1884] 1969. New York: J. B. Beers. Reprint, Cornwallville, N.Y.: Hope Farm Press.

History of Herkimer County, New York. [1879] 1980. New York: F. W. Beers. Reprint, Ovid, N.Y.: W. E. Morrison.

History of Montgomery and Fulton Counties, New York. [1878] 1979. New York: F. W. Beers. Reprint, Ovid, N.Y.: Heart of the Lakes Publishing.

History of Oneida County. 1977. Utica, N.Y.: Oneida County.

History of Seneca County, New York. 1876. Philadelphia: Everts, Ensign, & Everts.

History of Suffolk County, New York. 1882. New York: W. W. Munsell. [The page numbers in this reference are not consecutive; each town history starts over with 1. So the references read: Suffolk/town name:page number.]

History of Wyoming County. 1841. New York: F. W. Beers.

Hopkins, Daniel J., ed. *Merriam-Webster's Geographical Dictionary.* 3rd ed. Springfield, Mass.: Merriam-Webster.

Hough, Franklin B. [1853] 1970. *A History of St. Lawrence and Franklin Counties, New York.* Albany: Little. Reprint, Baltimore, Md.: Regional Printing Company.

———. [1854] 1976. *A History of Jefferson County in the State of New York from the Earliest Period to the Present.* Albany, N.Y.: Munsell. Reprint, Ovid, N.Y.: W. E. Morrison.

———. [1860] 1975. *A History of Lewis County in the State of New York.* Albany, N.Y.: Munsell & Rowland. Reprint, Merrick, N.Y.: Richwood Publishing.

Howell, George R. 1886. *Bicentennial History of Albany. History of the County of Albany, N.Y., from 1609 to 1886.* New York: W. W. Munsell.

Hurd, Duane Hamilton. [1878] 1978. *History of Otsego County, New York.* Philadelphia: Everts & Fariss. Reprint, Ovid, N.Y.: W. E. Morrison.

———. [1880] 1978. *History of Clinton and Franklin Counties.* Philadelphia: J. W. Lewis. Reprint, Plattsburgh, N.Y.: Clinton County American Revolution Bicentennial Commission.

Jackson, Kenneth T., ed. 1995. *The Encyclopedia of New York City.* New Haven, Conn.: Yale Univ. Press.

Johnson, Crisfield. [1877] 1991. *History of Oswego County, New York.* Philadelphia: L. H. Everts. Reprint, Salem, Mass.: Higginson Book Company.

———. [1878] 1979. *History of Washington County, New York.* Philadelphia: Everts & Ensign. Reprint, Interlaken, N.Y.: Heart of the Lakes Publishing.

Landon, Harry F. 1932. *The North Country. A History Embracing Jefferson, St. Lawrence, Oswego, Lewis, and Franklin Counties, New York.* Vol. 1. Indianapolis: Historical Publishing.

Lederer, Richard M., Jr. 1978. *The Place-Names of Westchester County, New York.* Harrison, N.Y.: Harbor Hill Books.

Lounsbury, Floyd G. 1960. *Iroquois Place-Names in the Champlain Valley.* Report of the New York-Vermont Interstate Commission on the Lake Champlain Basin. Legislative Document No. 9, pp. 23–66. Albany, N.Y.: State Education Department.

Lynch, Bernard, Irene M. Gibson, and J. Howard Pratt, eds. 1976. *Orleans County History.* Albion, N.Y.Mass. Eddy Printing.

McIntosh, W. H. 1877. *History of Monroe County, New York.* Philadelphia: Everts, Ensign, & Everts.

———. [1877] 1975. *History of Wayne County, New York.* Philadelphia: Everts, Ensign, & Everts. Reprint, Pultneyville, N.Y.: Dendron Press.

McMahon, Helen G. 1958. *Chautauqua County. A History.* Buffalo, N.Y.: Henry Stewart.

Melone, Harry R. 1932. *History of Central New York.* Indianapolis: Historical Publishing Company.

Milliken, Charles, F. 1924. "Ontario County Place Names." *New York State Museum Bulletin* no. 253: 103–10.

Minard, John S. 1896. *Allegany County and Its People.* Alfred, N.Y.: W. A. Fergusson.

Morgan, Lewis Henry. [1851] 1972. *League of the Iroquois.* Rochester, N.Y.: Sage & Brother Publishers. Reprint, Secaucus, N.J.: Citadel Press.

Munsell, W. W. 1886. *History of the County of Schenectady, N.Y., from 1662 to 1886.* New York: W. W. Munsell.

Murray, David, ed. 1838. *Delaware County. History of the Century, 1797–1897.* Delhi, N.Y.: William Clark.

Norris, W. Glenn. 1964. *The Origins of Place Names in Tompkins County.* Ithaca, N.Y.: De-Witt Historical Society of Tompkins County.

North, Safford E. 1899. *Our County and Its People; a Descriptive and Biographical Record of Genesee County, New York.* Boston: Boston History Company.

Noyes, Marion F., ed. [1964] 1980. *A History of Schoharie County.* Reprint, Middleburgh, N.Y.: Middleburgh Press.

Parker, Amasa J. 1897. *Landmarks of Albany County.* Syracuse, N.Y.: D. Mason.

Parker, Arthur C. 1925. "Indian Place Names of the Genesee Country." In *History of the Genesee Country.* Chicago: S. J. Clarke Publishing Company.

Peck, William F. 1895. *Landmarks of Monroe County, New York.* Boston: Boston History Company.

Peirce, H. B., and D. Hamilton Hurd. 1879. *History of Chemung County, New York.* Philadelphia: Everts & Ensign.

———. 1879. *History of Schuyler County, New York.* Philadelphia: Everts & Ensign.

———. [1879] 1982. *History of Tioga County, New York.* Reprint, Philadelphia: Everts & Ensign.

———. 1879. *History of Tompkins County, New York.* Philadelphia: Everts & Ensign. Reprint, Ovid, N.Y.: W. E. Morrison.

Pelletreau, William S. [1886] 1975. *History of Putnam County, New York*. Philadelphia: W. W. Preston. Reprint, Brewster, N.Y.: Southeast Museum.

Pool, William, ed. 1897. *Landmarks of Niagara County*. Syracuse, N.Y.: D. Mason.

Quinlan, James Eldridge. [1873] 1975. *History of Sullivan County*. Liberty, N.Y.: W. T. Morgan. Reprint, Rock Hill, N.Y.: Fallsburg Printing Company.

Roberts, Millard F. 1891. *Historical Gazetteer of Steuben County, New York*. Syracuse, N.Y.: Millard F. Roberts.

Roscoe, William E. [1882] 1994. *History of Schoharie County, New York*. Syracuse, N.Y.: D. Mason. Reprint, Bowie, Md.: Heritage Books.

Ruttenber, E. M., and L. H. Clark. [1881] 1980. *History of Orange County, New York*. Philadelphia: Everts & Peck. Reprint, Interlaken, N.Y.: Heart of the Lakes Publishing.

Selkreg, John H. 1894. *Landmarks of Tompkins County, New York*. Syracuse, N.Y.: D. Mason.

Shonnard, Frederic, and W. W. Spooner. [1900] 1974. *History of Westchester County, New York, From Its Earliest Settlements to the Year 1900*. New York: New York History Company. Reprint, Harrison, N.Y.: Harbor Hill Books.

Sias, Solomon. 1904. *A Summary of Schoharie County*. Middleburg, N.Y.: Pierre W. Danforth

Signor, Isaac. 1894. *Landmarks of Orleans County*. Syracuse, N.Y.: D. Mason.

Smith, H. P. 1884. *History of the City of Buffalo and Erie County*. Vol. 1. Syracuse, N.Y.: D. Mason.

———. 1885. *History of Broome County*. Syracuse, N.Y.: D. Mason.

———. 1885. *History of Essex County*. Syracuse, N.Y.: D. Mason.

———. [1885] 1981. *History of Warren County*. Syracuse, N.Y.: D. Mason. Reprint, Interlaken, N.Y.: Heart of the Lakes Publishing.

Smith, James H. 1880. *History of Chenango and Madison Counties*. Syracuse, N.Y.: D. Mason.

———. [1882] 1988. *History of Dutchess County, New York*. Syracuse, N.Y.: D. Mason. Reprint, Interlaken, N.Y.: Heart of the Lakes Publishing.

Stewart, George R. 1945. *Names on the Land*. New York: Random House.

———. 1970. *American Place-Names*. New York: Oxford Univ. Press.

Stone, William L. 1901. *Washington County, New York. Its History to the Close of the Nineteenth Century*. New York: New York History Co.

Storke, Elliot G. 1879. *History of Cayuga County, N.Y.* Syracuse, N.Y.: D. Mason.

Sylvester, Nathaniel Bartlett. [1878] 1979. *History of Saratoga County, New York*. Philadelphia: Everts & Ensign. Reprint, Interlaken, N.Y.: Heart of the Lakes Publishing.

———. 1880. *History of Ulster County, New York*. Vol. 2. Philadelphia: Everts & Peck.

U.S. Department of the Interior, U.S. Geological Survey. Geographic Names Information System, http://geonames.usgs.gov/geonames/.

Vasiliev, Irina. 1988. "The Naming and Diffusion of Moscows Across the United States." Masters thesis, State Univ. of New York at Buffalo.

Vedder, J. Van Vechten. 1927. *Official History of Greene County, New York, 1651–1800*. Greene County Board of Supervisors.

Weise, A. M. [1880] 1975. *History of the Seventeen Towns of Rensselaer County*. Troy, N.Y.:

J. M. Francis & Tucker. Reprint, Rensselaer County American Revolution Bicentennial Commission.

Williams, Edward T. 1921. *Niagara County, New York.* Vol. 1. Chicago: J. H. Beers.

Winsche, Richard A. 1999. *The History of Nassau County Community Place-Names.* Interlaken, N.Y.: Empire State Books.

Workers of the Writers' Program Works Projects Administration. 1941. *Johnstown in New York State's Mohawk Valley.* Johnstown, N.Y.: City of Johnstown.

Writer's Program of the Work Projects Administration. 1937. *Dutchess County.* Philadelphia: William Penn Association.

———. 1937. *Rochester and Monroe County: A History and Guide.* Rochester, N.Y.: Scrantom's.

———. 1939. *New York City Guide.* New York: Random House.

———. 1940. *New York. A Guide to the Empire State.* New York: Oxford Univ. Press.

———. 1940. *Pennsylvania: A Guide to the Keystone State.* New York: Oxford Univ. Press.

———. 1940. "A Survey of New York State Place-Names." Manuscript in the New York State Archives, Albany, N.Y.

Writer's Program of the Work Projects Administration in the State of New York. 1942. *Warren County. A History and Guide.* Glens Falls, N.Y.: Warren County Board of Supervisors.

Writer's Program of the Work Projects Administration of New York State research papers in the New York State Archives, Albany, N.Y.